BUCKEYE BROTHERHOOD

BUCKEYE BROTHERHOOD

How **OHIO STATE** Navigated a New World to Win a National Championship

BILL RABINOWITZ

TRIUMPH BOOKS

First Triumph Books paperback edition 2025

Library of Congress Cataloging-in-Publication Data available upon request.

This book is available in quantity at special discounts for your group or organization. For further information, contact:

Triumph Books LLC
814 North Franklin Street
Chicago, Illinois 60610
(312) 337-0747
www.triumphbooks.com

Printed in U.S.A.
ISBN: 978-1-63727-083-7
Design by Patricia Frey

All photos courtesy of AP Images unless otherwise noted

To Katie and Michael.
Watching you grow up into caring, passionate,
and hilarious adults has been the thrill of my life.

Contents

Foreword by Urban Meyer ix
Prologue xiii

1 Motivated by Tragedy 1
2 Climbing the Coaching Ladder 9
3 Welcome to Ohio State 17
4 A Special Recruiting Class 25
5 Success…and Heartbreak 31
6 NIL Changes the Game 43
7 The Courtship of Jeremiah Smith 51
8 One More Year 57
9 The Final Pieces 63
10 Offseason Improvement 73
11 "Natty or Bust" 81
12 Faith 95
13 Brick by Brick 101
14 Chasing Defensive Perfection 107
15 The Season Arrives 117

16 Disappointment at Autzen 127
17 Close Call in a Clunker 135
18 New-Look Line Delivers 141
19 Putting IU in Its Place 151
20 The Michigan Debacle. 161
21 The Fallout 171
22 The Turning Point 179
23 "No One Was Beating Us" 187
24 Dominant Redemption 197
25 "The Best Team We Played". 209
26 Scoop and Sawyer 219
27 A Terrible Start. 235
28 An Amazing Finish. .247
29 Celebration and Departures 255
30 What It Meant. 263

Acknowledgments. 271

Foreword

When I coached at Ohio State, I had a ritual at the end of team meetings. I'd say, "Long live," and the players would yell back, "The brotherhood!"

I've coached all around the country, and it's just different at Ohio State. The demands are different. The expectations are different. As a coach, every second of every waking moment, and even in your subconscious, you're thinking about the rivalry game, thinking about your team. It's not healthy, but I coached with fear. The glass always seemed half-empty. You're constantly worried about the what-ifs.

As someone from Ohio who grew up during the Ten-Year War with Woody Hayes and Bo Schembechler, I understand the passion people have for Buckeye football. Go to a spring game in Ann Arbor or at USC and then compare the attendance to an Ohio State one. I would hear people at other schools use the term "The brotherhood," but at Ohio State, it's real. When a former player comes to Ohio State, people stop. Coaches stop. Players stop. Everybody. That's what has always made Ohio State just a little bit different to me. Once you are part of the brotherhood, you're always part of the brotherhood.

That brotherhood was tested in 2024. The first test came right after the '23 season ended when Ohio State's juniors had to decide whether to go the NFL. I don't think the Buckeyes win the national title if most of those guys don't return. The Wolverines won in 2023 because they had a veteran team. Now Ohio State had one. There's a big difference between coaching boys and coaching men, and that '24 team had a bunch of men on it.

Then came the upset loss to the Wolverines. How intense is the pressure for that game? I still have nightmares just about the possibility of losing that game. I don't know what I would have done if we'd lost one. I can't even imagine it, to be honest. You start having these flashbacks that say, "This can't happen. Of all the choices in life, this isn't one of them."

But Ohio State did lose to the Wolverines in 2024, and it became Ryan Day's job to get the team to regroup before the College Football Playoff. Ryan was a GA for me at Florida in 2005. He impressed me even then with his football acumen. When I hired him at Ohio State after the 2016 season, he made our offense better. I was used to a run-first, pass-second team that would out-tough you at the line of scrimmage. With Dwayne Haskins Jr. at quarterback, we became really good in the passing game, too.

I knew I didn't want to coach at Ohio State forever. I didn't want the program to go outside the building for a coach and hire someone who would disturb what I believe is the best infrastructure in college sports. Not long after Ryan came to Columbus, I realized he would be an ideal successor. In Ryan's second year here, Mississippi State showed interest in him as its head coach. I told Ryan that I'd probably step down before long. I hoped that would be sufficient reason for him to stay. Ryan did stay and got the job when I retired.

I was a psychology major in college and relied on that knowledge as a coach. I remember my first year at Ohio State in 2012 when we were underdogs playing at Michigan State. In the team hotel, I asked players to raise a glass of water for a toast that promised they would give their hearts to the team. We won that game and went undefeated with the least talented team I had at Ohio State.

Ryan did a similar thing psychologically with the 2024 team. It's great to have a motivated team. The qualities of motivation are love, fear, and hate. Fear and hate are very powerful but unsustainable. What's even better than a motivated team is an inspired team. An inspired team is about ownership and love. If you get ownership and love, that team usually doesn't lose. If they do, it's just because they ran out of time. Ohio State was an inspired team in those four College Football Playoff games. It was a master class in psychology. It became an us-against-the-world, one-game-at-a-time mentality. There's nothing greater than coaching a pissed-off team. They were a pissed-off team with a mission, and it was great to watch. I was very proud. I'm a Buckeye, and when I see Buckeye Nation celebrating, it's a great thing.

Long live the brotherhood.

—Urban Meyer

Prologue

Scarlet-and-gray confetti covered the turf at Mercedes-Benz Stadium in Atlanta on January 20, 2025.

The scoreboard showed the final score of the 2024 College Football Playoff championship game: Ohio State 34, Notre Dame 23.

Ten long years had passed since the Buckeyes' last national title. They'd had so many heartbreaking near-misses in the intervening decade, half under Urban Meyer and half under Ryan Day.

But Meyer had won two national championships at Florida before arriving in Columbus. He won his Buckeye title in his third year at Ohio State. He didn't have the external pressure his successor did. Day entered the playoff with a 66–10 record in six seasons. That .868 winning percentage was higher than any coach in major-college football history except Knute Rockne. Yet the 45-year-old Day had become known more for OSU's failures than successes, especially the four straight losses to archrival Michigan that caused much of the fan base to turn on him.

Now, his clothes soaked from a Gatorade dousing, Day basked in the moment. So many emotions swirled in him. Joy. Pride. But mostly relief. Not as much for himself but for those around him. For his players, so many of whom had delayed going to the NFL to have one last chance at college glory. For his coaches and all the support staff that make a behemoth such as Ohio State function smoothly. And probably most of all, for his family. His wife, Nina, and children RJ, Grace, and Nia had bounced around the country for years as Day climbed the coaching ladder. They experienced the highs and lows while having no control over them. The vitriol they faced following an inexplicable loss to Michigan less than two months earlier had them ready to leave Columbus.

After Day conducted a postgame television interview, he finally got the moment he sought his whole career. His family approached and gave him an emotional embrace. "You did it! You did it! You did it!" Nina told him. Day replied, "We did it!" He knew only some of the cruelty they'd been subjected to, but he knew enough. This was not his victory alone.

In the joyous locker room, the thick smell of tobacco from victory cigars wafted in the air. The mantra for the season had been "Leave no doubt." After losing two games, the Buckeyes had plenty of doubters. But in their playoff run in the new 12-team bracket, they outscored four opponents 145–75. They had played the toughest possible opponent in every round and vanquished them all. Ohio State became the first team in history to defeat five Top 5 teams in one season. Day began training camp by telling his team that they had to build a foundation for success brick by brick, and they actually built a brick pyramid with cinder blocks outside the Woody Hayes Athletic Center. Now he had the final piece, a gold-covered one that he held above his head.

He had come to love these players. The seniors were his first recruiting class and had sweated and bled and cried as each previous season fell short of their goals. Their primary motivation during each round of the playoff was to win so they could play together again. They had not beaten Michigan. They had not won a Big Ten championship. This CFP was all they had. It was all or nothing. Day told his players throughout the playoff that they had an inspirational story to tell, but no one would care to listen unless they won it all. Now they had.

One thing he did not share with his players was that this date—January 20—had special significance to him. He had tried to put the anniversary of that painful date out of his mind as much as he could. But certain things are impossible to forget.

1

Motivated by Tragedy

All that remains are a few snapshots, both photographic and mental.

Ryan Day was eight years old on a rainy, foggy January 20, 1988, in Manchester, New Hampshire. People didn't talk much afterward about what happened. Such was the stigma then about suicide. Only as an adult did Day understand that his father had a mental illness that caused him to take his own life at the age of 31.

Ray Day owned and managed two 7-Eleven convenience stores. He and his wife, Lisa, were high school sweethearts. They had Ryan when Lisa was 21. Chris and Tim followed, two and four years later. Ryan said his dad was a good athlete. He remembers playing ball with him and his dad watching his T-ball games. He recalls that his dad had a lot of friends.

And then one day the police came to their house with the horrible news. "It was a shock to everybody," Day said, "and it was one of those things that nobody saw coming. That was one of the hardest parts of it all. There was just a range of emotions after—confusion, anger. Just a range of emotions."

It would take many years for Day to process his father's death. It wasn't discussed inside the home. It was just a deep, unspoken void. Ray Day didn't leave a note, so the reason he took his life remained a mystery. Chris Day became a police detective. He read the police report about his father's suicide. All it consisted of was one paragraph and some photos.

"Over the years," Chris Day said, "you're like, 'Why did this happen? Why did he do it? Why would he do it to the family? Was there something wrong?' You have all these questions, and you still do to this day."

What Ryan did understand quickly was that he was now the man of the house at 96 Bayberry Lane and had to act like it. His mom, he said, was devoted to her sons and would do anything for them. But she worked to support the family and therefore was gone a lot. That left it up to Ryan to provide guidance and often discipline to Chris and Tim.

Having to deal with such a tragedy could leave a young boy angry, bitter, and adrift. It could also make him more determined and mature because he had no choice. "I think I experienced all those things," Day said.

He got into fights daily, he said. He'd see kids with their fathers and resent that his was gone. Day wasn't isolated and didn't lack a support system. He was particularly close to his maternal grandparents, Joan and Paul McGaunn. Lisa was one of their five kids, and their house was the gathering spot for dinner every Sunday for about 20 relatives. His grandfather had New England Patriots season tickets. The Day brothers took turns going with him to games. Paul McGaunn worked in the hotel industry, eventually becoming senior vice president for Omni Hotels, and retired early. The McGaunn house was across the street from the brothers' Webster Elementary School. The Day boys would often have lunch with their grandparents.

"He preached family and really had to step into that [father] role when I lost my dad," Day said of his grandfather.

Manchester was a close-knit community, a New England city of 100,000 where many had roots there for generations. Day's ancestors came from Ireland. They settled first in Lowell, Massachusetts, and then moved north to Manchester. When Ryan was growing up, it was a city in transition. Its economy had been built around textile mills, but by then the mills were closing. Federal regulators shut down four banks in town. But Manchester wasn't as decimated economically as badly as some other northeastern cities. It was a popular destination for people moving north from Massachusetts, attractive in part because New Hampshire doesn't have sales tax.

Sports were a big part of life in Manchester, and for young Ryan Day it became his salvation after his dad's death. Day was a good student who took advanced honors classes, but sports became his passion. He was naturally a competitive kid. Now a fire had been lit.

"You would almost have to compartmentalize," Day said. "I'm going to go on the field and I'm going to play, and then I'll come back and deal with [life]. Sometimes when you're going through a tragedy at a young age, you learn to compartmentalize. That's how I dealt with it at a young age."

He felt a need to prove doubters wrong, and supporters correct. "It kind of burns deep," he said. "I don't think I'd think I'd be where I'm at now if that [suicide] didn't happen, if that makes sense."

His anger was close to the surface when he played. He argued with officials. In baseball, he threw bats and his cap. Losing was intolerable to him, something that has never changed. In the summer, his mom would take Day and his brothers to Sudden Pitch, a local sports complex. Their games were intense. Bloody noses and broken teeth and general mayhem were commonplace.

"My brother Tim barely has any teeth left because they were all knocked by Ryan or me just playing sports," Chris Day said. "It was hard love. But it was all lessons learned through sports. During those tough times, it was Ryan stepping in and being like, 'Hey, the only thing we have right now is sports.'"

Lisa Day bought summer passes for the boys to play golf cheaply at Derryfield Country Club, which, contrary to its name, is a city-owned public course. She dropped them off in the morning and the boys would play 36 holes.

Sports were also where Day found male role models. Day would play whatever organized sports were in season—basketball in the winter, baseball in the summer and football in the fall. "There were a lot of great coaches," Day said. "It was great to have that support system in place when I lost my father. I was able to choose the best attributes in each of those coaches. Obviously, it was tragic losing my father, but that was the silver lining."

Sean McDonnell taught and coached in the Manchester public schools before becoming the University of New Hampshire football coach. He grew up in upstate New York and was amazed by how much Manchester cared about sports.

"I coached football, basketball, and softball in the city for five years," McDonnell said. "The one thing I always tell people is that there was an unbelievable culture in the city of Manchester. For one, high school athletics. And two, Little League, Babe Ruth, Pop Warner, CYO basketball. Manchester was unique. Some of the best coaches I met in that city coached in Babe Ruth baseball and Pop Warner football."

Day's future mentor Chip Kelly, who grew up in Manchester, said that so much of life in the city revolved around sports. "It was awesome because it was just a sports town and we had so many coaches in youth sports—youth football, youth basketball, youth hockey, youth baseball," he said. "Everything seemed intertwined in that town and that led into your high school career. There was nothing better than playing for your high school in whatever sport it was."

PERHAPS MANCHESTER'S MOST prominent coach was Stan Spirou, the men's basketball coach of New Hampshire College (now Southern New Hampshire University). New Hampshire College was a Division II school, but it was the big game in town. Spirou was born in Greece and came to the U.S. at age nine. He got bullied because he knew no English.

Basketball saved him. He would take his ball and practice all day at a local park. He got good fast. That earned him respect and acceptance.

Spirou earned a basketball scholarship to Keene State College and became the head coach at Manchester Central High School. After leading Central to two state titles in four years, he was hired by NHC. He had a record of 640–341 in 33 years and was inducted into the New England Basketball Hall of Fame. Day went to NHC games, attended Spirou's summer camp as a boy, and worked them as a teenager. In a city as small and close-knit as Manchester, word spread quickly about that Ryan Day kid.

"You would talk to people who were always saying how good he was, how smart he was, how competitive he was," Spirou said. "His athletic IQ was above and beyond."

The Spirous lived about a mile from the Days. They had three kids, a younger son, Chuck, and twin girls, Kelly and Christina, who were a year older than Ryan. Kelly couldn't pronounce her twin's name correctly when she was young. She called her Nina. The nickname stuck.

Two decades before they married, Nina and Ryan met when they were on the same T-ball team. Though Nina and her dad insist she was better than Ryan then—he vehemently disagrees—what she remembers was his focus even at six years old.

"I was picking dandelions in right field, and he yelled at me," she said with a laugh.

That intensity would become Day's hallmark. He was an excellent athlete, though his brother Tim was more gifted. (Tim would play quarterback at the University of Massachusetts.) But to Ryan, sports wasn't just about playing. It was about competing and winning. "I was probably a year or two ahead of the people I was playing against in terms of anticipation, understanding the game, competitiveness, work ethic," he said. "I played the game really hard."

Day played positions at the center of the action. He was a catcher in baseball, a guard in basketball, and of course, a quarterback in football.

He became a quarterback by accident, though. He was a tight end and kicker in Pop Warner football. One game, he was set to kick an extra point when the snap went over the holder. Day picked up the ball, scrambled, and threw to a teammate in the back of the end zone for a two-point conversion.

"The next week I was quarterback and never played another position again," he said.

Day was a three-sport star at Manchester Central High School. He led the basketball team to the state semifinal. "Ryan was probably the hardest practice player I've ever seen," said Mike Fitzpatrick, then Central's basketball coach. "Our practices were very physical, primarily because of Ryan and guys competing with him. He was wired to play hard, whether it was practice or game, big game or small game."

Day's three-point shot at the buzzer rimmed out in a one-point loss to heavily favored Concord, which had future NBA player Matt Bonner. "Ryan made so many big shots over the three seasons he played for us that I thought for sure that was going in, and it almost did," Fitzpatrick said.

Day led Central to the state football title as a junior and was named New Hampshire's Gatorade Player of the Year as a senior after breaking numerous state passing records. But at just a shade over six feet, Day wasn't a blue-chip college prospect. His academic excellence earned him offers from Ivy League schools.

The University of New Hampshire, located in Durham 35 miles from Manchester, also recruited Day. McDonnell recalls coaching him at a camp in Londonderry and being amazed at how quickly Day learned new plays and could direct teammates—some from other high schools—on the field.

"I was very impressed with his presence and his understanding of the passing game," McDonnell said. "The other thing that jumped out at me was his leadership skills. He had that ability to have people magnetized to him and gravitate toward him. More importantly, he was able to lead them, and they believed in him. It was pretty cool."

Day was leaning toward going to one of the Ivy League schools until a phone call from Chip Kelly, then an up-and-coming UNH assistant coach. Kelly attended Manchester Central 15 years before Day. He knew Day well enough to appeal to his competitive spirit. The Ivy League then played only a regular season, lest a postseason interfere with academics. Kelly called Day at Central one day. Day answered it on the pay phone in the school cafeteria. Why would you want to play for a team, Kelly asked, that can't compete for a national title? "When you're in recruiting," Kelly said, "you've got to know what buttons to push," Kelly said. "I certainly knew what buttons to push in him because he's such a competitor." Day became a New Hampshire Wildcat.

NEW HAMPSHIRE WAS a middling Division I-AA (now Football Championship Subdivision) program when Day arrived. He was on a partial academic scholarship, not a football one. His career did not start well. He was buried on the depth chart and struggling with a stress fracture in his back that required him to wear a brace. One day in practice, McDonnell had the quarterbacks throw deep balls. Day had trouble cutting loose. He ripped off the back brace and threw with all he had. The pass bounced to the receiver.

"It was really embarrassing because I was so mad," he said. "I'm like, 'It can't get any worse than this.'"

Day had to learn patience as he grinded through six months of rehab and got in better shape by losing weight. Still, he wondered whether he was good enough to play for UNH and asked McDonnell that question. McDonnell reassured him that he wouldn't have recruited him otherwise. That was all Day needed to hear. Day competed with another quarterback who McDonnell said was probably more talented. But it was obvious who had taken command of the job.

"My wife saw him at our final scrimmage before we named him the starter," McDonnell said. "She said, 'I don't know anything about throwing and catching, but the team likes that No. 12 [Day] a lot better than the other kid.' She was right."

Day started for three years. Kelly was the offensive coordinator, and he was like a mad scientist at times. He adapted the scheme each week based on the opponent. One week, Kelly might use a Wing-T. The next, he might use a spread offense with five receivers. Against UMass as a junior, Day threw only seven times (though Kelly said it was because Day had a sore shoulder). The next week, he threw 65 passes, which still stands as a school record. That came in the highlight of Day's career. UNH trailed No. 2 Delaware 31–3 late in the third quarter when the Wildcats began their comeback. Kelly dialed up a trick play for a touchdown on fourth-and-19 to send the game to overtime. Day threw a touchdown pass to complete a 45–44 win.

"It was a wild game, a great atmosphere," Day said. "For us, over 20,000 fans was a big game. That was a big deal at the time."

Day's career did not end in a blaze of glory. UNH was 4–7 in his senior season and lost its last five games. The final game came in a 57–24 loss to Maine. Day threw for two scores to set a school record for career touchdown passes, but that was little consolation. Day knew he wasn't an NFL prospect. He realized his playing career was over.

"I remember being in my locker just sobbing," he said. "This is it. I'm never going to be able to play again in my life."

2

Climbing the Coaching Ladder

Even before he played a snap for the University of New Hampshire, Ryan Day knew he wanted to become a coach. Leadership came naturally. People had always told him coaching would be a good fit. Day told Chip Kelly that was his preferred path. Even as a bench-warming freshman at UNH, he spent hours in the football facility watching extra video and learning how coaches put together game plans.

"My GPA wasn't very good in the fall," Day said. "It was much better in the spring. But the best way to learn to become a coach is through apprenticeship, right?"

McDonnell had a major influence on Day. "He taught me about hard work and perseverance and toughness and grit," Day said.

UNH coaches were encouraging to Day about a coaching career, but they didn't sugarcoat it. They told him coaches didn't lead normal lives. Forget about hanging out at the neighborhood bar or a casual Tuesday night at the movies with a wife. To succeed would require long hours and plenty of sacrifice. He'd likely have to move repeatedly to climb the coaching ladder.

Day was undaunted.

"I remember waking up one day and said, 'That's it. I'm doing it,'" he recalled.

DAY CONSIDERS HIMSELF exceedingly fortunate to have found a wife who understands the sacrifice required for such a career. Their shared T-ball experience was the start of a friendship between Ryan and Nina. The Spirous were among the families in the Days' circle of friends. Chris Day and Chuck Spirou were best friends. Stan and Ryan shared a March 12 birthday. Every year, Ryan would go to the Spirou house and deliver a card to Stan. Ryan was friends with both twins but eventually became closer with Nina as they attended Webster Elementary, Hillside Junior High, and Manchester Central High School together.

"In eighth grade, I wrote a note to my sister telling her that I was going to marry him," Nina said. "Though we were just friends, we connected and always have. I can honestly say to this day that he was my best friend my whole life. Whenever anything went wrong in my life, I would go to him—even if I had a boyfriend, even if he had a girlfriend."

But they were not romantic until later. When Nina's boyfriend broke up with her shortly before her junior prom, Day took her as a friend. Nina played basketball at St. Michael's College in Vermont before transferring to UNH, though not because of Day. They were close friends in college and dated on and off, but Ryan was preoccupied with football and, well, was a college student who liked to have a good time.

"He got a lot out of his system, thank goodness," Nina said with a laugh.

Both Nina and Ryan sensed that they would end up together. "We were always great friends," Ryan said. "I always wanted to marry a good friend, someone you enjoyed being around."

Friendship eventually turned into romance. He loved her compassion, her loyalty, her love for her family, her sense of humor. He knew she'd be a great mom. "I liked her and then learned to love her as a friend and then love her as a wife," Ryan said.

They wouldn't marry right away. After Nina graduated, she took an advertising job in Boston and stayed there for two years. She was offered a job in Chicago and was tempted to take it. Ryan asked her to meet him in Manchester and pleaded with her not to go to Chicago and instead to give a serious relationship between them a chance. She agreed. She stayed in Boston. They've been a couple ever since.

Day's first coaching job was as a graduate assistant at his alma mater coaching tight ends. After a two-month stay at the University of Massachusetts, Day was hired as a GA at Boston College. Head coach Tom O'Brien was one of three Cincinnati natives on the staff along with Dana Bible and Don Horton. Another Ohioan, Jim Bridges, was from Cleveland.

As a GA, Day was low man on the totem pole, but he tried to make his mark. He did so in Boston College's final game in 2004. BC played North Carolina in the Continental Tire Bowl. BC led 27–24 in the fourth quarter. The Eagles' kicker had missed an extra point earlier in the game and was about to attempt a field goal. Day approached O'Brien, a tough former Marine, and suggested a fake field goal.

"I had a lot of balls to go to him and say that," Day said. "He kind of shook his head and walked away, and I'm like, 'Okay, that didn't go very well.' All of a sudden, I can see him thinking, and he walks back and says, 'We're going to fake the field goal.' I walk down and am like, 'Oh man, if this doesn't work…'" But it did work. BC's kicker ran 21 yards for a touchdown and the Eagles won 37–24 to cap a 9–3 season. Day appreciated that O'Brien credited Day afterward with the suggestion of the fake.

Boston College's likely bowl destination that season had been the Fiesta Bowl until a late loss to Syracuse. BC's opponent would have been

Utah, coached by Urban Meyer. Meyer's quarterbacks coach was Dan Mullen, who happened to be a Manchester native. Day had reached out to Mullen late in the season about joining Meyer's staff. Utah finished its undefeated season by winning the Fiesta Bowl, and Meyer was hired by Florida. Soon after, Mullen called Day asking if he'd be interested in coming as a GA. Day didn't hesitate to even learn details about the job before agreeing to take it.

"I literally just said, 'Yes,'" he said.

He called Nina, then his fiancée, and they rented a U-Haul and drove from Boston to Gainesville. That was not an easy year. Ryan and Nina took off work for one day to get married, but there was no time for a honeymoon. "We got married on a Saturday night and we had to be back in Gainesville by 10 o'clock in the morning," Nina said. "That's when I realized this profession is no joke."

Day got to work on time that Sunday. Florida was hosting a high school camp, and Meyer rode over in his golf cart. "He said, 'Why have you been gone so long?'" Day recalled with a laugh.

Back then, programs were limited to one GA on offense and one on defense. "Can you imagine?" said Ohio State strength coach Mickey Marotti, who was then with Meyer at Florida. "I just remember [Day] running around all over the place. He's a hard-ass worker, and the kids respected him. He ran scout team in practice."

Ryan Stamper was one of those scout team players. He would go on to join Meyer's staff at Ohio State before moving to the Jacksonville Jaguars, for whom he's a national scout. "What stood out to me was that he was really smart," Stamper said. "I was a young freshman, but I could tell he had a brilliant mind. Just like now, he was always a good dude. He never really screamed when we messed up and always kept his composure."

Meyer considers Mullen one of the brightest offensive minds with whom he's worked. They installed the spread offense at Florida, and Meyer was impressed that his young grad assistant wasn't out of his depth. "When you talk to high, high-IQ football people, you remember it,"

Meyer said. "And I remember Ryan was right there and his opinion was valued, even as a graduate assistant back then."

There were times Day wondered if Meyer even remembered who he was but believed he made an impression. That was his goal. As he ascended in coaching, he advised young coaches to work so hard that they leave a hole when they leave.

But the workload left little time for a personal life. Nina recalls calling her twin, Kelly, and her parents daily crying, questioning why she agreed to become a coach's wife. Grad assistants made next to nothing. Nina worked at a hospice, but the job didn't pay much. She said her parents had to support them financially, which continued for the first five years of their marriage.

"They bought us groceries, gave me gas money," Nina said. "They literally gave us the shirts off their backs so that we could survive."

The workload made Day question his chosen profession. "I worked a year there, and there was a point where I wanted to quit," Ryan said. "That was a brutal year. That was a tough, tough year."

But it ended well. Day got a call from new Temple head coach Al Golden to interview for the wide receivers coach job. "Ryan comes on his interview, and basically everything he owned was in a duffel bag," Golden said.

Golden offered him the job. A plum one, it was not. Temple went 0–11 in 2005, which was par for the course for the Owls.

"I remember going into Urban's office and saying I have an opportunity to be the wide receivers coach, a full-time job, at Temple," Day said. "And in only the way he could, he says, 'Oh, that's an awful job. But you've got to go.' He wasn't going to sugarcoat it."

FOR THE NEXT eight years, Day went back and forth between Temple and Boston College, with two stints at each as he gained responsibility and became an offensive coordinator under Steve Addazio, who coached under Meyer at Florida. During that time, Ryan and Nina had their three children—first RJ, then Grace and Nia, all two years apart. The longest period at one place was at BC from 2007–11 as wide receivers coach. The Days' Boston-Philadelphia shuttle was almost interrupted in 2009. Chip Kelly was the Oregon coach and revolutionizing college football with an ultra-fast-tempo offense that left defenses exhausted. Kelly offered Day the quarterback coach/offensive coordinator job, and he had all but accepted it. At Day's grandfather's birthday party, the cake was decorated with Oregon's green-and-yellow colors. But RJ was only one year old, and the idea of moving across the country and away from family and friends gave Ryan and Nina second thoughts. He turned down the job.

"I remember [Chip's] answer," Day said. "He said, 'That's why I love you. I understand why.'"

Instead, Kelly hired Mark Helfrich, who coached against Ohio State in the 2015 CFP championship game. Ponder that possible alternate history in which Day is on the opposite sideline in that game. "It would have been a different path," Day said. "That's for sure."

The next time Kelly offered Day a job, though, he took it. Kelly was the Philadelphia Eagles' coach in 2015, and he hired Day as his quarterbacks coach. Kelly was in his third season in Philadelphia. It would be his last. The Eagles traded or cut several key starters before the season. New quarterback Sam Bradford was inconsistent and suffered a season-ending injury in Week 10. The season went south. Kelly was fired with one game left in the season with the Eagles at 6–9.

"Nina and the kids found out on the TV," Day said. "I wasn't even able to tell them [first]. I remember walking around with Nina, and we were just trying to figure it out. What are we going to do next?"

Even though Day said the Eagles offered to honor his contract and keep him, when Kelly was hired by the San Francisco 49ers, Day agreed to rejoin him. The 2016 season was a disaster. The 49ers went 2–14. They won their opener against the Los Angeles Rams and then lost their next 13 games before beating the Rams again. The 49ers' quarterback was

Colin Kaepernick, who became a national lightning rod for his decision to kneel during the National Anthem as a protest against racism.

Kelly again was fired, and Day was without a job. The Day family was at a crossroads. By Nina's count, she had moved 11 times in 15 years. They craved stability. RJ told his dad he was tired of always being the new kid in school. RJ wanted to go to a place where his family could stick around for more than a year or two.

"We grew up in a town where nobody moved," Day said. "If you move down to Boston, it's like on the other side of the world."

Now they were across the country in limbo. "Nina is a twin," Day said. "She comes from a big Greek family. They're very, very close, so there was a lot of sacrifice there."

When Ryan got a new job, Nina would have to stay with the kids until they could sell the house and buy a new one. "When you do that for back-to-back years, that can wear on the family because there's so much time when you're not with them," Day said. "You're not there for dinners. You're not there for a lot of stuff. It doesn't seem like much, but before you know it, it can get away from you fast."

Ryan and Nina had always been a team and made decisions together. "I don't think Nina always felt, especially early on, like she had a lot of say, but she did, and it was frustrating," Day said. "It was difficult. There were days we looked at each other like, 'What are we actually doing? Does this make sense for us and where we want to be?' You can find yourself lost at times, lost in the washing machine of football, like, 'Where am I going next? What is our home base? Where is our support system? Who are your friends?' because you're moving all across the globe."

That stress can make a marriage closer or cause it to fray. Ryan said it made his tighter because they knew they had to rely on each other.

Ohio State was in the College Football Playoff that year. The Buckeyes faced Clemson in one semifinal while Alabama played Washington in the other. RJ told his dad, as only an eight-year-old can, he had to get a job at one of those schools. If only it were that simple.

But Ohio State's game was a disaster. The Buckeyes lost 31–0, the only shutout in Meyer's coaching career. Afterward, he vowed changes. Meyer had already touched base with Day before the CFP because Meyer was concerned about the offense under coordinator Ed Warinner. Day considered that phone call just a backup plan for Meyer in case the game didn't go well. As the game unfolded, Day turned to Nina and said their next stop was likely to be Ohio State. Meyer indeed targeted Day. He'd kept tabs on Day's career when he coached under Addazio at Temple and Boston College. Meyer visited the Eagles when former Heisman Trophy winner Tim Tebow was briefly coached by Day in Philadelphia and sat in meetings.

"In a roundabout way, I stayed very close with what he was doing because I had a lot of respect for him as a young coach," Meyer said. "I wanted to hire someone I knew and someone who knew the style I wanted to play in offensively," Meyer said. "Ryan was with people who were like-minded. He knew Dan Mullen. He worked with Steve Addazio. I was very close with Chip [Kelly]."

Sure enough, Meyer hired Day and former Indiana coach Kevin Wilson to revamp the Buckeyes' offense. "He was excited," Meyer said. "He wanted to go win. Losing eats away at your soul. They had two tough years [in the NFL], and he was ready to go win."

It wasn't just the two years in the NFL that were tough. Since Day became a full-time assistant coach in 2006, his teams had a combined record of 67–80. He was headed to a place where winning was a little more demanded.

3

Welcome to Ohio State

Ryan Day had never been to Columbus before coming to Ohio State in 2017. He had gone to Cleveland and Cincinnati on recruiting trips as an assistant coach but hadn't stepped foot in the state capital.

For several months, he would be on his own. Nina remained in California to prepare for moving. Before settling in Columbus, Nina flew with RJ, Grace, and Nia to see her family. She remembers the kids screaming the whole flight to Boston. When they landed and saw her parents, the stress of the flight and another new beginning came flooding out.

"I was just bawling my eyes out," Nina said.

Ohio State's second game that season didn't reassure the Days about their decision to come. That was the infamous game in which Oklahoma quarterback Baker Mayfield, the eventual Heisman Trophy winner, dissected No. 2 Ohio State in a 31–16 win and then planted the OU flag in the Block O at midfield of Ohio Stadium. Day remembers more that Ohio State's offense scored only three points in the first half and one touchdown total.

"A low point," Day said. "It took a while to get myself out of that one because you start to question yourself a little bit. As a dad and a husband, it's like, 'What are we doing as a family right now?' Things just don't seem to be going well for us. You get yourself up off the ground and you move forward. But that was a tough loss because we played poorly on offense."

That was the first time that RJ Day, then nine years old, understood how unacceptable losing was in Columbus. He heard negative comments from teachers and classmates at school.

"I was in fourth grade, and just seeing the fans' reaction to a loss, I'd never seen that," he said. "We were 2–14 with the 49ers and 7–9 with the Philadelphia Eagles. Losing to me was just another thing until I got here. You realize this is not normal. Even in Philly, those fans get kind of crazy, but it was nothing like these guys."

A big comeback win over Penn State was followed by a blowout loss at Iowa, knocking the Buckeyes out of College Football Playoff contention. Day's introduction to the Michigan rivalry was an odd one. "I remember everyone saying, 'Well, this game is different,'" Day said.

Just before kickoff, quarterback J.T. Barrett's knee was injured when it was hit by a camera. The culprit was never identified. Meyer was livid. Barrett gutted it out into the second half before giving way to redshirt freshman Dwayne Haskins Jr. Joe Burrow and Haskins competed to be Barrett's backup that year, a battle that ended when Burrow broke a bone in his hand during training camp. Against Illinois the week before the Michigan game, Haskins fumbled when sacked during the second half of the game, a blowout played in a rainstorm. Day reamed him out for his lack of ball security. Haskins was temporarily benched.

"We challenged Dwayne, like 'You've got to grow up,'" Day said.

Haskins returned and led OSU to a touchdown against the Illini, which gave him and his coaches more confidence when he had to replace Barrett in Ann Arbor. He led Ohio State to a 31–20 comeback win. The Buckeyes then defeated Wisconsin in the Big Ten championship game behind Barrett, who played six days after arthroscopic knee surgery. Ohio State finished its season with a victory over USC in the Cotton Bowl.

THE NEXT SPRING was an eventful one at quarterback. Barrett had finally graduated after a career that seemed to last a decade. Thanks to his performance in the comeback win over Michigan, Haskins entered March with a leg up on Burrow, but Day was enamored with both.

"Dwayne at that time was much further along as a passer, but man, Joe had something about him," Day said. "If you were just watching practice, you said it wasn't that close at the time. Dwayne was better. But Joe had this fire in him. There's competitiveness in him. The guys loved him. If you were going to do a tire pull in mat drills, you weren't beating Joe Burrow. And he was very intelligent. I absolutely loved him. It killed him to leave. He was in tears."

But Burrow hadn't overtaken Haskins in the spring. He'd spent two years as a backup and had already earned his degree. That allowed him to transfer and be instantly eligible in that pre-transfer portal era. (A non-graduate would have had to sit out a year.) Burrow transferred to LSU. He did okay in Baton Rouge.

Burrow's departure saddened Day, but it had removed the biggest potential drama he'd face as summer approached. Or so he thought. In July, news broke about domestic abuse allegations against wide receivers coach Zach Smith by his estranged wife, Courtney. One of the major questions was the extent to which Urban Meyer knew about the allegations and actions he took, or didn't, as a result. Smith is the grandson of Earle Bruce, who was OSU's coach when Meyer was a graduate assistant. Meyer revered him as a mentor and hired Smith after becoming coach in late 2011. Meyer later admitted giving Smith too much of the benefit of the doubt because of his relationship with Bruce.

On August 1, three days before the start of training camp, Ohio State placed Meyer on paid administrative leave. Athletics director Gene Smith needed to name an acting coach. He had several obvious candidates.

Defensive coordinator Greg Schiano had done the nearly impossible by turning around a moribund Rutgers program before a failed head coaching stint with the Tampa Bay Buccaneers. Wilson had been Indiana's head coach for six seasons.

It was a stunner when Smith chose Day to fill in for Meyer. "He had no dirty laundry," Smith explained.

Schiano had been on the verge of becoming the Tennessee coach in November 2017, even signing a memorandum of understanding. But a vocal segment of the Volunteers' fan base and even some Tennessee politicians protested. They used as a reason—or excuse—an alleged link between Schiano and the Jerry Sandusky sexual-abuse scandal at Penn State. Schiano had been a Nittany Lions assistant but denied knowing about the abuse. No evidence ever surfaced indicating knowledge, but that didn't stop the protests, and Tennessee pulled out of the deal with Schiano.

"There was nothing, but still [there was] the perception," Smith said.

Wilson's time at IU ended amid allegations of insensitive treatment toward injured players. In Smith's mind, he needed someone to fill in who was squeaky clean. Day was, in part because he was a virtual unknown to most people outside of the Woody Hayes Athletic Center.

But Smith had already become impressed by Day's intelligence—both intellectual and emotional—and by how quickly he'd developed a rapport with OSU players.

"He established a relationship with the players that was phenomenal," Smith said. "I felt at the time that we've got to hold this team together. That was a critical time. Things could fall apart because the head coach is not there on a daily basis. This was preseason camp, and it's a hard part of the season.

"I knew he had a great support staff with our trainers and strength coaches and everyone else around them. But I needed a guy who was relational, and I felt he was the best one of them all. Not to say Kevin or Greg were not, but they had some dirty laundry."

Day was as surprised as anyone else to be chosen. He had been summoned to Smith's office along with Schiano and Wilson and esteemed defensive line coach Larry Johnson, whom Smith had also considered. Day said that when Smith told them that Meyer would "just step away for a little while" and named him acting coach, he looked around like, "He's picking me?' It kind of caught me off guard."

Nina was shopping at Kohl's with her kids trying to stuff her daughter Nia's foot into a sandal when her phone started blowing up. "What in the heck is going on?" she thought. Ryan hadn't even had a chance to call her when the news broke. She hurried the kids to the car and heard it about it on the radio.

"When he finally called me, I was like, 'Not to be mean, but why you?'" Nina recalled with a laugh. "It was just confusing and exciting. No one even knows who he is. I remember people saying, 'Who the heck is Ryan Day?'"

Day had no time to worry about that. When training camp started, he said, he took it minute by minute, just trying to put one foot in front of the other. He leaned on strength coach Mickey Marotti, who really served as a de facto head coach in the offseason. He relied on the assistants.

"I've got to give Greg Schiano, Kevin Wilson, and Larry so much credit because they never flinched," Day said. "It was very easy for them to say, 'Well, why not me?' And they helped in a big way. They were extremely helpful in getting that up and running."

TRAINING CAMP ENSUED with no quick resolution regarding Meyer's status. Finally, after a marathon day of deliberations by the school's board of trustees on August 22, Ohio State suspended Meyer—and Smith—for the first three weeks of the football season.

Day, who had never been a head coach, had been thrust into that role. The first two games were breezes. The No. 5 Buckeyes routed Oregon State 77–31 in the opener and then drubbed Rutgers 52–3. Next up was No. 15 TCU. Though technically a neutral-site game at the Dallas Cowboys' AT&T Stadium in Arlington, Texas, this was really a road game.

Day understood how pivotal that game was, not only for OSU's season, but his career. He had no idea at that point that Meyer would step down at the end of the season. He did recognize this was his one chance for a signature win. Get it, and he might be deemed a rising star. Lose, and he might not get another chance.

The game went back and forth. Ohio State got two defensive touchdowns to take a 26–21 lead late in the third quarter. As the Buckeyes got ready to kick off, several OSU players ran to Day, pointing out that a TCU player was on his back deep in the end zone. Day's first thought was that someone had shot the player. Instead, it was a fake that the Horned Frogs almost pulled off. The kickoff went to the left and that returner started upfield before throwing the ball to the player who'd been playing possum. He caught it and ran to the end zone. But the pass had gone a few yards forward and wasn't a legal lateral. The score was nullified, and Ohio State pulled away for a 40–28 victory.

"If they don't call that flag, if that doesn't happen, I don't know what happens in that game," Day said.

Meyer returned the next week and coached the rest of the season. A disastrous 49–20 loss to Purdue, the only loss that season, derailed OSU's chance to make the playoff. Meyer, then 54, was in his seventh season as Ohio State coach. He was weighing stepping down and told Smith that. "I'm not built for longevity," Meyer said, "and 55 is kind of the time I wanted to move on."

Meyer is friends with Oklahoma's Bob Stoops and was impressed with how seamlessly the Sooners orchestrated their succession when Stoops retired and Lincoln Riley took over. That didn't require wholesale personnel changes. The program's infrastructure stayed intact. Meyer wanted Ohio State to follow that same path.

"I love Ohio State," Meyer said. "Ohio State's home. I would feel awful if all of a sudden that place started to go backwards. It's the best infrastructure in all of the sport, from the academics to the training room, weight room, and recruiting."

Both Meyer and Smith viewed Day as the obvious successor, though it was Smith's call. He had a list of outside candidates and talked to colleagues about them. But he said he didn't seriously consider any of them enough to warrant an interview. "I came to the conclusion that Ryan was the guy," Smith said.

Ohio State's program wasn't broken. The support staff with people like Marotti, recruiting head Mark Pantoni, and others was strong. A coach from outside might want to bring his own people and that would be needlessly disruptive. To Smith, Day had passed what served as a three-game audition to start the season "exceptionally well."

Day's more relaxed personality would be a nice change from Meyer, who believed making people uncomfortable was a necessary safeguard against complacency. But working every day like it was fourth-and-1 was exhausting. People inside the Woody needed to be able to catch their breath. Meyer was respected, not beloved. Day was well-liked. When Smith is in his hiring process, he ignores a candidate's references. Instead, he talks to those who interact with the candidate on the job. He wants to know if an equipment manager felt valued or demeaned by the candidate.

"The thing I loved about Ryan in that regard was his empathy, his respect for people," Smith said. "It was genuine."

Though Meyer was leaning toward stepping down, the decision was tentative until the night before the press conference. Meyer called Day at his home to tell him his decision was final. The Day kids were still small enough to all fit on their parents' bed.

"Ryan was like, 'Are you sure, coach?'" Nina recalled. "He was almost like trying to get him not to do it."

But Meyer was sure. Then Smith called Day to formally offer him the job.

"[Ryan] gets off the phone and I'm crying because I know from that moment on, our life was never going to be the same," Nina recalled. "I was overwhelmed by it all. I couldn't believe it. The kids were excited. "We had no idea what we were getting ourselves into."

4

A Special Recruiting Class

The first recruit to commit to Ohio State under Ryan Day was a local kid. Jack Sawyer wanted to be a Buckeye as long as he could remember. He grew up in the Columbus suburb of Pickerington, about 20 miles east of Ohio State's campus. His mom, Michelle, painted young Jack's bedroom scarlet on top and gray on the bottom with an Ohio State banner in the middle. Jack came out of the womb seemingly smiling. When he was a toddler, he'd greet everybody in his neighborhood with a wave and a grin. Everyone started calling him "Happy Jack."

"Still to this day," Sawyer said, "I think if I saw some of those neighbors, they'd be like, 'Happy Jack! How's it going?'"

His parents were athletes, and it was clear that Sawyer was gifted, too. Pickerington is known for producing way more talent than a suburb of 25,000 had any right to. Its youth sports programs were intense. Pickerington would also produce two other starters on the 2024 team—linebacker Sonny Styles and defensive tackle Ty Hamilton. Sawyer was in sixth grade when the 2014 Buckeyes made their improbable run to the first College Football Playoff title. All he and his classmates talked about were running back Ezekiel Elliott and quarterback Cardale Jones and all the stars on that team. One day, Sawyer thought, "That could be me."

It wasn't unrealistic. A defensive end, Sawyer became a starter at Pickerington North in his freshman season. Colleges began offering him scholarships that year. When Ohio State offered him one, it wasn't the joyous event Sawyer envisioned. Urban Meyer was not one to blow smoke, and he certainly didn't that day.

"He sat me down in his office and pretty much told me he doesn't know who the hell I am, but his coaching staff seems to think I could be a great player there," Sawyer said. "He almost offered me like he was mad he had to do it. I was 15 at the time, I think, and I'm like, 'Damn, this dude doesn't even want to offer me, but he feels obligated to. This is awkward.'"

Meyer told Sawyer he wanted him to return in a couple months and compete at OSU's summer camp. Sawyer trained seriously for the first time, and his performance showed.

"I crushed it," he said.

He said Meyer watched every rep that defensive line coach Larry Johnson ran. Whatever reservations Meyer had when he offered Sawyer the scholarship vanished. Sawyer came to like Meyer and his bluntness and looked forward to playing for him. But Day was involved in his recruitment as well. Sawyer and Nina bonded over their love of Swedish Fish.

When Meyer stepped down, Sawyer, just a sophomore, didn't waver. Being Day's first recruit was a point of pride to Sawyer, who would ascend to five-star status and become the ringleader in assembling OSU's 2021 recruiting class.

"I can remember long talks with TreVeyon [Henderson] and a lot of the guys," Sawyer said. "I know it's a cliché, but our class was super-tight. In our group chat, we were always joking, texting, and goofing around. It was cool to see that transfer into all of us committing and having that bond before we even stepped foot on campus. It felt like we'd all been friends for years."

A GENERATION AGO, Sawyer would have been one of many Ohioans in Ohio State's recruiting class. But demographic shifts in population have changed that. Only six of the 24 signees in the 2021 class were from Ohio. Sawyer was the only one who made a significant impact. Ohio State has recruited nationally for a long time. Several members of Woody Hayes' 1968 title team came from elsewhere. But Meyer accelerated the trend, and Day has continued it.

Ohio State's 2021 recruiting class came from 14 states. Wide receiver Emeka Egbuka and defensive end J.T. Tuimoloau are from the Seattle area. Running back TreVeyon Henderson and defensive tackle Tyleik Williams are from Virginia. Defensive back Jordan Hancock grew up in Georgia. Offensive lineman Donovan Jackson is from suburban Houston. Cornerback Denzel Burke is from Arizona. One recruit came from abroad. Punter Jesse Mirco, who transferred after the 2023 season, was another product from the ProKick academy in Australia. (The 2021 class also included brilliant receiver Marvin Harrison Jr. and 2023 starting quarterback Kyle McCord, who were teammates at St. Joseph's Prep in Philadelphia.)

Egbuka, whose father emigrated from Nigeria and became a civil engineer for the U.S. Defense Department, suggested that his son use a decision matrix to help make his decision. Emeka listed about 20 categories—academics, skill development, etc.—and ranked the top schools on his list. Ohio State prevailed.

Though Jackson is from Texas, his dad, Todd, is from Cleveland and his mom, Melanie, is from Cincinnati. Donovan remembers that in kindergarten all his classmates were Texas or Texas A&M fans. He asked his mom which one he was. She told him he was a Buckeye. She even carries around an actual buckeye in her purse. But Jackson's parents didn't pressure him to sign with Ohio State. He intended to stay in the South. Jackson's recruiting visit in 2019 changed his mind. He felt a sense of comfort at OSU he didn't find anywhere else. He committed the next day.

Hancock grew up in suburban Atlanta as a Buckeye fan because of OSU's history of producing NFL cornerbacks. "I just always loved Ohio State," he said. "The tradition, the Buckeye leaves—you won't find that anyplace else."

He was planning to commit to Ohio State in early 2020, but his mother, Benita, was diagnosed with breast cancer and required radiation treatment. Hancock decided he should stay closer to home. In March, he committed to Clemson, which is about 90 minutes away.

"He was actually the strongest person in the whole family when I was going through this," Benita said in 2023. "He was the main one that said, 'We can beat this.' He's such a competitor, and he brought that mentality, like, 'You may be down, but we're going to beat this.'"

Benita did beat it and was deemed cancer-free in May. With his mom healthy again, Hancock decided with his mother's blessing to decommit from Clemson and pledge to join Ohio State.

OHIO STATE'S 2021 class bonded under adverse circumstances. Because COVID-19 prevented on-campus official visits, recruits in that class had to get to know each other and OSU's coaches virtually through Facetime calls and a group text chain.

"That was crazy," Day said. "We spent all this time on Zoom, just constantly meeting with multiple guys on calls because that's all we had. There were a lot of guys who stepped on campus for the first time when they reported to the apartments [as freshmen]."

Ohio State also got some good fortune with that recruiting class, specifically with Williams. The Buckeyes were his second choice. Williams wanted to stay in the South and play for Alabama. But another lineman the Crimson Tide recruited, Tim Keenan, committed before Williams did. When Williams called Alabama to say he was ready to pledge, he was told it was too late. Williams was disappointed but not devastated. He had developed a good relationship with Johnson and trusted that the coach would develop him. A Buckeye he became.

Day recalled Williams telling him the week before the spring game in 2021 that he looked forward to being in the iconic Horseshoe for the first time. Day was startled by the comment until he realized that Williams hadn't had a chance to come to campus because of the pandemic.

Burke didn't even take an unofficial visit to Columbus. He said he hadn't met any of the other recruits in person until he enrolled. But he knew Ohio State's secondary billed itself as the best in the country—"BIA" (Best in America) is its motto—and that was enough for him. "I wanted to compete against the best, play at a very high level every week, and compete for a national championship," Burke said. "I prayed a lot and trusted in my faith that everything would work out how it did work out," Burke said.

Recruitment during COVID had plenty of hurdles, but it did have a benefit for OSU's recruits. "It opened the way to more communication solely because we couldn't go anywhere else," Jackson said. "Other schools tried to reach out to some of us, but we were so close-knit in our group chat and our coaches did such a great job recruiting everyone that we all knew we wanted to go to Ohio State. We wanted to play high-level football together."

The last piece of the recruiting puzzle was Tuimoloau. He was the No. 2 prospect nationally according to 247Sports. He was also a star basketball player, and he fit football recruiting visits around his AAU basketball schedule. As an elite prospect, he had leverage other recruits didn't. He and his family were determined to be thorough with the recruiting process. It dragged out so long that COVID-related restrictions were lifted enough for him to take an official visit to Ohio State in June 2021. Ohio State coaches wore Tommy Bahama Hawaiian shirts to the airport to greet the Tuimoloau family to show kinship with its Polynesian heritage. The Tuimoloaus took an early-morning flight and were groggy when they landed. When they saw OSU coaches, they were flattered by their garb, but they were so disheveled that they ducked into a bathroom to make themselves look more presentable.

"We thought it was pretty cool, especially knowing there weren't too many Polynesians on the team," Tuimoloau said. "It was actually a shock as well. They were the first team to actually greet me in the airport."

When he got to the Woody, he was impressed by how close OSU players seemed to be. He noticed that veteran players looked out for the young players. Playing for Day and Larry Johnson also appealed to him. "Having coach Day and coach J are in my opinion the greatest D-line and head coach duo. Having those two coaches there meant a lot. I felt they were going to help me become a better player and a better man."

Two weeks after his visit, Tuimoloau committed to Ohio State. Now all he and his fellow recruits had to do was live up to the hype and bring home a championship. That would take longer than any of them imagined.

5

Success...and Heartbreak

Meyer's final game was Ohio State's 28–23 Rose Bowl win over Washington on January 1, 2019. In the locker room, Meyer took a whistle from around his neck and put it around Day's in a ceremonial passing of the torch. The players erupted in cheers.

Day's first Ohio State team was a juggernaut, but only after he made a crucial decision regarding the quarterback position during the first days of his tenure. Dwayne Haskins Jr. had such a tremendous season as a first-year starter in 2018—50 touchdowns and 4,831 passing yards—that he decided to enter the NFL draft and was picked in the first round by the Washington Redskins. He later moved to the Pittsburgh Steelers before his life was cut short by a tragic offseason accident in spring 2022.

Ohio State's backup quarterback in 2018 was Tate Martell, who in high school in Las Vegas had been the Gatorade National Player of the Year. But he was generously listed at only 5-foot-11, and Day didn't have enough faith in his passing ability to go into the next season with him as the heir apparent.

Fortunately for the Buckeyes, Georgia's Justin Fields entered the transfer portal. He had been the No. 2 player nationally in his recruiting class. Day made a push for Fields after getting to Ohio State in 2017 but arrived too late to make much headway then. With Fields now available, Day pounced. "It was like, "All right, all systems go," Day said.

Signing Fields jump-started Day's head coaching career. Martell transferred to Miami and then to UNLV, failing to leave a mark at either place. Imagine how different the Day era might have been if Martell had been the OSU quarterback in 2019. Instead, it was Fields, who lived up to his billing as both a passer and runner. He threw for 41 touchdowns in 2019, with only three interceptions. He also ran for 10 scores and almost 500 yards. Future first-round pick Chris Olave was one of four receivers with at least 30 catches. K.J. Hill broke the OSU record for career receptions. Defensive end Chase Young had 16½ sacks to lead a stifling defense under new defensive coordinator Jeff Hafley.

Ohio State won each game by at least 24 points, and usually much more, until Penn State tested them in a 28–17 win in OSU's 11th game. Against Michigan, Dobbins scored four touchdowns in a 56–27 rout. It was OSU's eighth straight win in The Game. Ohio State's dominance in the rivalry seemed secure for the foreseeable future, "seemed" being the appropriate word.

In the Big Ten championship, the Buckeyes finally got a scare. They'd beaten Wisconsin 38–7 in late October, but the No. 10 Badgers took a 21–7 halftime lead in Indianapolis. Ohio State then outscored Wisconsin 27–0 in the second half for a 34–21 win. That set up a showdown against Clemson in the College Football Playoff semifinal at the Fiesta Bowl. The Tigers featured quarterback Trevor Lawrence, the only player ranked ahead of Fields in their recruiting class and a future No. 1 overall NFL draft pick.

The Buckeyes dominated early, taking a 16–0 lead in the second quarter. With five minutes left before halftime, defensive back Shaun

Wade sacked Lawrence on third down. But on replay review, officials ruled Wade was guilty of targeting, a reversal OSU fans still dispute.

Buckeye Nation remains even more indignant about a later reversal. Clemson scored after Wade's targeting call and took a 21–16 lead in the third quarter. Lawrence threw to wide receiver Justyn Ross, who caught the pass with cornerback Jeff Okudah draped on him. Ross took three steps with the ball before Okudah stripped it. Safety Jordan Fuller picked up the ball and weaved into the end zone. The ruling on the field was a catch and strip for a touchdown. But it was overturned on replay review. Day put his hands on his head in disbelief. Ohio State regained the lead before Clemson scored on a four-play, 94-yard drive to go back ahead with 1:49 left. Fields led the Buckeyes to the Clemson 23 before throwing an interception in the end zone on a miscommunication with Olave to seal Clemson's 29–23 win.

"There are games that you can't get over," Day said. "That one took me a long time to get over. I'm over it now, but just barely."

If Ohio State had won, the Buckeyes would have played LSU and Joe Burrow. The former Buckeye had a season for the ages in Baton Rouge, and that Tigers team ranks among the best in college football history.

"I remember during the TCU game in Jerry Jones' stadium, they put the LSU game up on the video board, and all the Buckeye fans were cheering like it was the Buckeyes," Day said. "They were still pulling for Joe. We pulled for Joe the entire season, and he had a magical season. But it sure would have been fun to play him."

THE CLEMSON LOSS would be the first of several devastating losses that would characterize Day's first five years as coach. In 2020, Day had to fight just to have a season. After COVID-19 struck in March 2020, everything, including sports, came to a halt. On August 11, new Big Ten commissioner Kevin Warren declared that the season would be canceled, even though the Southeastern Conference, the Atlantic Coast Conference, and the Big 12 said they would play. But advances in testing and pressure by

Ohio State (led by Day), Iowa, and Nebraska convinced the Big Ten to relent and have a late, shortened season played mostly without spectators. Day tested positive for COVID and had to miss a victory at Michigan State. Larry Johnson filled in as acting coach. The Michigan game was canceled because of an outbreak among the Wolverines, though at least one interested party is skeptical.

"But then [they] practiced and went about their business the next day," Nina Day said. "So I guess 12 hours made a huge difference."

Michigan suffered through a 2–4 season in 2020. At the next summer's Big Ten media days, Wolverine players acknowledged that OSU would have crushed them if that game had been played.

"During that time, if there was an outbreak, the games had to be called [off]," Ryan Day said. "But there certainly was always a concern that competitively a team would be able to bow out of a game if they didn't feel it would be a good game for them. Whether that was the case or not, we'll never know. You'd like to take people at their word, but I know that any time you found yourself in those situations at that time, I think everybody was always skeptical of whether a team could actually play or not. Could they actually field a team?"

Ohio State won all five regular-season games in 2020. The Buckeyes trailed Northwestern at halftime of the Big Ten championship game before running back Trey Sermon went wild. He finished with a school-record 313 rushing yards in a 22–10 win. The Buckeyes then got revenge against Clemson. They blew out the Tigers 49–28 in the CFP semifinal in New Orleans. But Fields took a nasty hit to the ribs in that game. He barely practiced before the national championship game against Alabama. Several other Buckeyes were also hurt or out with COVID, and Sermon broke his collarbone on his first carry. That Crimson Tide team was perhaps Nick Saban's best, and the 52–24 Alabama rout could have been even more lopsided.

Ohio State and Michigan met in 2021 with both teams 10–1. (The Buckeyes lost to Oregon at home in the season's second game.) Wolverines coach Jim Harbaugh had gotten the turnaround he needed to save his job, but he had zero wins against the Buckeyes in five prior matchups. He finally got one. It was a perfect storm in the worst way for Ohio State. Illness had swept through the team in the week before the game. Snow in Ann Arbor hampered Ohio State's explosive passing game led by C.J. Stroud. Michigan's defense, particularly star defensive end Aidan Hutchinson, dominated Ohio State's offensive line. Michigan's offensive line battered Ohio State's defense in a stunning 42–27 victory. It was an ass-kicking few expected.

The next year, Ohio State expected revenge in Columbus. It didn't happen. The Buckeyes dominated the first half but led only 20–17. Then Michigan held OSU's offense to a field goal in the second half. Ohio State's defense was repeatedly victimized by big plays as Michigan pulled away for a 45–23 win.

The rivalry had turned. Ohio State fans wondered how it could have happened so quickly. Many believed they got their answer the next year when the Connor Stalions scandal broke. A Naval Academy graduate, Stalions was ingenious at deciphering opponents' plays. But college football has a rule that prohibits teams from sending staffers to scout opponents in person or hire someone to tape an opponent's signals. Stalions clearly did. How much did that play a role in Michigan's wins in 2021 and 2022? That's impossible to know for sure. But long before anyone outside of Michigan's program knew of Stalions, Ohio State suspected something was amiss in those games.

Day said he studied film from that game and said it's clear Michigan knew what was coming from Ohio State's offense. "How they got them obviously is part of the [ongoing as of July 2025 NCAA] investigation," Day said, "but they certainly did have our signals. When you know it's a run or you know it's a pass, it completely changes the game."

The 2022 loss in Columbus was particularly painful. Stroud was a strong Heisman Trophy contender heading into that game. His hopes died when the Buckeyes managed only a field goal in six second-half possessions. "When you watch the film, they had the perfect defenses on," Day said. "You're watching the sideline, and they're pointing to the sky when we're throwing it."

He said tight end Cade Stover came to the sideline and said Michigan called out a screen pass play before it happened.

"I feel awful for the guys during those games," Day said. "For C.J. Stroud, it might have cost him a Heisman Trophy. As a coach, you always feel responsible to put your guys in a situation to be successful. Looking back on those games, that didn't happen on offense. That's what we believe to be true. After studying it, that was what we concluded."

Day said he is reserving some judgment until the NCAA releases the findings of its investigation. If Michigan deciphered OSU's signals from the sideline or from TV copies, that's legal. If Stalions did as suspected and advance scouted or paid others to do it, as has been alleged, that's quite different. That, Day said, "just undermines the integrity of the game."

Urban Meyer, who became an analyst for Fox after retiring from Ohio State, said he got into arguments with his colleagues about how damaging the sign-stealing was to Ohio State's chances in those games.

"They'd say, 'C'mon, coach, everybody does it,'" Meyer said. "I'm like, 'What are you talking about?' I've never even heard of that, where someone is at the game videoing on the sideline and then there's a whole data analysis center where people are working. That's illegal.

"Did that help them win a game? Why would you do it [otherwise]? You're jeopardizing everything. Your career is over. And you're going to tell me it's not that important? Then why are you doing it? Why would you jeopardize everything you've ever worked for and stand for to do it?"

Meyer was a minor-league baseball player before going to college. He compared the advantage Stalions gave Michigan to a hitter who knows what pitch is coming. You've still got to hit the ball, but it's a helluva lot easier.

OHIO STATE'S 2021 loss to Michigan ended their CFP hopes. It didn't in 2022. The Buckeyes got a reprieve when Utah upset USC in the Pac-12 title game to give OSU a spot in the semifinals against No. 1 Georgia in Atlanta on New Year's Eve.

The underdog Buckeyes were inspired and controlled play most of the game, leading by 14 twice. But as was the case against Clemson in 2019, the breaks went against the Buckeyes. The biggest came when star receiver Marvin Harrison Jr. was knocked out of the game after a hit on a pass in the end zone that was ruled targeting on the field and then reversed. Ohio State had to settle for a field goal instead of a touchdown. Still, the Buckeyes had a chance to win despite playing with a makeshift skill-position group around Stroud because of injuries. Trailing 42–41, the Buckeyes drove into Georgia territory before Noah Ruggles missed a 50-yard field goal as the clock struck midnight on the year and Ohio State's season. If the Buckeyes had won, they'd have been prohibitive favorites to beat TCU, which upset Michigan in the other semifinal, in the national title game. Georgia crushed TCU 65–7.

Ohio State and Michigan were undefeated heading into their 2023 showdown. Stalions was gone after his sign-stealing had been exposed, but this was Michigan's best team under Harbaugh. The Wolverines had largely done what Ohio State would do in 2024 by retaining most of their key seniors who'd been eligible to go into the NFL draft. But Harbaugh wasn't on the sidelines for half of the regular season, including the Ohio State game. Michigan self-imposed a three-game suspension on Harbaugh at the start of the season because of alleged recruiting violations being investigated by the NCAA. The Big Ten suspended Harbaugh for the last three games of the regular season because of the Stalions scandal. Co-offensive coordinator Sherrone Moore filled in for Harbaugh.

The turmoil off the field had little effect on the Wolverines' performance. That continued against the Buckeyes. Stroud's successor, Kyle McCord, threw an early interception that set up a Michigan touchdown, and Ohio State played uphill most of the game. Trailing by six, the

Buckeyes drove into Michigan territory in the final minute. But McCord was hit as he threw to Marvin Harrison Jr., and the pass was intercepted to preserve Michigan's 30–24 win. The Wolverines went on to beat Alabama and Washington in the CFP to win the national championship.

Ohio State was relegated to the Cotton Bowl against Missouri. McCord entered the transfer portal nine days following the Michigan loss after asking Day for both an assurance that he would be the starter in 2024 and a hefty NIL deal. Still trying to process the Michigan defeat, Day wasn't prepared to do that. McCord left. The bowl game was supposed to be an opportunity for backup Devin Brown to stake an early claim for the quarterback job for 2024. Instead, he left early after being injured. True freshman Lincoln Kienholz, who didn't enroll until after spring practice, could do little behind poor offensive line play. The defense eventually wilted in a 14–3 loss.

"It was painful," said athletics director Gene Smith. "Everybody was in a bad mood—the coaches, the players, the support staff. I was. I remember in my head saying to myself, 'We've got to do better.'"

Smith had only limited time to oversee that himself. In August 2023, he announced he would retire mid-year in 2024 after 19 years at Ohio State in which he cemented his legacy as one of the most influential college athletics directors in history. Ohio State's new president, Ted Carter, directed the search for a successor. In mid-January, OSU announced the hiring of Texas A&M's Ross Bjork as Smith's successor.

For Nina Day, the disappointing end to the season, including watching Michigan win the national title after the Stalions' scandal had been exposed, left a bad taste in her mouth.

"Having an idea of what was going on behind the scenes, I said to Ryan numerous times that college football is not what I want to be associated with anymore," she said. "We pride ourselves on having morals and values, and he's in a profession that does not value that in a lot of ways. It's just hard to succeed in an environment when everybody's not playing by the rules."

BEING THE HEAD football coach at a program like Ohio State is highly stressful. The same goes for the coach's wife. When Day succeeded Meyer, numerous charities asked him for his support and involvement. One cause was close to Ryan and Nina's heart—mental health. But to jump in fully, he would have to do something he'd avoided for decades.

"I knew he had to get there in his mind for that to happen," Nina said. "At that point, it still wasn't known what happened to his dad. Everyone knew his dad died, but not how. We still hadn't really talked about it [publicly], so I knew it was going to be a slippery slope with that. It took time. [But] I just wanted to do something we were both passionate about that's impacted both of us and shaped our lives."

After his father's death, Ryan did not get much professional psychological help. He went to a therapist only a couple times, he said. Nina has battled anxiety her whole life. For much of the time, it was untreated.

"I knew I felt a certain way but really didn't know why," she said. "I'm obviously Type A and [have] OCD. I just thought, 'This is the way I am and this is normal and everyone feels like this.' My parents are super supportive, but back then they had no idea. People just didn't talk about mental health or mental fitness, so I just dealt with it."

As an adult, Nina grew frustrated because she felt she was suffering in silence. Until she did research and educated herself, she couldn't understand why her symptoms persisted. Being a coach's wife added to her stress. Nina is a private person by nature. She is not drawn to the spotlight. She hates large crowds.

"I tell people all the time I am so not cut out for this life," she said with a laugh.

The Days wanted to help remove the stigma that surrounds mental health. Their first major initiative was to support Nationwide Children's Hospital's "On Our Sleeves" program, now known as the Kids Mental Health Foundation. That included providing a toolkit called "Day Time Break" that served as a resource for educators, parents, and caregivers to help identify and aid adolescents with mental health challenges. Nina said in 2021 that one million kits had been distributed. The next year, the Days gave $1 million for the Nina and Ryan Day Resilience Fund for research and treatment for students and adults at the OSU Wexner Medical Center and College of Medicine. Much of the work on research has been led by Dr. K. Luan Phan, chair of the OSU department of psychiatry and behavioral health. It is aimed at understanding the causes of mental illness and treating it before it becomes worse.

"A big part of mental health is building resilience," Ryan Day said. "In physical health, you think about your immune system. You think about physically getting strong by running and getting your aerobic shape up. But what about mentally and having a plan for when something doesn't go well?"

Regular college students deal with stress daily. They're gone from home for the first time, have academic responsibilities without parents overseeing them, and are being treated as adults. It can be particularly stressful for football players at a high-pressure place like Ohio State. They were all stars of their high school teams. Now they are competing daily with a roster full of stars for playing time at a place where losing is unacceptable. Almost every Ohio State player experiences adversity in his career.

"If you were to take the average college freshman dealing with the average college stress, then you multiply it and put it in a very public-facing arena, it can be a lot," said Dr. Jamey Houle, OSU's lead sports psychologist.

Unlike a generation ago, Houle said, current athletes must deal with criticism on social media. Add in the expectations in an NIL era when players are no longer viewed as amateurs, and the advent of sports betting, and the vitriol can be intense. "People can DM them, get directly to them, and say some pretty hateful things," Houle said. "It feels like a conglomeration of things that the average student wouldn't have to deal with."

Day's advocacy for mental health has proven invaluable for several players. Harry Miller medically retired from football because of mental health issues. Before the 2021season, Miller told Day he intended to kill himself. Day put Miller in touch with medical-health professionals. Miller credited them with saving his life. Day said other players have come to him for help or had teammates do it on their behalf. Ohio State has a counselor, Dr. Charron Sumler, who directly works with its football players.

"I felt it was good to see that college football players, who are big and strong and everyone thinks they have it all together, are just like everybody else, to normalize the conversation," Day said. "Like Nina says, there was a time growing up where people would suffer in silence, and there really wasn't a lot of conversation about things like this. And for me to talk about it was a little therapeutic. It was good to get it out there a little bit. What I found was the amount of people that would come up to us and the feedback we'd get from so many in the community."

Houle is grateful that the Days have been prominent supporters of mental health. "He has one of the highest platforms in the entire state, if not the country, as the Ohio State football coach," he said. "To have him advocate for something that still has a stigma associated with it shows leadership. It shows the ability to be vulnerable and say, 'This is something that I've gone through in my life. This is something that is normal, that we all have it.'"

6

NIL Changes the Game

Ohio State's 2021 recruiting class was the last before name, image, and likeness (NIL) rights were finally granted to college athletes. It was a game-changer. When NIL came into existence on July 1, 2021, the rules barring players from making money from their identity were suddenly gone.

In 2011, the NCAA placed OSU on probation after its tattoo-and-memorabilia scandal. It cost Jim Tressel his job as coach after he lied on an NCAA form about knowing of the transgressions. Five players got suspended. The biggest star, quarterback Terrelle Pryor, left Ohio State for the NFL. That scandal now seems quaint. One of the other players, running back Daniel "Boom" Herron, couldn't help but make a quip about the new landscape under NIL. "Scandal is the new normal," he said.

Yes, it was. But no one really knew what the new landscape would look like. Battered by a series of losses in court, the NCAA mostly threw up its hands. College leaders hoped Congress would pass federal legislation. No such luck. It was left to the states to come up with their own rules. Ohio scrambled to pass a law quickly.

But with states passing their own laws, the rules regarding what was permissible and not permissible remained murky for the next three years. It wasn't until June 2025, when federal judge Claudia Wilken approved a settlement in the *House v. NCAA* case, that standard guidelines regarding NIL were adopted nationally. That enabled college programs to pay athletes directly instead of using third parties to do so.

From 2021–2024, collectives were the mechanism by which athletes were paid. For Ohio State, the two main collectives were THE Foundation and The 1870 Society. THE Foundation, a nonprofit, was founded by Brian Schottenstein and Cardale Jones. Schottenstein's extended family is one of the wealthiest and most influential in Columbus. Schottenstein grew up a huge Buckeye fan and befriended wide receiver (and now wide receivers coach) Brian Hartline when they were OSU students in the early 2000s. Schottenstein said that when it was clear NIL would become a reality, Hartline encouraged him to get involved. Schottenstein is close friends with Jones, the unlikely star of Ohio State's 2014 national championship team. The former third stringer led the Buckeyes that postseason following injuries to Braxton Miller in the summer and to J.T. Barrett against Michigan. The 1870 Society, a for-profit organization, was founded by IT entrepreneur Aidin Aghamiri, an OSU grad. Athletics director Ross Bjork said that about $12-15 million was raised through the collectives for the 2024 team.

"I'm amazed by how much we grew and how organically our brand got out there in just three years," Schottenstein said. "We have thousands of donors across the world. It was truly amazing to see the support we got."

Much of the money came from personal appeals by Day to donors. Day said that when he solicited them, many had a hard time grasping the new rules—or lack thereof. "I think in general the idea of boosters and companies paying players was just so frowned upon that it was hard to change people's mindset," he said. "We explained the landscape is changing and here's how it works."

Donors would have more access to the team than before, Day explained. "I think once we educated a lot of these folks, they wanted to help out," he said.

THE COLLECTIVES WERE separate from the university but worked with them. At Ohio State, the point person for NIL is Logan Hittle, who truly worked his way up from the bottom. A self-described average high school football player in Zanesville, Ohio, Hittle took a job as a janitor at the Woody Hayes Athletic Center just to get his foot in the door. He cleaned toilets, waxed floors, and took out trash—whatever it would take to build relationships and earn respect. Hittle then walked on to the football team. His only action came on the final kickoff of a 76–5 win over Miami University in 2019.

"It was pouring down rain, and there were probably 300 people there, and it was probably all the parents of the kids that were [finally] getting in the game," Hittle said of the remaining crowd at Ohio Stadium.

After graduation, Hittle got a job as associate director of student-athlete development before he was promoted to the NIL role. When recruits visit, he gives a presentation that highlights opportunities they'll have to capitalize on NIL. Ohio State is uniquely positioned that way. Columbus is the 15th-largest city in the country, trailing only Chicago in population among Midwestern cities. In Ohio, Columbus is a magnet for people leaving cities and towns in decline. Ohio State also dominates the state in football appeal like no other program in a highly populated state. Texas, California, and Florida each have several schools with large fan bases. The University of Georgia in Athens is an hour away from Atlanta. Columbus has the NHL's Blue Jackets and the MLS' Crew, but the Buckeyes are the most popular team in town.

"That's our pitch to student-athletes," Hittle said. "It's one of the fastest-growing cities in the Midwest. It's got over 30,000 businesses, Fortune 500 companies, the largest living alumni base in the country. We have the largest fan base of any college in the country for football. All those things added up, it's going to give you more opportunities statistically than any school in the country."

Hittle said OSU's collectives raised three times as much in 2024 as they did in 2021. That left Ohio State capable of spending to attract and retain players. But even for a program with the resources OSU has, NIL presents major challenges as well as opportunities.

MARK PANTONI CAN attest to that. He is one of the pillars of Ohio State's program. Pantoni started college as a pre-med major at the University of Florida and has bachelor's and master's degrees in applied physiology and kinesiology. But he became enamored with the football program at Florida under Urban Meyer and volunteered in the athletic department. He advanced quickly and became a key figure in the Gators' recruiting department. When OSU hired Meyer in 2011, Pantoni followed to be the point person for Ohio State's recruiting. He was adept at forming relationships with prospects and was tireless in watching game video—whole games and not just highlights—to help determine which players OSU would pursue.

What started as a two-man department has swelled as college programs increasingly resemble NFL teams' front offices. Pantoni is now Ohio State's general manager, player personnel. In a sign of his importance, OSU increased his salary from $350,000 in 2024 to $900,000 in 2025. In the new NIL world, Pantoni spends little time talking to high school prospects. He now deals with their agents. Yes, high school recruits have agents. Some are NFL-certified. Pantoni finds it more straightforward to deal with them. Often, those agents aren't taking a percentage of a recruit's deal for signing, instead taking the long view of building a relationship for more lucrative contracts in the future. Then there are the uncertified agents.

"I like to say they have an 'online support management' degree," Pantoni said. "They kind of are 'playing' agent. They're a little bit more difficult because they're charging 10-20 percent in commission, and their sole focus is shopping as many guys as they can to get them the most amount of money, and not for the right reasons."

Gene Smith and many others called the landscape before the House settlement the Wild West. It forced programs to be more discerning in their recruitment. It wasn't just about selling your program, your coach, your culture, or your tradition. From Ohio State's end, it wanted to make sure recruits weren't coming to Columbus as a cash grab. Day said that recruits whose primary goal was to maximize NIL probably weren't a great fit for the culture he wants. But still, the money component loomed large. Where there's money, inevitably the possibility of corruption exists.

"There needs to be some structure," Pantoni said before the House settlement was finalized. "There's zero regulation now."

That was the world in which he and OSU had to operate in 2024. The NCAA's oversight committee, Pantoni said, is composed of athletics directors and commissioners. "Nothing against them," he said, "but professionally they just don't have their boots on the ground and understand by making a rule all the repercussions that come from it."

He cited having a transfer portal opening in December, which has become the most chaotic time of the calendar in what was once one of the quieter periods. National Signing Day used to be in early February. Now almost all signings come in the early signing period in mid-December. First-round College Football Playoff games in 2024 were December 20 and 21. There was almost no time for sleep.

Cheating has always been a part of college football. It became brazen. "Just publicly, schools are tampering with our guys," Pantoni said. "You have agents that are not regulated by any means who send lists of their clients and it's like a menu. 'Just tell us who you want, and we'll make sure they get into the portal for the right price.'"

Some liken it to free agency in professional sports, but that's not an apt comparison. Free agency in pro sports is highly regulated through a collective-bargaining agreement. In the NFL, for instance, drafted rookies are bound to their teams for at least three years. The transfer portal allows players multiple opportunities a year to seek a new home. Unfortunately, many seeking greener pastures—in the figurative and literal sense—are disappointed. Many are left without a home when the roster musical chairs end.

For colleges, it makes roster management a constant chore. Established players want to be compensated. Up-and-coming players want to be paid for their potential. Freshmen want to be paid just to sign. Ohio State has the resources to compete with anyone both in terms of athletic department revenue and NIL opportunities through associated collectives. Bjork said at Big Ten media days in July 2024 that about $20 million was spent to get or retain players on Ohio State's roster. That comment made headlines, but Bjork said it was misconstrued.

"I regret the way it was portrayed, not the fact the number was out there because there are a lot of [programs] that have [similar] numbers out there," Bjork said. "The way it was portrayed is that we bought the team this way. The $20 million was the total value of what the athletes were able to either earn on their own or that our collectives put together or actually true sponsorship value when a company approached an athlete and said, 'We'd like to do an NIL [deal].'

"It wasn't that we sat in a room with Gene and Ryan and said, 'We have to have $20 million. Let's build $20 million and deploy that.' It wasn't that way. That's how it got portrayed, and that would be on me to not clarify that."

Said Day, "It's our job to help them get market value. How do you find market value? Unfortunately, these guys talk to agents and talk to other schools to figure out what they're willing to pay, and you do the best you can to bridge those gaps. That's really how we handle it. We talk to agents. We talk to marketing people. We try to figure out what that number is, knowing it's a floating target."

FOR THE FOUNDATION, Jones was the one who had direct contact with players. He became a folk hero in Ohio because of the 2014 championship and has a knack for connecting with people from all walks of life.

"Whenever I go somewhere with him," Schottenstein said, "it's 'Cardale time,' because when he's walking from Point A to Point B, he'll probably be stopped a few times along the way by people wanting autographs or to say hi to him. He always makes a point to stop and not just move on."

Jones said there are essentially three NIL categories: one for recruits, one for younger players who haven't established themselves, and one for established starters. Pantoni said Ohio State's preference is to direct NIL to veterans who've already earned it, though exceptions must be made for the best recruits. He compared it to the NFL in which most rookie contracts pale in comparison to the more lucrative contract a veteran earns after his rookie contract expires. But every case is different. To a player who comes from a disadvantaged background, NIL money probably matters more than to one who had a privileged upbringing.

Jones grew up poor in Cleveland. He understands the pressure players face in maximizing their earning potential. Jones also knows that not everyone close to the player has the athlete's best interest at heart.

"I don't put this on the recruits at all," he said. "I wish these agents would guide these guys a little better than they're doing and not just cash in on a payday. It's hard for a coach to come in a kids' living room and say, 'Hey, turn down that $1 million and come here for $200,000,' and all this kid knows is struggle. It's simple to him. One million dollars versus $200,000 is a huge difference. I'm not saying the gap may be that big. But the kid thinks, 'The more I have, the better I can take care of my family and myself.' I don't knock these kids at all for having the mindset of going wherever the most money is going to be."

On signing day in December 2023, the NIL issue would loom large.

7

The Courtship of Jeremiah Smith

Ohio State wide-receivers coach Brian Hartline first saw Jeremiah Smith when the receiver came to an OSU camp from Miami after his freshman year of high school. Even then, Smith's talent was undeniable, and Ohio State offered him a scholarship. "I fell in love with his quietness, his mindset, his approach," Hartline said. "And yeah, he checks some athletic boxes."

Hartline's affection for Smith as a player and person only grew during his recruitment. He said Smith's parents raised him the right way. Hartline once asked Jeremiah if his grades were slipping. "Hell, no," Hartline said Smith replied. "My dad's gonna kick my ass [if they do].' That's the mentality. He was just raised to do things right. When? Every time. He was raised to outwork people. When? Every time. Coupled with his blessings, it's just been an awesome experience to see him grow."

Smith didn't seem destined to be a phenom when he first became interested in football. He was cut from the Miami Gardens Vikings team when he was seven. Soon after, he began having epileptic seizures, which lasted more than a year before he outgrew them. Once they subsided, he tried out again for the Miami Gardens Vikings and made the team. His dad put Jeremiah and his younger brother through workouts two or three times daily at hilly Vista View Park.

"My mom used to get mad at my dad: 'Why are you working them out so hard?'" Jeremiah said with a laugh. "But my dad always wanted us to be the hardest-working men in the room. That's where I get it from—my dad pushing me to the limits."

It helped that his older cousin, Geno Smith, excelled at West Virginia and became an NFL quarterback. "I went to a game of his at the age of seven when they played in the Orange Bowl against Clemson and won," Smith said. "Seeing him on the biggest stage performing the way he did, I was like, 'This is something I really want to do in my life and take it to the next level.' He definitely was a big influence."

Jeremiah Smith developed into the No. 1 recruit in the 2024 recruiting class, a 6'3", 215-pound beast with rare strength and speed and hands. He was considered a once-in-a-generation wide receiver prospect. Hartline, who spent six of his seven years in the NFL with the Miami Dolphins, developed a close relationship with the Smith family. That proved essential. Recruiting in Florida is cutthroat, and the Miami Hurricanes have been desperate to return to the college football elite. The "U" once dominated the sport but haven't been the same since losing to Ohio State in their epic BCS championship game in 2003. Hartline was able to sell the Buckeyes' success under him in developing receivers. Chris Olave, Garrett Wilson, Jaxon Smith-Njigba, and Marvin Harrison Jr. were all first-round draft picks.

"Jeremiah is not a kid who was ever caught up in the bells and whistles with the recruiting process," Mark Pantoni said. "His main focus was all football and how he's going to be developed and who he's going to be playing with. Hartline did an incredible job building a relationship with him, his family, and the people around him."

JEREMIAH SMITH COMMITTED to Ohio State in December 2022. He would have to wait 12 months to sign. As the December 2023 signing day approached, rumors swirled that Miami was courting him with a generous NIL pitch. Head coaches from not only Miami but Florida and Florida State also paid visits to Smith.

"I knew there was stuff going on," Hartline said, "but Jeremiah told me the entire time, 'Coach Hart, I'm good. Don't worry about what you're reading. Nothing's changing.'"

Hartline said it got the point that he told Smith he wouldn't keep pestering him because he didn't want to seem like a worried girlfriend. Hartline considers himself a no-bullshit guy and likes that Smith is the same way. He tried to ignore the noise.

"There were some things and funny business and all kinds of things that were trying to go on on signing day, and I was getting informed," Hartline said. "But J.J. always told me one thing, and I had no reason to think otherwise. That's just the relationship we have."

But Smith had just turned 18 and had plenty of voices in his ear. Other schools were telling him Ryan Day and/or Hartline might not stay at Ohio State. "The night before signing day was crazy because you have Miami and all the other schools coming at me, texting me, my family, my dad," Smith said.

The next morning, Smith acknowledged, he did waver a bit. He asked himself if he really wanted to go to school way up north in Ohio. Would he prefer to stay home and play for Miami? He said NIL wasn't a major factor. "I knew I would get money anywhere I would have gone," Smith said.

Inside the Woody, there was deep concern that Smith would flip his commitment. Day called Smith's dad and Geno Smith trying to get reassurance. "Right before we were supposed to do the [signing day] press conference," Day said, "I was told that he's probably going to say he was going to Miami, but he wasn't going to sign anything officially until later on that night."

Day started the press conference and was clearly a bit distracted. Finally, Pantoni signaled to Day from the back of the room that Smith announced he would be a Buckeye, after all. Day sighed, smiled and said, "Really?" before jokingly buckling his knees in relief.

"I just knew the decision for me was to come to Ohio State," Smith said.

THAT WASN'T THE only drama on signing day. Ohio State's second-ranked commitment, defensive lineman Eddrick Houston from Georgia, was reportedly wavering. Crystal-ball forecasts suddenly predicted that Houston would sign with Alabama. That would have been a huge blow. The Buckeyes had already lost a top lineman, Justin Scott, in part because of NIL factors and because of concern that septuagenarian line coach Larry Johnson would retire early in Houston's college career.

"There were a lot of questions at the last second about what was going to happen," Day said. "Alabama made a late pitch to him, and we had a hard time getting in touch with him that morning."

That's because Houston had shut off his phone a couple of days earlier. "I deleted all social media because I wanted the decision I make to be between me and the Lord," Houston said. "I was just really praying, asking what's the best fit for me."

Houston was still weighing his decision at Buford High School, where he was scheduled to announce his decision. He said he intended to stick with his Ohio State commitment but needed to hear that Johnson would stay. A phone call was arranged with Johnson and Day, who left the press conference for 17 minutes. The conversation reassured Houston. He was in the fold.

"It was an interesting conversation because he had been committed for such a long time," Johnson said. "We knew he was coming, and then at the last minute, in the last hour, somebody got into his brain. That's what [some] adults do. They put it on pause, and it shouldn't have been on pause because he wanted to be here."

When Houston finally turned his phone back on, he had more than 200 text messages and voicemails, including about 50 increasingly frantic ones from Ohio State. When he arrived on campus in January, he felt compelled to apologize for his radio silence. "That's the first thing I did," Houston said. "I told them I'm sorry for giving you that little panic attack, but my heart's always been here."

Day returned to finish the press conference, but the drama wasn't quite over. Hour after hour passed before Jeremiah Smith finally sent his signed letter of intent to Hartline at about 10:00 PM.

"My agent wanted to make sure everything was in writing," Smith said.

"That was a long, long, drawn-out day," Pantoni said. "You're always nervous until it's official when the paperwork comes in."

Jeremiah Smith would make the wait well worth it.

8

One More Year

On the quiet plane ride home from Dallas after the Cotton Bowl loss to Missouri, Ohio State's underclassmen eligible for the NFL draft knew they had a decision to make. The deadline for entering the draft was days away. They had gone 11–2 in each of their three seasons. At most programs, that would be cause for celebration. At Ohio State, it was a disappointment because it included the three losses to Michigan and no Big Ten or national championship.

Still, their ultimate goal was to play in the NFL, and now that was within reach. Marvin Harrison Jr. was considered a no-brainer to leave, given his status as the top non-quarterback in the draft. Arizona took him with the fourth overall pick. Defensive end Michael Hall Jr., who had a baby son, also left and was taken by Cleveland in the second round.

None of the other underclassmen were projected as first-round locks. But even mid-round NFL draft picks make enough money to set them up for life. A fourth-round draft pick in 2024 could expect to sign a contract worth about $4.5 million, including a signing bonus above $500,000.

Draft-eligible players can receive a grade from the NFL of the range in which they'd likely be selected. Jack Sawyer said he'd been deemed a probable third or fourth rounder. Sawyer was tempted, but he told Day before the Cotton Bowl that he was staying. His parents had encouraged him to consider turning pro, but his heart was still at Ohio State. There was unfinished business. He felt loyalty to the program and to Day and Larry Johnson to return. He set his sights on persuading his teammates to come back also.

"I told people, 'Look, if you guys decide whatever is best for your career and future isn't to come back, I completely understand, respect that and wish nothing but the best for you," Sawyer said. "'But I want you guys to understand that we could do something bigger than ourselves, something that we could be able to come back and show our kids one day, something we could tell—a story of loyalty bigger than yourself.' I think that really resonated with a lot of guys."

It did.

"I think Jack did a great job of talking guys into coming back," safety Lathan Ransom said. "I think him being an Ohio guy, it meant a lot to him."

Ransom had endured two serious injuries in his Ohio State career, so nobody would have blamed him if he didn't want to risk another before going to the NFL. Ransom—his first name is a combination of his father Nathan and mother Linda's names—played with a recklessness for his body from the time he first played the sport. His dad said Lathan earned the nickname "Lights Out Lathan" for his ferocious hits at a young age despite having a lean frame.

"My dad did such a great job of instilling in me, being a smaller guy, that if you get to the ball-carrier faster than he gets to you, you'll win that battle 95 percent of the time," Ransom said. "I still play that way, always going to the ball full speed fearlessly."

He played seven games as a true freshman in 2020 and was a part-time starter the next year. But in the Rose Bowl against Utah, he broke both the tibia and fibula in his left leg when he was inadvertently leg-whipped by a teammate in kickoff coverage. In the hospital after having surgery, he tested positive for COVID, delaying his departure back to Arizona. OSU athletics director Gene Smith arranged for a private plane to fly him home.

Ransom wondered whether he'd ever be the same player. "I feel that's natural to have when you have such a horrific injury," Ransom said. "There's definitely that doubt in your mind. I questioned why this would happen to me."

Ransom attacked his rehab hard and was ready for the start of the season. His first play that year was a big hit for a third-down stop on star Notre Dame tight end Michael Mayer, who outweighed Ransom by about 50 pounds. Ransom became a semifinalist for the Thorpe Award, which is given to the country's top defensive back. But his 2023 season was cut short by a non-contact Lisfranc foot injury against Wisconsin in November. He couldn't play against Michigan or in the Cotton Bowl. That left him hungrier than ever for his fifth and final season as a Buckeye.

Nose tackle Ty Hamilton grew up in the same Columbus suburb of Pickerington as Sawyer. They were friends from the time they were pee-wee football teammates and then high school rivals. Hamilton had already been at Ohio State for four years, including redshirting as a freshman. He considered turning pro. But when Sawyer made the case for returning, he was swayed. "He was the first guy to announce he was coming back, so after that, we all got together and talked about why we wanted to be here," Hamilton said. "We described it as reloading the clip."

Some were easier to persuade than others. Offensive guard Donovan Jackson came the closest to departing. He'd been given a draft projection that had him selected as early as late in the first round. "Coming off the Missouri game, that was obviously frustrating," he said. "Emotions were running high, and I was like, 'Dude, I'm done. I'm going to the NFL.'"

He went back home to Houston after the game and told Day he was leaving. He told Sawyer the same thing. But as the days passed, he had second thoughts. "Every day I woke up and knew that decision didn't rest well with me," he said. "It was like I was fighting myself over the decision to leave."

He had papers to sign to make his decision official and a deadline to fly to begin training for the draft. He said his mom could see the anguish on his face one day as they ate breakfast. She told him it was okay to change his mind. A weight had been lifted off his mind. He told her he wanted to return to Ohio State. He called Sawyer to deliver the news.

"I felt relief," Jackson said. "I knew that was the right decision. We had such a talented class and really had nothing to show for it, for the most part. We wanted to run it back one more time and get after it."

The others followed. Defensive linemen J.T. Tuimoloau and Tyleik Williams, running back TreVeyon Henderson, wide receiver Emeka Egbuka, and cornerback Denzel Burke all announced that they'd return. "For me, hardware and legacy is a big thing," Burke said. "Being able to be remembered forever was a big thing for me. My brothers [on the team], they wanted me to come back, and coach Day wanted me to come back. Just for my love for him and the love for my team, I wanted to do that."

To be sure, the NIL component made returning viable financially for many of them. "What was special about that was that before NIL, being a kid from Tucson, Arizona, my parents weren't able to come to many games," Ransom said. "My sister didn't get to come to a game until this past year. For them to come see me play meant so much to me."

The players also had another financial incentive to stay. Another year of development could enhance their draft stock. Linebacker Cody Simon, for instance, was told he probably wouldn't be drafted and announced before the Michigan game that he would return. But their decisions were not rooted mostly in money, they said.

"For those guys, they love this place so much," Day said, "They love the university, love the program, love their brothers so much. I think they couldn't come to grips with the fact that they'd have nothing to show for it. I don't think they could live with themselves."

Said Ransom, "It was the brotherhood. We all had personal goals that we've had since we were young kids," Ransom said. "We always had a dream of playing at the next level. We all put that aside to achieve something bigger."

9

The Final Pieces

The return of so many veterans gave Ohio State a strong foundation for 2024, but the Buckeyes still had holes to fill. The most glaring was at quarterback. Kyle McCord was off to Syracuse, and Devin Brown's injury in the Cotton Bowl prevented him from staking a claim to the job. As Day analyzed different candidates, Will Howard stood out to him. He liked that he'd led Kansas State to a Big 12 championship. He liked that he was a mobile runner with a sturdy 6'4" frame, which would give Ohio State a dimension it hadn't really had since Justin Fields. When he called Howard and started talking Xs and Os, he was impressed by his knowledge. Howard dissected one play against TCU in such detail that Day felt he was talking to an NFL quarterback.

"At that moment, I was like, 'Oh, this guy's different. He's very, very mature,'" Day said.

Howard grew up in Downingtown, Pennsylvania, as the oldest of Maureen and Bob Howard's four kids. He was named William Thomas after two of his mother Maureen's brothers, one older and one younger, who died as newborns. "Whenever I hear my mom or grandma talk about it, it felt like I was carrying something a little bigger than myself," Howard said. "I have to carry on their legacy with me."

As a baby, Howard had trouble staying asleep. Maureen was a pediatric physical therapist who used to work in a NICU unit, so she was an expert in getting babies to sleep. Will was a big baby and outgrew what his parents used as a swaddle. Maureen designed a sturdier outfit that provided more support. It worked. In fact, it became the prototype for what eventually became the Howard family business—Baby Merlin's Magic Sleepsuit. The family sold the company to a Boston firm in 2021.

Will showed his athleticism early. His parents bought a Little Tikes basketball hoop when he was a toddler. He amazed them by sinking 30 baskets in a row. Growing up, he played basketball, baseball, and football. Like most Pennsylvania football players, Howard was a Penn State fan and dreamed of playing for the Nittany Lions. As a sophomore at Downingtown West, Howard showed enough potential that Penn State began recruiting him. But when Howard broke his right wrist during his junior season, PSU's interest cooled. Then Howard later broke his left wrist dunking a basketball in gym class, further hurting his recruitment.

"I just felt helpless," he said.

Howard sent a highlight tape to Kansas State because most of the staff had previously coached at North Dakota State. Howard, a Philadelphia Eagles fan, liked their quarterback Carson Wentz, a North Dakota State product. Kansas State liked the tape and offered a scholarship. But Manhattan, Kansas, was 18 hours from home. He went on a campus visit almost as a lark. Maureen didn't even bother to go. But Howard loved his visit and committed to Kansas State two months later.

Howard enrolled in January. In early March, COVID-19 hit just as spring break started. When players were finally allowed back on campus in June, they had to live alone. Howard's goal at the start of training camp was to make the 70-man travel roster. But he played well enough to win the backup job behind starter Skylar Thompson.

When Thompson was injured early in the season, Howard took over. He wasn't close to ready. Kansas State lost its last five games. Howard was miserable. His mom visited a few times, and he became emotional every time she left. As a sophomore, Howard again filled in for Thompson because of injury. He consented to play in a fifth game against Texas, which burned his redshirt, because coaches told him they wanted him to start building momentum for his junior season. Then Kansas State signed former Nebraska quarterback Adrian Martinez out of the transfer portal.

Howard felt betrayed. He knew he'd be a longshot to win the job over Martinez, and he didn't. But Martinez suffered a midseason injury and Howard took over. He led Kansas State to the Big 12 title game where the Wildcats upset No. 3 TCU. Howard entered the 2023 season feeling that he finally was the guy. But Kansas State signed dynamic in-state four-star quarterback Avery Johnson, and after Howard threw three interceptions in a loss to Oklahoma State in early October, coaches gave Johnson a look in the next two games. Howard retained the job and the Wildcats went 9–4, but by season's end, Howard was ready to move on.

The question was whether that would be to the NFL or to another college. Howard got a draft grade that indicated he'd be a later-round pick if selected at all. When he entered the portal, he viewed his destination as what he called a rocking chair decision. He wanted to go somewhere he could make an impact big enough to talk about when he was 80 years old sitting in a rocking chair. When Ohio State showed interest, he knew joining the Buckeyes would give him that chance. But Day didn't want to pull the trigger on Howard until Brown had a chance to prove himself in the Cotton Bowl against Missouri. Howard watched that game in a bar with two close friends. He told them he was likely headed to Ohio State. But Howard wasn't happy that OSU laid an egg against Missouri. The Tigers had beaten Kansas State in 2023 on a 61-yard field goal, and he wanted OSU to beat them, regardless of how that might affect his chances to come to Columbus. But the outcome pretty much sealed the deal. Six days after the Cotton Bowl, Howard committed.

Day did not promise him the starting job.

Said Howard, "He framed it as, 'We believe you can be the guy to takes us to the national championship, but you're going to have to come earn it. We're not going to hand it to you. You're going to have to win the job, and you're going to have to win the team over.' Nothing was guaranteed."

There was an NIL component, of course, but Howard said that was a minor consideration. "It was not about that at all for me," he said. "If I would have been in it for the money, I probably would have committed to Miami well before I even talked to Ohio State."

He said the Hurricanes had offered him a comparable package that Cam Ward took, which was reportedly about $2 million. But he sensed something special brewing in Columbus and wanted to be a part of it.

QUINSHON JUDKINS FELT the same way. He grew up in Pike Road, Alabama, outside of Montgomery. Quinshon was born bow-legged and tripped over his feet so often as a toddler that he compensated for by walking on his tiptoes. That gave him unusually muscular calves as a young boy. One day when his mom, Teva, took him to Walmart, a man noticed his legs and told her he was destined to be a football player.

That stranger was prescient. But Quinshon's football debut as a boy was inauspicious. The first time he touched the ball, he ran all the way to the end zone—the wrong end zone. Once he was pointed in the right direction, he was hard to stop. But his childhood wasn't without adversity. When he was eight, Teva, then just 34, needed open-heart surgery following a heart attack caused by an undiagnosed birth defect. Her recovery was long and difficult, but it made the bond between mother and son even stronger.

Quinshon became a coveted recruit, and he was such a good student academically that Yale was among the schools he considered. He chose Ole Miss, which recruited him the hardest. Judkins became a star as a freshman, running for 1,567 yards and 16 touchdowns. After his sophomore year, he was looking for a change for reasons he prefers to keep private. In this era of unfettered social media, it's easy for reputations to be sullied, fairly or not.

"We were told he was toxic in the locker room, he was not a good teammate, he was selfish," Day said. "That's all the feedback we were hearing. None of that was even close to being true. I don't know how that [criticism] happened. One of the things he wanted to do when he got here was to quote-unquote clean his name because of the things that were being said. I gave Teva our word that we were going to do that."

Judkins visited Ohio State only two days after he entered the transfer portal. "I immediately fell in love with the school, the program, the culture, how everybody took pride in what Ohio State means," Judkins said. "We talked about relationships and what I could do on the field, but Ohio State is a place that I'll forever be a part of. That brotherhood is real. It was a great situation. I ended up committing the same day. I didn't even want to take a visit anywhere else."

That night happened to be the night Michigan won the CFP championship by beating Washington. Judkins announced on social media that he'd committed to Ohio State just as that game ended, giving Buckeye fans a needed salve. "A lot of people reached out and were like, 'Man, you made my night,'" Judkins said.

The idea of playing in the Big Ten had a special allure for Judkins for an interesting reason. He loved hearing Gus Johnson on Fox's broadcasts. But Fox didn't broadcast SEC games. Knowing that Johnson would call some of Ohio State's games was a bonus for becoming a Buckeye. "I didn't really talk about it a lot, but it's one of those moments you always wish to experience," Judkins said. "To have him call one of my games was a special moment."

One issue that could have been a deal-breaker became no issue at all. At Ole Miss, Judkins was a workhorse. At Ohio State, he'd have to share the load with TreVeyon Henderson. They had a friendship dating from their recruitment days. They talked about winning a national championship together and how a tandem system would benefit them in 2024 and in the NFL by reducing wear and tear on their bodies.

"We both have great energy—just two selfless guys," Judkins said. "We both had the same goal in mind, which was to be relentless in helping our team win. That's why we worked so well together."

Judkins also bonded quickly with Howard. When Judkins first got to Columbus, his car hadn't arrived, so Howard gave him rides to the Woody. "We just talked about the schools we came from and were just so psyched and happy to be in a situation like this," Judkins said. "I remember we just looked at each other like, 'Let's go fucking do this shit!'"

SETH MCLAUGHLIN CAME to Ohio State a defeated man. Or at least a defeated football player. He'd accomplished a lot at Alabama. McLaughlin was the lowest-rated Alabama recruit in 2020, an afterthought in Nick Saban's No. 2–ranked class. He was so unimposing physically that star running back Najee Harris asked him if he was a walk-on. "He was like, 'Who the hell are we recruiting these days?'" McLaughlin said with a laugh. But McLaughlin developed. He beamed when after he'd had a few good practices, Harris approached him and put his arm around him as a sign of respect and acceptance. In the classroom, McLaughlin was brilliant. He graduated in 2½ years with a 4.0 grade point average as a finance major and later earned his master's in hospitality management.

McLaughlin started eight games in 2022 and played well. He expected to build on that the next season. Instead, it turned into a nightmare. He had some errant snaps working with quarterback Jalen Milroe. The issue came to a head in Alabama's CFP semifinal loss to Michigan at the Rose Bowl. On the final play of the Tide's 27–20 overtime loss, Milroe was stuffed on fourth down after taking a low snap. When McLaughlin returned to Tuscaloosa, he needed a police escort to get back to his house after his address was leaked on social media.

"I got out of Tuscaloosa pretty quick," he said.

McLaughlin had about six potential schools in mind when he entered the transfer portal. Ohio State wasn't one of them. The Buckeyes hadn't recruited him out of Buford High School in Georgia even though McLaughlin's predecessor at center there was Harry Miller, a five-star recruit for Ohio State.

He didn't think the Buckeyes were an option this time around, either. He knew Carson Hinzman had started for the Buckeyes in 2023 and figured Hinzman would again in 2024. But Hinzman had struggled taking over for Luke Wypler, who'd surprised and disappointed coaches by entering the 2023 NFL draft. Coaches benched Hinzman for the Cotton Bowl loss. McLaughlin didn't know that when offensive line coach Justin Frye reached out to him after he entered the transfer portal. Frye told him he'd compete with Hinzman for the job and would be expected to serve as a mentor for him. On McLaughlin's visit, Frye gave a detailed presentation of OSU's scheme and how he could help him improve. It rekindled the spark in McLaughlin.

"Once I got here," McLaughlin said. "I was like, 'Damn, I don't even want to leave,' because I was so excited to get back to working at football."

ALABAMA FANS MIGHT have wanted McLaughlin gone. The Crimson Tide certainly didn't want Caleb Downs to leave. Downs' football pedigree was impeccable. His father, Gary, was an NFL running back for seven years. His brother, Josh, is a wide receiver for the Indianapolis Colts. His uncle was star cornerback Dré Bly. The Downses haven't limited their success to athletics. Downs' sister, Kameron, is in medical school at Wake Forest.

"My dad taught us when we were kids the word, *Kaizen*, which is a Japanese word for continuing improvement," Downs said. "Our family has continued to live by that, and that has allowed us to push and grow in a lot of ways."

Gary Downs, who became a track coach after his NFL career, had his sons and daughter running hills in the suburban Atlanta neighborhood when Caleb was four. Caleb didn't understand it or like it then, but he wasn't going to quit and watch his siblings do it alone. He and Josh, who's almost three years older, went at it as only brothers can, with the usual effect of toughening up the younger one. From the start, Caleb was a star in football. In his first game as a six-year-old, he scored touchdowns the first six times he touched the ball.

"I didn't understand it at that point, but I was like, 'Well, that was pretty easy,'" Downs said.

He became a five-star safety ranked as the No. 8 overall recruit nationally in the 2023 class. He seriously considered Ohio State then. "When I watched Caleb in high school, he was one of the best high school players I've ever seen," Day said.

After Downs chose Alabama to play for Saban, he became an instant star. He led the Crimson Tide in tackles and was an All-American. He was close to a perfect player—gifted athletically with uncommon sense of purpose and work ethic.

"He was just so consistent," McLaughlin said. "He had a plan to go about his day. After every single practice, without fail, you'd see him in the cold tub for 10 minutes with headphones on, locked in. You don't see a lot of freshmen locked in with an intentional mentality when they walk in the facility every day. Usually, it takes two or three years to develop that mentality. He stepped onto campus with it."

Nine days after Alabama's CFP loss to Michigan, Downs attended what he expected to be a routine team meeting. At first, it didn't register when Saban, probably the most accomplished coach in college football history, told his players that he was retiring. A couple of players wondered if Saban was joking. He was not.

"It was a difficult pill to swallow," Downs said. "I didn't see it coming, didn't want to see it coming."

After a week of deliberation, Downs entered the transfer portal. Ohio State and Georgia were the top contenders. Downs did not grow up a Bulldogs fan, but he is from Georgia and Kirby Smart's team had won the previous two national championships. His position coach, Travaris Robinson, had left the Crimson Tide for Georgia. The smart money was on the Bulldogs. Ohio State knew it had to impress Downs when Day, Knowles, cornerbacks coach Tim Walton, and new safeties coach Matt Guerrieri met with him at his home. Knowles said it almost felt like a job interview, except that Downs was the employer. Knowles took out his laptop and explained in detail Ohio State's defense—its scheme and what they envisioned Downs' role to be in the red zone and in other situations.

"He's there with his notebook, taking notes, asking questions, always serious, just ultra-focused," Knowles said.

The meeting was a success. Downs knew the Buckeyes had a loaded, senior-laden roster returning. He wanted to surround himself with similarly talented players. Ohio State's scheme also intrigued him. Smart was Saban's defensive coordinator at Alabama and ran a similar scheme. Downs wanted to learn a different defense. He also remembered liking Columbus when he visited as a recruit. "I just wanted to be a Buckeye, honestly," he said.

Ohio State's NIL inducement wasn't a major factor, he said. "As a kid, the biggest goal is to get to the league," Downs said of the NFL. "Making money now is cool, but that's not the end goal. The end goal is to have a successful career in the league, play a lot of years, and do everything God has blessed me to do."

Except for Downs, there were questions marks about all the transfers. Would they deliver as hoped? Would they fit Ohio State's culture? To a large degree, Ohio State's season would ride on those questions.

10

Offseason Improvement

The core of the Ohio State team had remained intact, and the Buckeyes had added key transfers. Now the veterans had a request for Mickey Marotti, the team's head strength coach. Marotti was Urban Meyer's right-hand man dating back to their time with the Florida Gators and remained with the Buckeyes when Day succeeded Meyer. In many ways, he was the Buckeyes' head coach in the offseason because of his daily involvement with players.

"Mickey is sort of the glue around the culture in and out of the building," Ross Bjork said. "He sets a great tone of, 'Hey, we're going to be intense.'"

The seniors' message to Marotti about the 2024 offseason conditioning program was simple. "I remember we as leaders," Jack Sawyer said, "and guys who came back having a real talk with coach Mick saying, 'Look, we want it harder than it has ever been. If it even looks like we're thinking of taking a shortcut on anything, jump on us harder than you jump on a freshman because we're not leaving anything to chance this year. All our chips are in the middle of the table, and it's our last shot, no matter what.'"

Marotti agreed. He told them that if that was his mandate, they couldn't challenge him on it. Sometimes, Marotti would chew out Sawyer, linebacker Cody Simon, or another leader just to send a message to the rest of the team, even if they'd done nothing wrong.

"Being an older guy who'd played a lot of games," Lathan Ransom said, "I just didn't want any stones unturned. And I was tired of hearing we're not tough enough or that we're soft."

Ransom also helped set the expectations for the Buckeyes defense. Ohio State's goal every year is to live up to the standard of being Silver Bullets, a nickname given to the Buckeyes' dominant defense in the 1990s. In the first meeting of offseason conditioning, Ransom said that the goal for the 2024 defense was not just to be the best defense in the country.

"I told coach Mick and the team that we're going to be the best defense to ever come through Ohio State," Ransom said.

With so many veteran players, Marotti wanted to emphasize the mental side of toughness. They'd been through years of physical development. There was only so much they could do to enhance that. Marotti told the older players that he would devise a plan to ensure accountability. Unlike the image of a strength coach as drill sergeant, Marotti was collaborative with the players, a nod to their experience and his overall regard for them. He and Day met with leaders to help plan the next workouts. They had meetings to discuss how they could make the culture of the program even stronger.

Punctuality was one measure. Marotti has a rule that players must check in 25 minutes before the start of their scheduled lift. If they're late, they can't lift and must make up the session on the weekend with their presumably pissed-off teammates having to come in to oversee it. If they were one of the 20 or so players on the leadership committee, they'd be stripped of that honor.

Caleb Downs found out quickly how inflexible that standard was. As a high-profile transfer, Downs was intent on showing his new teammates how mature and responsible he was. One day soon after arriving,

Downs overslept for his 6:30 a.m. workout. "I'm used to getting there early, but I didn't know you had to get there 25 minutes early or they sent you home," Downs said. "I had to be there at 6:05 and got there at like 6:06."

Downs ran into the Woody, only to be told to leave. "I was like, 'No, you can't be serious,'" he said. "That was a sad day. I drove home and sat in the car for like 25-30 minutes, feeling sorry for myself. Just being the new guy, I wanted to be a stand-up guy for my teammates, not wanting to seem like I didn't care. I wanted to earn the respect of my teammates."

Ohio State's offseason conditioning under Marotti has always emphasized competition. He raised it to a different level. "We made everything competitive," Marotti said. "If you could think of it, it was competitive."

Marotti pitted older players against each other instead of having young players get their welcome-to-college moments by getting dominated by veterans. Donovan Jackson, for example, was pitted against defensive tackle Ty Hamilton. "I had no choice but to get better because Ty pushed me in every way," Jackson said. "Ty is a freak of nature in terms of training, so I had to bring my 'A' game every day or be embarrassed by him. That made both of us better."

For Seth McLaughlin, the workouts were a reality check in two ways. First, he was impressed by how seriously the seniors took them. He knew a lot of them could have been training for the NFL draft in some warm-weather spot knowing that a big payday was just ahead of them. Instead, they were grinding in the middle of a dreary Ohio winter in the hopes of winning a national title that had eluded the Buckeyes for a decade.

"That was definitely an inspiring thing," McLaughlin said. "When a guy like that says something, you listen because you know they didn't come back for no reason."

The actual weight and conditioning work was jarring for McLaughlin. OSU's workouts were much different than Alabama's. McLaughlin's grip strength, for example, was weaker than Ohio State players' because that wasn't something Alabama emphasized. Marotti makes everything a competition, and McLaughlin was often pitted against Carson Hinzman, who excels in the weight room.

"He was kicking my ass," McLaughlin said. "I felt I had to completely relearn football. I felt like a freshman again, coming from a guy who's won two SEC championships and as a starting center had blocked countless first-round draft picks at a high level. In January and February, I was like, 'What the hell am I doing? Am I even going to play football again?' It was an interesting experience, for sure."

McLaughlin found his footing as winter workouts continued, and that made him feel that he had earned respect from his new teammates. For Will Howard, offseason conditioning was a challenge for a different reason. He'd been in the transfer portal for six weeks and put on "portal weight" while in limbo. Howard weighed over 250 when he first tipped the scales at OSU.

"I was a little chubby," Howard said. "I came in and my ass was throwing up damn near every workout—not every workout, but there were definitely a couple of times I blew some chunks out there on the field."

WHILE HOWARD, MCLAUGHLIN, and the others were enduring Marotti's offseason conditioning, Day twice had to hire an offensive coordinator. Day loved being the play-caller. It was his calling card. He enjoyed the Xs and Os chess game. But in the NIL/transfer portal era, he knew he had become more of a CEO and oversee the whole program from more of a macro view. Finding himself immersed at 10:00 PM on weekdays of game week trying to decide what to call on third-and-seven was not a wise use of his time. In 2023 he promoted Brian Hartline to offensive coordinator because of Hartline's success as wide receivers coach. But Hartline wasn't ready to call plays then. After the Missouri disaster, Day was intent on finding an experienced, play-calling coordinator. He hired Bill O'Brien, who had NFL experience and had masterfully coached Penn State for two years following the Jerry Sandusky child-abuse scandal that forced legendary coach Joe Paterno's firing in 2011. O'Brien left State College to become head coach of the Houston Texans, which lasted until 2020. He was Alabama's offensive coordinator for two seasons.

"When he came in for those couple weeks, he was hitting the ground running, and everybody was really excited about him," Day said.

But then Boston College coach Jeff Hafley, the former OSU defensive coordinator, left to become coordinator for the Green Bay Packers. O'Brien, a Boston native, quickly surfaced as a candidate. After those two seasons at Alabama he had previously returned to the Boston area as offensive coordinator and quarterbacks coach for the New England Patriots in 2023. The lure of returning home proved too hard to resist, and O'Brien took the job. The timing was not ideal. Spring practice was to start in less than a month. Whoever Day hired would have to be a quick study. There was an obvious candidate.

CHIP KELLY HAD been on Day's original list of offensive coordinator candidates in January because...of course. Kelly and Day had remained close after last coaching together with the San Francisco 49ers in 2016. This was not merely a coaching relationship. It was a tight friendship. Day and Kelly had summer homes next to each other and would go boating together. Nina Day and Kelly's wife, Jill, are good friends.

As a coordinator candidate, Kelly was an obvious, if overqualified, choice. No one could match his resume. After 14 (nonconsecutive) years as a New Hampshire assistant, including his last 10 seasons as offensive coordinator, Kelly was hired as Oregon's offensive coordinator. Defenses had few answers for his ultra-fast-tempo offense. In two seasons as coordinator, the Ducks led the Pac-10 in scoring and total offense.

In 2009, coach Mike Bellotti became Oregon's athletics director, and Kelly succeeded him. His first team went to the Rose Bowl, where it lost to Ohio State in what was perhaps Terrelle Pryor's finest moment as Buckeye quarterback. The next season, Kelly led undefeated Oregon to the national championship game and was voted national coach of the year. The Ducks lost 22–19 to Auburn in the title game on a last-second field goal. In 2011, Oregon won the Pac-12 title and beat Wisconsin in the Rose Bowl. In 2012, the Ducks' only loss was to Stanford. Oregon finished the season ranked No. 2 after winning the Fiesta Bowl.

The Philadelphia Eagles then hired Kelly. His first two teams finished 10–6, losing in the wild-card round the first year but failing to qualify for the playoffs in the second. The next season was the ill-fated one after Day had been hired as quarterbacks coach when quarterback Sam Bradford was injured and the season went south. After his disastrous 2–14 season with the 49ers, Kelly took a year off before he was hired as UCLA's coach in 2018. He was unable to replicate his previous college success with the Bruins, who have long been in the football shadow of crosstown rival USC. His best record in six seasons at UCLA was 9–4 in 2022.

During practice for UCLA's 2023 LA Bowl appearance, Bruins quarterbacks coach Ryan Gunderson left to become Oregon State's offensive coordinator. Kelly filled in for Gunderson and loved it. "I had not been in a position room since I became a head coach in 2009," he said. "You go in and out of those rooms, but you're not in there day-to-day."

Jill Kelly told him that he seemed happier being immersed in coaching quarterbacks, and he agreed. He loved getting back into the nitty-gritty of coaching players closely and not just overseeing a program. "The role of a head coach has changed drastically," Kelly said. "You're a fundraiser, and you're wearing a lot more administrative hats, and you're not coaching. I got into this because I love coaching."

Though reports of a potential amicable divorce between Kelly and UCLA circulated for months, Kelly wasn't ready to leave when the Ohio State began its coordinator search that ended with O'Brien's hiring. "I was still trying to make sure we had a recruiting class at UCLA and take care of my coaches," Kelly said. "I wasn't really thinking about [the OSU job], but then when he called the second time, it just seemed things were more aligned at that point."

He reportedly interviewed for some NFL coordinator jobs, but when Day reached out again, he jumped at it. Ohio State offensive line coach

Justin Frye had been on his UCLA staff. He knew Jim Knowles and Larry Johnson. He talked with O'Brien about OSU's staff and players. "OB was like, 'Chip, I was only there for three weeks, but I absolutely loved those guys,'" Kelly said.

Still, it's highly unusual to leave being a head coach at a Power 4 school to become a coordinator at another program. "I wouldn't have gone to any other college," Kelly said. "I would not have taken another college job."

Kelly had always been Day's mentor. Now he would be his coordinator. Neither man was concerned about the role reversal. They discussed how it would work. "We weren't going to let any of that affect our relationship and our friendship," Day said, "because it's my responsibility to be the head coach. It's his responsibility to be the coordinator, so that was understood."

"I had no problem with it," Kelly said. "I just need things black and white. I'm a black-and-white guy."

Day was thrilled to be reunited with his mentor. He had hired Jim Knowles to be what he termed the head coach of the defense two years earlier. Now he had an eminently qualified and trusted coordinator for the offense. During his hiring pitch to Kelly, Day discussed the OSU roster position by position. He knew the ingredients were in place for a title run. Kelly was the final piece.

"I said that we have a team to go win the national championship," Day told him. "It's not going to be easy, but how cool would it be for us to come together and win a national championship together?"

11

"Natty or Bust"

With a loaded roster, Ohio State opened spring practice with lofty expectations. As if there was any doubt what the measure of success for the 2024 team was, Denzel Burke dispelled that early. "It's definitely natty or bust, man," the cornerback said on March 7. "That's our mentality. No excuses. We've got to win it all."

Burke did not begin his interview session that day intending to make that declaration. But he is a candid guy. "I was just responding to the question, and it was the first thing that came to mind," he said.

He saw eyeballs get big. "I was like, 'Well, y'all are going to have to hold me to the standard,'" he said. "I obviously didn't know how the flow of the season was going to go, but we all had a goal, and we weren't going to let anything get in the way of it."

Ryan Day didn't chastise Burke for his comment, though he wishes he'd have been little less forthcoming. "I just felt he was playing into the narrative, which is not a great idea," he said. "I think you need to focus on winning the first game and not worry about that narrative. But I think for Denzel in that moment, he was trying to explain why he decided to come back and forgo the NFL and show what the expectations were of him and his teammates. So that was his decision to make. It all worked out in the end, but we were trying to avoid those types of conversations, not add to them."

Though Ohio State had an undeniably talented roster, Day did have questions about his team. In the two months since Will Howard arrived from Kansas State, Day had become impressed by his intelligence and work ethic. Howard also has the type of upbeat, engaging personality that causes people to gravitate toward him.

"I pride myself on that," Howard said. "I'm not going to be too good to talk to anybody. I want to be a good person. How you impact people around you is how you're remembered in life. I try to live out every day trying to make everyone around me feel good."

Howard is a natural leader, but he couldn't carry himself right away as if he was the starting quarterback. He knew he had to earn respect from teammates with his work. He'd been on the other side of it when Adrian Martinez transferred to Kansas State. Howard admired how Martinez handled it and wanted to be the same way. Howard treated players for meals and got to know them away from the football facility.

"It's a tough line to walk," Howard said. "You want to be that guy. You want to earn the respect. You want to tell these people to know they can count on me. But you also don't want to step on anybody's toes and be overconfident and piss anybody off."

Howard threaded that needle well.

"Will is an offensive lineman in a quarterback's body," right tackle Josh Fryar said. "He's so personable to everybody. He got along with everybody in the locker room."

But Howard still had to perform on the field. He had shed weight, but everything was new to him—scheme, coaches, and teammates—and it showed. Day had the quarterbacks rotate taking snaps with starters and backups, and Howard didn't separate himself.

"It wasn't as if you walked off the field saying, 'He can't do it,'" Day said. "It's just that there were certain times when you'd see a play it would give you pause and concern because he had very little experience in the style of offense. There was just concern that he would be able to pick it up fast enough to play at a high level in the fall."

But Howard remained the clear front-runner for the job. Devin Brown, who was ahead of Kyle McCord for the job in 2023 before a couple of bad practices late in training camp, remained inconsistent. Some days, Day thought Brown was ready to make a push. But Brown couldn't sustain that momentum. The quarterback who did impress when he got reps with the starters was freshman Julian Sayin. Two months earlier, he signed with Alabama as the No. 1 quarterback nationally in the 2024 recruiting class. But just as was the case with Caleb Downs, Nick Saban's retirement caused him to enter the transfer portal. The Buckeyes already had Air Noland as a quarterback recruit, but Sayin was too good to pass up even though Day said he told the quarterback's family that Ohio State's NIL coffers were exhausted.

"I was clear at that point that we had very little or no NIL left," Day said. "I was very honest and transparent about exactly what this would be this season because I've gone through this before with quarterbacks. There are four other guys in the room. There's nothing guaranteed. There's no NIL. I think Julian's family, his mom in particular, really appreciated the honesty and the transparency."

Sayin showed quickly why he was such a highly rated prospect. "He had some really good days," Day said.

Said Kelly, "I think Julian is a special player. He's got an unbelievable release, has smooth a stroke as you can. I think he's really quick of mind. I think Julian's a really, really talented football player and a great kid."

But as a true freshman, Sayin was always a longshot. It was always Howard's job to lose. He told Day during their discussions before he committed that he wanted to be coached hard. Howard had developed thick skin through his adversity at Kansas State. He recognized that he had to get better if he was to lead OSU to a championship and improve his NFL draft stock. Howard struggled in particular with the deep ball. As a big quarterback, he sometimes had issues with his footwork. He also wasn't used to the speed of Ohio State's receivers.

"I was taking three steps and two hitches at K-State to throw the go ball," Howard said. "I did that the first time during spring ball with Jeremiah, and I threw it like 10 yards behind him. Coach Day is like, 'What the fuck are you doing?' I was like, 'Oh man, that's what I was taught [at Kansas State].' He's like, 'You can't get away with that here.'"

Day is a perfectionist when it comes to coaching his old position. He knows one bad play can change a game. By making practices harder than games, Day believes it forces his quarterbacks to be resilient and tough.

"He is never satisfied," Howard said. "Even if you throw a touchdown, if it's not the right read or you used the wrong footwork, he's going to get on your ass, and that's just how it is. He's a yeller. He definitely is pretty high on the volume in practice. If you take a drop and he wants that ball out, he's yelling, 'Ball!" right behind your head, making sure you're getting that ball out on time. If not, he's going to rip your ass. 'What the hell are you doing? Are you fucking stupid?' There were times in the spring where I was like, 'Man, do I even know how to freaking read a coverage? Do I know how to throw a football?' He was getting on me so hard, but I needed it."

Howard came to appreciate that bluntness. He recognized that playing quarterback at Ohio State comes with so much responsibility, on and off the field. He wasn't in Kansas anymore.

THE OTHER BIG QUESTION entering the spring was the offensive line. Still fresh on everyone's minds was its underwhelming play in 2023, particularly its awful performance in the Cotton Bowl loss to Missouri. Ohio State ran for only 97 yards in 33 carries in that game. The only certainties were Josh Simmons at left tackle and Donovan Jackson at left guard. Josh Fryar was the incumbent at right tackle, but Day wondered whether he could play consistently well enough on a championship team. A handful of players—namely Tegra Tshabola, Luke Montgomery, and Austin Siereveld—auditioned for jobs.

Seth McLaughlin quickly became the front-runner at center over Carson Hinzman, who also saw time at guard. Day liked McLaughlin's confidence, the way he made the blocking calls and communicated with the other linemen. Bad snaps proved not to be an issue. Ohio State coaches learned that when Alabama went to a silent snap count in loud stadiums, the Crimson Tide didn't have a signal before the quarterback clapped for the snap. Most teams, including Ohio State, have theirs yell something before the snap to give the center a trigger to get ready to hike the ball. Without that, it's akin to trying to hit a golf shot without a backswing.

Fryar did enough to keep the right tackle job, but the right guard spot remained up for grabs. It was only shortly before the spring game did a potential favorite emerge in Tegra Tshabola.

Tshabola was born in the Democratic Republic of the Congo in central Africa. His family immigrated to the Cincinnati area, where it had relatives, when he was four. He's the youngest of seven siblings. Tshabola remembers watching a football game on TV when he was in kindergarten, intrigued by this sport he'd never seen. He and his siblings would play backyard football with neighborhood friends for hours. He was hooked. It helped that he grew so quickly. By the seventh grade, he was 6'3" and weighed at least 260 pounds. *By the seventh grade.*

"And at that point, I was the fastest kid on the team," Tshabola said.

Opposing teams in his youth leagues would regularly question his age. Tshabola made sure his coaches had a copy of his birth certificate. He became a coveted recruit even before he enrolled at Lakota West High School in West Chester. Kentucky offered him a scholarship when he was in junior high. But Ohio State was his dream school. He watched YouTube videos of OSU legends. When he got to see the inside of the

Woody during a recruiting visit, he was mesmerized by the pictures and videos showing the Buckeyes' tradition and history.

"I was like, 'There's no way I don't want to also become a part of this,'" Tshabola said.

Like most offensive linemen, Tshabola had to watch and learn when he first got to Ohio State. For the first time, he was blocking players he couldn't overpower. He redshirted and then took 32 offensive snaps in five games in 2023. He considered 2024 to be a pivotal season. But he bounced around at different positions during the spring, primarily competing with Fryar at right tackle.

"I didn't really get an opportunity to practice at right guard until the last two days before the spring game," Tshabola said. "Coach Kelly was the one who wanted to see what I could do at guard. I want to say it was the last contact day before the spring game and I played guard, and he was like, 'Yeah, you're staying at guard. We need a big body that can move people.'

"We didn't really have a guard at that point. That's why coach Kelly was like, 'Let's see what he can do. He hasn't really had a chance to show himself here at this position.' It was literally just one practice."

Kelly said that the decision for Tshabola to be the starter was Day's and Frye's. But he was in Tshabola's corner. Though as a young lineman, Tshabola lacked consistency, Kelly said the number of mistakes decreased throughout the spring.

"I said, 'Bro, I think you've got a bright future in this game,'" Kelly recalled. "Sometimes, it's just making sure guys believe in themselves. I truly believe that. I'm a direct person who doesn't BS, and I think Tegra's going to be really special. He moved so well for such a big guy. Football was important to him, and he wanted to be good in it."

Tshabola would certainly have ups and downs during the season, but he had become a piece of the offensive line puzzle.

THE TIGHT ENDS were another position group trying to find their identity. It was one that Keenan Bailey was determined to instill. Even though he was not yet 30, Bailey had been on the Buckeyes' coaching staff longer than anyone but Larry Johnson.

Bailey had been a junior at Notre Dame who knew then-Ohio State running backs coach Tony Alford from Alford's time coaching in South Bend. Bailey would drive to Columbus to help Alford. Meyer saw something in Bailey and wanted him to intern at Ohio State but couldn't guarantee an internship would be open the next year. So Bailey scheduled 24 credit hours at Notre Dame, all from Monday to Thursday, and then drove to OSU and stayed with the Alford family for three nights a week so he could graduate early. That was his foot in the door.

Bailey then advanced steadily until Day named him tight ends coach in 2023. He was blessed that year by having Cade Stover. "Farmer Gronk" was the most productive pass-catching tight end at Ohio State in decades and a John Mackey Award finalist. But now Stover was off to the NFL, and Bailey knew he had to piece together his unit by committee. He started by issuing a challenge. Really, it was more of a putdown.

"In my very first tight end meeting, I just plainly put it on the board: You guys are the least talented unit at Ohio State. Like not close," Bailey said. "Everyone was looking at me sideways, like, 'That's fucked up.' And I'm like, 'That's the truth.'"

In the tight ends room, he had Gee Scott Jr., a converted wide receiver. He had sophomore Jelani Thurman, who had barely begun to tap into his potential. He had Bennett Christian, who was suspended for the 2023 season for taking a supplement that contained a banned substance. He had Patrick Gurd, a walk-on.

Bailey needed someone who could block the "C" gap on the perimeter of the line against defensive ends. He scoured the transfer portal looking for candidates. The one who caught his eye was just down the road, though few knew who Will Kacmarek was. He wasn't even a starter at Ohio University. But Bailey saw video of Kacmarek "just mauling dudes." A former OSU walk-on receiver, Sam Wiglusz, had transferred to Ohio and vouched for Kacmarek to Bailey. When Kacmarek went into the portal before Ohio State's Cotton Bowl game against Missouri, Bailey told Day he wanted Kacmarek. Day was skeptical. How could a backup at Ohio University help Ohio State? Bailey held firm.

"He's what we need," he told Day. "We need a mauler. We need someone to change the culture [and add] toughness."

Day acceded, and Kacmarek became a Buckeye. He fit what Bailey wanted. If his unit was the least talented on the team, he wanted it to be the toughest and most aggressive. In that first meeting, Bailey showed his players a montage of the "Bad Boys" Detroit Pistons, who were the bullies of the NBA in the early 1990s. He later showed them Mike Tyson knockouts and UFC tap-outs. In on-field drills in the winter, tight ends usually balanced blocking and receiving drills. Bailey insisted that it all be spent on blocking. Footballs never left the bag. In spring practice, Bailey told them that if a fight started, his unit better have instigated it.

"I cannot lie to you, the tight ends were annoying in practice," linebacker Sonny Styles said. "They were all going super hard every single play and blocked you all the way through the whistle. "I remember in [training] camp, I swear the DBs and tight ends hated each other. When the tight ends would go up against the linebackers, they're going to block us, but they weren't going to bury us into the ground. We hold our own. But they'd catch the nickels or the corners on one of the edges and just bury them. They would do it time after time, and the DBs would get all mad."

SONNY STYLES WAS making his own transition. The son of former OSU linebacker Lorenzo Styles Sr. (and brother of Ohio State DB Lorenzo Styles Jr.), Sonny was supposed to be one of the crown jewels of the Buckeyes' 2023 recruiting class. But Sonny—only his closest female relatives call him by his given name Alex—was mature beyond his years physically and mentally. When he decided to reclassify and enroll in the summer of 2022, he was already 6'4" and about 220 pounds at age 17.

He saw action as a safety as a freshman and started in 2023. But as he continued to fill out, he and OSU coaches decided to move him to the weakside (Will) linebacker, which figured to be his position in the NFL. "It was definitely a bit of an adjustment," he said. "You have to see things faster and be able to react to all the different run concepts, like the pulling guards and things like that. It was great to have coach Laurinaitis as my coach. He's just got so much knowledge. Obviously, he's a super-decorated player from his team at Ohio State and the NFL."

For James Laurinaitis, coaching at his alma mater was a dream come true. As a boy in Minnesota, he was so obsessed with football that at parent-teacher conferences, his parents would regularly be asked if James could talk about anything besides the sport. He had been a three-time All-American at Ohio State and had a successful eight-year NFL career. After his retirement, he became a sports radio talk show host. But the itch to get back in the game persisted.

"My wife, Shelly, always thought I'd be a great coach and thought I should do it," he said. "She always said you have a lot to give to this world outside of just your opinion on sports. You should go impact these young people."

For a couple of years, it never got past the talking stage. "I felt I was getting to a point where I needed to jump in and try to check that box or else I was going to live with regret," he said. "The people I knew in the business might get fired out of it."

His old Ohio State roommate, Marcus Freeman, finally gave him a shot when he got the Notre Dame job in 2023 and offered Laurinaitis a graduate assistant position. The next year, Ohio State called. Defensive coordinator Jim Knowles had linebackers as his position group and wanted someone who could take over that responsibility. In February 2024 Laurinaitis was officially promoted from grad assistant to linebackers coach.

"I've always felt this is a calling that God has put in my heart to try to help young people, through the game I love, accomplish their dreams just like I got to accomplish mine," he said. "I do it for the love of the game and being a part of something way bigger than yourselves. I wanted to impact these guys."

LAURINAITIS AND RECEIVERS coach Brian Hartline weren't the only former Buckeye players on the coaching staff. Tim Walton had joined the Buckeyes in 2022 to coach the cornerback position he'd played as a Buckeye in the early 1990s. After a successful NFL coaching career spanning 11 seasons between 2009 and 2021, Day lured him back. His rationale was similar to Laurinaitis'.

"I like this better because you get to impact lives," Walton said. "You meet the guy at 16. If they end up coming to your school, you could end up with five, six years with a guy. They're still learning. They're still impressionable, so you can make an impact on the foundation they have at that point.

With Burke and Davison Igbinosun, Walton had talented veterans at cornerback. But the corners found out quickly they had their hands full trying to cover OSU's receivers, especially the newest one. Jeremiah Smith showed early that he was the generational talent he was touted to be. He simply skipped the growing pains that come with the territory for an 18-year-old going against players three or four years older.

"The way he practiced, the way he made plays, his attention to detail, was just tremendous," Day said. "We've always had good receivers, but the combination of size and strength and speed was unlike anything we've ever had."

Ohio State already had senior Emeka Egbuka, who would break the OSU record for career catches and become the first Buckeye taken in the 2025 NFL draft. The Buckeyes had Carnell Tate, who would become perhaps the best No. 3 receiver in the country. They also had Brandon Inniss, who'd been a five-star prospect a year earlier and was ready for a significant role. But Smith was simply different.

"Every day was a jaw-dropping play," Styles said. "We've had guys like Marvin [Harrison Jr.], who was one of the best players I've been around, if not the best. He made stuff just look so easy. But Jeremiah, some plays, it was like this dude's just not from this earth."

In the summertime, he would continue to impress with his off-field work. The Buckeyes have an annual competition on their ecobikes. It's an exercise that requires raw strength. A lineman almost always wins it. In 2024, Smith did.

"He's never been late," Brian Hartline said. "He's never had an academic issue. He's never had anything. He's always on top of his stuff."

Mickey Marotti awards "Iron Buckeye" honors to the very top achievers in his summer conditioning program. Smith became the first OSU freshman ever to earn that.

"He's the most impressive young player I've ever seen," Kelly said.

DAY HIMSELF HAD to take on an additional role in spring practice. During spring break, which came after only two practices, running backs coach Tony Alford quit to take the same job at Michigan. Day was at Clemson on a recruiting visit with his son, RJ, who had developed into a college prospect as—of course—a quarterback when Alford called to inform him. "It was a short conversation, as you can imagine," Day said. Alford had been on thin ice at Ohio State. His salary had been cut, and he was serving on a one-year contract. But the timing of his departure and the destination left a sour taste. "There were enough reasons for him to leave, but I think for him to leave and to go there caught everybody off guard," Day said. "But he had to do what was best for him."

Day himself coached the running backs during spring practice while he searched for Alford's replacement. Ohio State interviewed up to 10 people, but Oregon's Carlos Locklyn separated himself from the pack.

"He was really, really prepared," Day said of the interview. "Lock had a PowerPoint presentation with all his drills. He had done a lot of research on Chip. He had done a lot of research on me. He had read Jim Tressel's *The Winner's Manual*. You could tell he was not only prepared but wanted the job. And he took a lot of pride in relationships, did a great job in recruiting, was very organized."

Locklyn's coaching path was unconventional. His original career was in law enforcement, with some duties so top-secret that he still can't reveal details. A Montgomery, Alabama, native, Locklyn played running back and then defensive back at Tennessee-Chattanooga. He liked law enforcement but believed he could influence more people as a coach. He volunteered at several high schools in Memphis before the University of Memphis let him assist for no pay in its weight room after his law-enforcement shifts. He eventually worked with the running backs and quickly developed a reputation because of his passion. Eventual Florida State coach Mike Norvell and Oregon coach Dan Lanning were on that Memphis staff. Locklyn got jobs with both as he climbed the coaching ladder.

Locklyn knew both TreVeyon Henderson and Quinshon Judkins before coming to Columbus. Judkins is also from Montgomery. Locklyn recruited Henderson while at Florida State. Locklyn prides himself on coaching his players hard and without much subtlety.

"The first day in the room, I kicked everybody [else] out and sat Q and Tre down and said, 'Look, there's a new sheriff in town. This is how stuff is going to be run. Y'all are going to learn how to play as one. It doesn't cost you nothing to celebrate another man's success. If y'all trust what I'm telling you, both of y'all will win the national championship, you're still going to rush for 1,000 yards, and you're still going to hear your name called early in the NFL draft.' And they said, 'Coach Lock, we trust you.'"

Chip Kelly, Ohio State's next-newest coach, was already struck by how close OSU's players were. "A lot of teams talk about a brotherhood," he said. "But the brotherhood at Ohio State is real. It is truly a brotherhood. Those players truly care about one another. I watched how easily Will Howard, Seth McLaughlin, Q [Judkins], and Caleb Downs transitioned in. It was seamless. You could tell that the players—the transfers and current players—had great respect for each other and that grew into love for each other."

That bond was enhanced in the spring and summer playing a sport that bears little resemblance to football—golf. "I think it's just the competitive nature of us trying to conquer a game that's so hard," Denzel Burke said. Egbuka and Lincoln Kienholz might have been the most well-rounded athletes on the team and were considered the team's best golfers, along with Howard and offensive lineman Toby Wilson.

The Buckeyes continued working with Marotti the next couple of months before training camp started. Marotti and his wife, Susie, traditionally host an end-of-summer get-together at their house for the team's leaders. Usually, he said, players come almost as a courtesy. They'll eat and hang out for a little while and then leave. This year, the players didn't want to leave. He could see how much they liked being around each other and respected each other. At the end of the evening, Marotti told his wife, "There's something different [about this team], just different."

12
Faith

There was something different about this Buckeye team. What many of the players would say made it different was their spiritual faith. As a public institution, Ohio State is secular. Unlike some coaches who openly proselytize, Ryan Day, who is Catholic, does not. But in 2024, several Ohio State players became prominent in expressing their Christianity and the role it plays in their lives. Many checked into their training camp hotel wearing "Jesus Won" T-shirts. On August 26, several participated in an on-campus baptism of about 60 students.

These players believed their faith was an essential part of their journey in college. Gee Scott Jr. might be the perfect representation of that. Scott was a wide receiver from the Seattle area ranked as the No. 37 overall prospect nationally in the 2020 class. But his early years at Ohio State were bumpy.

"He was always in conflict with somebody in the building," Mickey Marotti said. "With his position coach or why he wasn't playing more or 'Why did you pick him to be front of the line and not me?' Everything was questioned. Everything."

Scott doesn't dispute that. "He's spot on," Scott said. "That's absolutely true."

Scott was going through change in his football and non-football life. He decided, after discussing it with his father and with former NFL cornerback Richard Sherman, who's a family friend, that he had more potential as a tight end. That required changing his body and having patience. He redshirted his first year. In 2021, he injured his hamstring and missed spring practice. That July, his mother died. Scott was filled with regret. He said he was close to his mom but didn't believe he was there for her as much as he should have been, that he took things for granted.

"It was absolutely devastating," he said.

Scott became estranged from his father around this time. They didn't talk for more than a year. Football was no refuge. He was still buried on the depth chart and unhappy about it. Before the Oregon game that September, Scott walked out of practice. "It got to the point where I almost hated being there," Scott said.

During Ohio State's off week in October, Scott decided he was done. He got in his car and headed toward Seattle. He was in rural Indiana when he parked at a convenience store to rest. Someone in the store called the police because they suspected suspicious activity.

"Here I am, a black male," Scott said. "I was driving a red Challenger with 5 percent window tints. I'm in dreadlocks. I'm probably in an all-white town. That could have gone a various amount of ways."

Instead, it turned into a life-changing event. The officer who responded, Rob Moore, repeatedly asked Scott what was going on. Scott then unburdened himself. He told the officer everything that was going wrong in his life. About his mom dying. About being unhappy with football.

"I started crying to this guy," Scott said. "At the end of me ranting, he told me to come with him." The rest of that day and night, Scott rode with Moore as he did his job. They even got pizza with his son. Moore encouraged Scott to return to Ohio State. Scott slept in his car that night then returned to Columbus. The only coach Scott had been in contact with was running back coach Tony Alford, who encouraged him to talk to Day.

"I didn't really want to do it because it made me a little bit embarrassed," Scott said. "I didn't want to come into the facility, but I ended up doing it. I sneaked through the back door."

Scott said he didn't know what to expect from Day. At that point, he was so disillusioned that he wasn't even scared of being kicked off the team.

"I didn't care at all," Scott said. "But he was so welcoming. He said, 'Anything I can do to help you, I'm here for you. I don't think you're crazy. You're just fighting mentally.' He ended up bringing in his wife, Mrs. Day, and we had a conversation. He figured she'd be able to help me with the stuff I was going through as well. I'm forever thankful for him being who he was in that moment of my life."

Gee's father put it even more bluntly. "He saved my son's life," Gee Scott Sr. said of Day.

Day said he didn't want to kick Scott off the team because even though his emotions could get the better of him, he knew Scott was a caring young man. "I knew there was a good person in there," Day said.

Scott's life and football career did not turn around right away. He had never been a drinker, but he sampled the nightlife scene for the next year. He found it unsatisfying. When he'd look in the mirror, he wasn't proud of what he saw. In the 2022 Michigan game that year, with Ohio State trailing 24–20 in the third quarter, Scott headbutted a Michigan player on the sideline after a play. He got the predictable hate from angry fans after the game.

"A lot of things that happened on the field were symbolic of where I was in my life," Scott said. "I did struggle with anger issues. In that moment, that was just a part of my character. He was probably jawing at me and said some things I didn't like to hear. At that time in my life, that's how I would handle conflict."

Scott did not grow up in a religious home. At one point during his tailspin, he considered himself an atheist. "In my mind, I was like, 'If there's actually a God, why would he do these things to me?'" Scott said.

At the beginning of 2023, he decided to put his reservations aside. He bought a Bible. He randomly picked a church. "I was like, 'God, if you're really there, I'm not doing the whole Christian thing, but I just want to know for real,'" Scott said. "It began a journey from literally that moment. In the next couple of weeks, my life began to dramatically change. I received a peace in pursuing Christ that I've never received in my entire life. Not from any alcohol. Not from any relationship. Not from any amount of money. Not from any touchdown."

All his life, he felt like a square block trying to fit into a round hole. Now he finally felt like a circle that fit into a round hole. His anger issues gradually dissipated. Scott was finally at peace.

AT THE END of his sophomore season, TreVeyon Henderson was also lost. He grew up in Hopewell, Virginia, about 20 miles from Richmond. Henderson described his hometown as a violent place with shootings commonplace. His mom, LaKeesha Hayes-Winfield, was determined that her three sons not become statistics. She earned an accounting degree while working two jobs and made academics a priority for her boys. She even offered $100 for straight-A report cards.

TreVeyon is the middle of her three sons, all of whom are athletes. TreVeyon's brother, Ronnie Walker Jr., played at Indiana and Virginia. TreVeyon became a five-star recruit after averaging 12.2 yards per carry while gaining 2,424 yards and scoring 45 touchdowns as a junior to lead undefeated Hopewell to a state title.

Virginia canceled high school sports in 2020 because of the pandemic. Henderson stayed in shape by having weights from the high school delivered to his backyard despite his mom's semi-joking complaints that his workouts were tearing up the grass. Henderson always had an eye toward a post-football life. He read books about finance and investing. Even before NIL came into effect, Henderson saved some of his scholarship stipend and invested it in the stock market.

Henderson enrolled at Ohio State with expectations befitting a recruit of his stature. He certainly fulfilled them at the start of his career. He turned a swing pass into a 70-yard touchdown against Minnesota in the 2021 opener. Henderson broke two-time Heisman Trophy–winner Archie Griffin's freshman rushing record by running for 270 yards against Tulsa. But he tailed off late that freshman season because of nagging injuries.

His sophomore season was derailed by injuries. He broke a bone in his foot early in the season and had ligament damage. He tried playing through it, but after gaining only 19 yards in 11 carries in a November game against Maryland, he didn't play again, including the loss to Michigan. During media day interviews before Ohio State's heartbreaker against Georgia, Henderson sounded frustrated and discouraged. He later admitted to having suicidal thoughts.

Finding God, he said, helped save him. "I remember being in that state, hurting and so depressed," Henderson said on The Walk Foundation podcast. "I was idolizing football. I was idolizing this game, and I'm so thankful the Lord saved me from serving false idols, saved me from allowing this game to rule over my life and allowing him to rule over my life."

SCOTT AND HENDERSON weren't alone. Emeka Egbuka, Will Howard, Caleb Downs, J.T. Tuimoloau, and Jack Sawyer were among many others whose religious faith deepened and were eager to share their view.

"It was at this university where I first met God," Egbuka said during the championship celebration in Ohio Stadium. "He met me where I was in the darkness and pulled me into a new life, into a life of light."

Public displays of faith weren't new at Ohio State. C.J. Stroud was outspoken about his faith. So was Kamryn Babb, a wide receiver who endured multiple ACL tears. But the 2024 Buckeyes had many players who wore their religious convictions on their sleeves. That's not always popular.

Some look askance at players who are so devout. But the Buckeyes believe it was vital as they endured the ups and downs of the 2024 season.

"I think it was very important," Howard said. "It wasn't everything, and not every single guy on the team was participating in Bible studies or was super into it. But we were praying together before every game. We were praying together after every game. That was a big focal point for us.

"The way I look at it, Jesus is the way, the truth, and there is no other way. Obviously, that's a point of contention in normal everyday life. But I feel in the game of football, when you use it for the right things, it's such a positive force that can bring calm and peace over you."

Egbuka said his faith was the primary reason he chose to return for his senior season. "The biggest attribute I was looking to refine in my senior season was my faith in God," he said at the NFL combine. "That comes first and foremost before anything on the field. I spent a lot of time in prayer. I felt like He was leading me back to Ohio State for something bigger than football. As players, we had amazing moments where we were able to share the gospel of Jesus Christ and secure our faith in Him. We had experienced a bit of a revival on campus. There were people getting baptized left and right. We were able to share our testimonies, and it was a beautiful thing to be a part of."

Day stressed that religion was not pushed on anybody. "It's more about everyone's individual journey with faith," Day said. 'There are other religions that are represented on the team. I always try to say, 'If there's something you need or if you feel we need to provide something, please let us know.' It's always optional.

"But like I say to a lot of the guys, it'll be the best 15 minutes of your week if you listen to someone [preach] because it's usually a great message about life."

13

Brick by Brick

Ryan Day began training camp feeling good about his team. "I felt we had had what we needed," he said.

But he didn't want his team to look too far ahead when it opened camp on August 1. The "Natty or Bust" talk was counterproductive. Day wanted something that could be a tangible reminder for his players to stay in the moment. The Michigan game, Big Ten championship game, and College Football playoffs were months ahead. The Buckeyes' nonconference schedule was unimposing, and the temptation might be for minds to wander.

Day decided that something tangible to demonstrate that would be useful. Ohio State bought bricks—actually small cinder blocks—from a local construction company. Day told his team they would build a pyramid outside of the Woody Hayes center near the practice fields with those bricks, with the final spot on top reserved for winning the national title. He told the team that the bricks during the grind of training camp were essential in building the season's foundation. Believing they could ratchet up the intensity for only the bigger games or the CFP was a recipe for failure, Day believed. It became a post-practice ritual. Day handed a brick to a player who'd had a good day and asked him to add it to the foundation. It would ultimately consist of more than 100 bricks. Bricks placed on the pyramid after practice were painted black. Bricks after victories were red. CFP bricks would be gold.

For Jack Sawyer, training camp started with a figurative brick on his shoulder. In early June, Sawyer awoke at 4:55 AM before a scheduled 6:30 weightlifting session. He drank a glass of water and decided to get some extra rest on his couch. Sawyer fell back asleep. By the time he heard his alarm, it was 6:01. He didn't even put his shoes on before dashing to his truck.

"I'll never forget the way my heart sunk down to my feet when I woke up and it's light outside, and I've got to be there at 6:05," Sawyer said. "I probably broke every speeding law known to man trying to get to the Woody."

The drive normally took Sawyer seven minutes. It was 6:05 when he parked. But by the time he entered the building it was 6:06. He was one minute late for his check-in 25 minutes before his session. Mickey Marotti would not budge from the zero-tolerance policy he and players had agreed upon.

"Coach Mick is like, 'Nope. Sorry,'" Sawyer said. "I remember as a grown man, 22 years old, leaving the Woody having to cover my face so people didn't see me crying because I feel that fucking bad. One of the most embarrassing days of my life. I felt I let my team down."

Said Marotti, "I fucking laid into his ass, excuse my French. He was a blubbering mess. I'd never seen a human being cry as much, because it meant so much to him. All he wanted to do was come back, beat the team up north, be a captain, and win a championship."

Marotti wouldn't let Sawyer try to explain why he was late. The reason didn't matter. But Marotti told him how he responded would. "I said, 'You have an opportunity to change history because you have to be the best leader now,'" Marotti recalled.

Sawyer had been on the team's leadership committee. He was booted from that. In his makeup workout session overseen by teammates that weekend, he was so determined to show contrition that he completed what usually takes 45 minutes in about 20. "I was trying to prove a point that I'm not messing around," Sawyer said. "That was a mistake. I couldn't breathe for 20 minutes after it."

Sawyer figured his dream of being voted captain was gone, but he was determined during training camp to do everything in his power to give himself a chance.

AS CAMP PROGRESSED, it became clear that Will Howard would win the quarterback job. The Buckeyes held a quarterback school in May, and that helped Howard correct some footwork issues that affected his accuracy. He'd mastered Ohio State's playbook and developed chemistry on and off the field with his teammates. By the time, Day had a meeting with all the quarterbacks to tell them Howard had won the job, it was stating the obvious instead of a revelation.

"I don't think it caught anybody off guard," Day said.

One position battle was settled, but the offensive line wasn't. Complicating matters was a wave of hand, foot, and mouth disease that swept through the unit. Defensive lineman Hero Kanu is believed to have contracted the first case, and Carson Hinzman, his roommate, got it next. Hinzman then unknowingly started a chain reaction throughout the offensive line. The illness causes blisters to form on, well, hands and feet and in the mouth, often with an accompanying fever and sore throat.

"It would take a few days at least to go away, and then it could resurface," Day said. "It cost a couple guys a week, a couple guys 10 days. One guy would clear up and then here comes another guy. That's a long time when you're talking about preseason camp."

The illness forced the offensive line to leave its meeting room and set up shop on the indoor Woody practice field so players could space out. It felt like the COVID days of social distancing. With so many linemen out, players shuffled in and out of practice, and it was hard to develop any continuity. But backups who were able to practice got first-team reps they otherwise wouldn't have had. That would pay off down the road. Donovan Jackson then pulled his hamstring, which would cause him to miss the first two games of the season, stretching the depth even more.

ON AUGUST 17, Ohio State named its captains and Block O recipient. Ohio State established the Block O in 2020 to honor the legacy of Buckeye legend Bill Willis, who was one of the Black players who integrated pro football. Cody Simon was awarded the Block O, which was no surprise. For the fifth-year senior, it was a cherished honor. His father, Michael, is a West Point graduate who works in real estate. His mom, Amy, works in client management for Morgan Stanley. Growing up in New Jersey, Cody tried to emulate his older brother, Shayne, who played for Notre Dame and Pitt.

"When people say I'm mature or calm or poised, that's more of a compliment to my brother," he said. "He's the one who led the way for me, showed me the ropes, showed me how to work hard and how to be a good leader."

Part of the 2020 recruiting class, Simon was a part-time starter the next year. But he tore his labrum in high school and by the end of the 2021 regular season, it became intolerable. "It was like hanging by a thread," he said. "I could barely lift my arm over my head."

He finally had surgery before Ohio State's Rose Bowl win over Utah. In that game, linebacker Tommy Eichenberg had 17 tackles and then kept the job for the rest of his career. Simon never considered transferring. He believed Ohio State had a unique culture. He wanted to be a part of it and enhance it however he could.

"Tommy had worked and earned that spot, and I didn't do enough to get that spot back," Simon said. "My focus was then to always be ready, no matter what."

Even as a part-time player in 2023, Simon finished fourth on the team with 57 tackles. Simon excelled academically, graduating in 2023 as a Big Ten Distinguished Scholar with a degree in finance. Gene Smith and his wife, Sheila, give an award to one student-athlete, regardless of sport, they believe best display leadership, academic success, and character. They gave it to Simon.

He was the first of Ohio State's seniors to announce he would return in 2024, revealing that before the Michigan game.

"The way he leads by example," Mickey Marotti said, "the way he leads vocally, the way he leads with his energy, the way he brought everybody together, he was the glue, especially on defense, but more so on the team."

The same day he was named the Block O recipient, which meant he would wear the number 0 in 2024, Simon also was voted one of OSU's four captains. The others were Emeka Egbuka, TreVeyon Henderson, and, yes, Jack Sawyer. He had redeemed himself after being late by one minute for that June workout.

"Thankfully, my teammates saw the way I showed up to work every day following that incident with fire and drive," Sawyer said. "It was special that they voted me a captain. It's a day I'll never forget."

14

Chasing Defensive Perfection

Jim Knowles knows that his coaching journey is an improbable one. The middle of three kids of a Philadelphia policeman, he grew up in row houses on the north side of the city. Think of the movie *Rocky*, which is set in Philly, and you get the picture.

"It was a concrete jungle," he said. "There was no grass. We used to go play football at a place we called 'The Greens.' We called it 'The Greens' because it was the only green around. We probably walked a mile to get there. It was just like the front lawn of some business. It wasn't even a park, but we thought it was the greatest place in the world."

Football, he said, saved his life when he was an impressionable young boy playing in youth leagues. The coaches were policemen, firemen, or maintenance men, Knowles said. They told the kids if their grades or behavior wasn't up to snuff, they wouldn't be allowed to play. "I found out later when I got to know those guys as I got older and had a few beers with them that was all bullshit," Knowles said with a laugh.

Knowles was a good student at the Catholic schools he attended. He scored in the 99th percentile of a standardized test, which qualified him for an academic scholarship to St. Joseph's Prep, the same prestigious Philadelphia high school Marvin Harrison Jr. and Kyle McCord would attend. Every day, he took the subway and a bus to get to school. His mom, who'd been a homemaker, got a job so the family could pay the ancillary costs of St. Joseph's.

Knowles said he was a good kid, but trouble was never far away in his gritty neighborhood. He believes he was arrested three times, mainly for being in the wrong place at the wrong time. The most serious came shortly before his high school graduation. He was on a street corner outside of a bar because, as Knowles said, there was a bar on every corner. A fight inside the bar spilled outside.

"The police come rolling in like they were storming the beach at Normandy," he said. "That's the way it was in Philly. They came running in and I got hit by a cop across the nose with a nightstick, just trying to get away from the action, not doing anything. I got busted up pretty good."

The cops threw him in a car and took him to the hospital, where he was arrested. His nose was broken, and he spent several days in the hospital. He attended his graduation in a tuxedo wearing sunglasses to try to conceal his injuries. The charges were later dismissed, and he later got some money—he guesses it was $18,000—from the city for wrongful arrest.

Knowles was a good football player, and with his grades, Ivy League schools recruited him. He was the first person in his family to attend college. He picked Cornell because he believed it to be the least elitist of the Ivys. It didn't hurt that the new Big Red football coach was Maxie Baughan, who had been a star rookie linebacker on the Philadelphia Eagles' 1960 NFL championship team.

"Maxie ended up coming to our little row house, and that was pretty cool for my father," Knowles said.

Cornell had been a losing program, but in Knowles' senior season, it went 8–2. Knowles was on a defense that posted three shutouts; he was voted a second-team All-Ivy League defensive end. Ivy League graduates are more coveted than Ivy League football players, so Knowles thought he was ready to get on with his life.

"I was just tired of being poor," he said. "Like any good Ivy League graduate, all I cared about was making money."

He took a job with Prudential Insurance and moved to New York City before being transferred to Boston. Prudential had entered the managed care business and Knowles was involved in the financing and marketing of it. He didn't hate the job and was making almost $100,000. But he missed football. He remembers going to a high school practice and standing outside the fence and just smelling the grass. Football grass. He sent a letter to Bob Colbert, who'd been an assistant coach he was close to at Cornell, saying he was interested in getting into coaching. Two weeks later, Baughan offered him a job coaching running backs for $3,000 a year, a bed in the locker room, and three meals a day at the cafeteria. Knowles knew nothing about coaching running backs. He took the job anyway.

CORNELL WON THE Ivy League championship in Knowles' first season. He thought he'd won the jackpot. Reality then hit. Baughan left under murky circumstances after that 1988 season. His successor didn't last long. The instability shook Knowles, who contemplated going to law school. But he stuck it out under Jim Hofher and Cornell shared the Ivy League title in 1990. He remained at Cornell until 1996. He sensed that if he stayed any longer, he'd be pigeonholed as an Ivy League coach. He got a job at Western Michigan under Gary Darnell and then at Ole Miss under David Cutcliffe.

In 2004, he applied for the head job at Cornell but couldn't get a sniff in the initial hiring process. Knowles agreed to take a job at Nebraska under Bill Callahan coaching linebackers. He got to Lincoln and was about to sign his contract when the Cornell athletics director called him. Cornell's top candidates hadn't panned out, and he was circling back to Knowles.

Knowles was head coach for the Big Red for six years. His teams went 26–34. Knowles said he was in discussions with Cornell about a contract extension when Cutcliffe, who'd become head coach at Duke, offered him the defensive coordinator job. Knowles had grown tired dealing with the non-football aspects of being a head coach. He just wanted to coach. On the field, there was immediate feedback. You succeeded or you didn't. If you didn't, you had to adjust. Knowles loved the chess match part of the game. Every Sunday during the season, he'd start from scratch devising a game plan for the week. His players would practice all week and then the games would come and take on a life of their own and Knowles would have to adapt. Starting at Western Michigan, Knowles discovered he had a knack for being creative in moving players around to confuse offenses. He loved disguising pass rushes, for example, causing quarterbacks to pause in confusion for the split-second that could be the difference between a completion and a sack.

But Knowles also understood that coaching isn't only about Xs and Os. Knowles is hard on players on the practice field, and he knew they'd tune him out unless they formed a connection and had mutual respect. Knowles would be creative in meetings to keep them fresh, occasionally playing a version of *Jeopardy!* or other game shows to teach the playbook.

At Duke, Knowles was part of a staff that turned around a program that had long lived in the shadow of Blue Devils basketball. In his final season in Durham, Knowles' defense ranked 21st nationally in yardage allowed. That caused Oklahoma State coach Mike Gundy to take notice. He interviewed with Gundy and about 10 other coaches and staffers in a hotel room for three hours talking Xs and Os. He never even saw the campus in Stillwater before he was sent back home and told to wait. He got the job.

In the Big 12 then, defense seemed like an afterthought. It was like a different world for Knowles. "I was not familiar with the Big 12, and the Big 12 at the time was still chucking it all over place," he said.

He used the scheme he had at Duke in his first season and got exposed. Like at his previous stops, Knowles didn't have blue-chip players. He had to be creative. The Cowboys improved defensively in each of the next three years. In 2021, Oklahoma State's defense ranked fourth nationally in total defense. Only two other Big 12 defenses ranked in the top 30.

THAT 2021 SEASON was a disaster for the Ohio State defense. Jeff Hafley, the coordinator behind the elite 2019 unit, left after that year to become head coach at Boston College. Day hired Kerry Coombs as his replacement. The charismatic Coombs had been a successful cornerbacks coach under Urban Meyer at Ohio State before going to the Tennessee Titans. As OSU's defensive coordinator, though, Coombs wasn't successful. After the Buckeyes' loss to Oregon in the second game of the 2021 season, Day stripped play-calling duties from Coombs and gave it to defensive backs coach Matt Barnes. The change only helped marginally. Ohio State finished 59th in total defense and 38th in scoring defense.

Day, who was still the offensive play-caller, wanted to hire what he would term a head coach for the defense. Knowles' Oklahoma State contract was expiring, and he'd just hired an agent for the first time. By the end of the season, offers started pouring in. Knowles now had a substantial body of work. He didn't need to submit to an intense interview like the one he had for the Oklahoma State job. He and Day talked on the phone a few times for a few hours total without meeting in person before Day offered the job.

"He had done more with less," Day said. "I felt like based on where we were at, we needed somebody to come in and look at it from a different point of view. I talked to David Cutcliffe. I talked to a lot of people I respected and felt like he was the right guy."

At Ohio State, Knowles finally would get to work with players who'd been elite recruits. It took time for it to mesh. Knowles had made his bones being creative with lesser talent. With the Buckeyes, he almost always had superior talent to the opponent. He didn't have to take as many risks with scheme. On his first play in the 2022 opener against Notre Dame, Knowles called for a cornerback blitz. The corner didn't get to the quarterback, who threw a short sideline pass. The receiver, Lorenzo Styles Jr. (who'd later transfer to Ohio State and switch to defensive back), broke a tackle by safety Josh Proctor for a 54-yard gain. Against Michigan that year, the Wolverines repeatedly burned Knowles' defense for big plays.

"After that first year," Knowles said, "when we gave up way too many explosive plays in the big games, I just said to myself that we have really good players. We can't give up explosive plays. There's no reason to take unnecessary risks. It's not like we have to create something. The players are elite. Put them in good position and they'll make plays. I had to really adjust to that."

His Buckeye defenses improved year by year. As the 2024 season approached, he knew he had all pieces in place for a special defense. Jack Sawyer and J.T. Tuimoloau were five-star recruits who by the end of their junior seasons were playing like it. Between them were nose guard Ty Hamilton and Tyleik Williams, who played the 3-technique position (lining up between the offensive guard and tackle).

Hamilton and Williams, who dubbed themselves TnT, were happy to cede the spotlight to others. But they would be the foundation of Ohio State's defense. Hamilton's older brother and role model, DaVon, was a star for the Buckeyes who also largely flew under the radar. He was so unassuming that when Ohio State listed him as "Davon" on its website bio, he didn't bother telling anyone until he was a senior. DaVon was a third-round draft pick by the Jacksonville Jaguars in 2020, the year Ty arrived at Ohio State.

"I talk to him pretty much every day, just picking his brain," Ty said. "I'm thankful to have him."

Ty played on rival youth teams and high schools in Pickerington with Sawyer. Running back was the first position for both until they outgrew it. Hamilton was only a three-star recruit and redshirted as a freshman during the shortened 2020 COVID season. He committed to Ohio State as a defensive end, but Larry Johnson told him that as he filled out, he'd grow into becoming a defensive tackle.

"He never wavered," Johnson said. "He never said, 'Coach, I'm going to go somewhere else.'"

Hamilton played in only three games and took 25 snaps in 2020. The next three seasons, he became an important player in Johnson's line rotation, getting more snaps each year. In the weight room, Hamilton was a force. At Ohio State's 2024 pro day, he bench-pressed 225 pounds 35 times, which was more than anyone at the NFL combine lifted and six more than any defensive tackle.

In his entire Ohio State career, Hamilton never missed a practice, which is almost unfathomable for a position that often requires fending off double-team blocks. "You've got to have a high pain tolerance to play the position I'm at," Hamilton said. "You just have to be able to go out there and suck it up. As long as there ain't nothing broken, you can still go out and play."

Such toughness and durability earn trust and respect, and Hamilton had done that.

"Jack and J.T. were the outgoing leaders of the D-line, Jack more than J.T," Mickey Marotti said. "And Tyleik never shuts up. But Jack and J.T. would never do anything unless they cleared it with Ty. I called Ty 'Don Corleone, the Godfather,' because of the way he presented himself, the way he works, the way he grinds. He never says a word, wasn't highly recruited like those three, lived in the shadow of his brother. And then each year, he came out of his shell. By the end, he was the vocal leader of those guys."

TYLEIK WILLIAMS' JOURNEY to Columbus was a lot farther than Hamilton's, in more ways than one. He grew up in Manassas, Virginia, with four siblings. His dad was a presence in his life but didn't live with him. His mom, Gloria, worked to support the family as a Walmart manager.

"That's my *why*," Williams said. "She's probably the closest person to me, and I love her. I don't know how to put it into words. She's like my other half."

Despite her best efforts, the family occasionally found itself having to stay in homeless shelters. Marotti said that in his experience, people who grew up in those circumstances are guarded, have a chip on their shoulder, and find it hard to trust. "He's the complete opposite," Marotti said. "Outgoing and funny and aware. Street smart and smart smart. I think he's one of the smartest players on our team."

Williams said he resolved early not to let his circumstances affect his attitude. "Growing up, I went through a lot, and I just tried to stay positive all the time," he said. "I try to keep a smile on my face and keep others around me happy."

Like Hamilton, Williams' first position in football as a kid was running back. He also played linebacker. That's how he believes he developed remarkable quickness for someone his size. "I was always in spots where you had to be quick, and I think the football just came along with it when I got bigger," Williams said.

Williams got bigger than Ohio State wanted by the time he got to Columbus. Virginia canceled its 2020 high school sports because of COVID-19, and Williams let himself go that fall. When he arrived in Columbus in January, he weighed 365 pounds. Ohio State team dietitian Kaila Olson put Williams on a diet, and he lost weight to about 320 pounds pretty quickly. Early in his OSU career, Williams struggled with consistency. Even with the weight loss, his conditioning wasn't great. He finally blossomed as a junior in 2023 when he led all Buckeye linemen with 54 tackles, including 10 for losses. Williams was determined to build on that in 2024.

The back seven of the defense looked as imposing as the defensive line. The Buckeyes were confident Sonny Styles could make a smooth transition from safety to linebacker next to Cody Simon. Davison Igbinosun and Denzel Burke were multiyear starters at cornerback. Caleb Downs was already an established star as a sophomore. He and fellow safety Lathan Ransom had already bonded.

"Two alpha males, two competitors," Lathan said of himself and Downs. "When he came into the room, I was extremely excited and blessed because he was a guy I was able to compete against at the highest level every day and be able to push each other. That's what built our friendship, being dudes that would get there early, watch film together, would stay after practice and do a bunch of extra drills together. Whether it was games or practices, we were always trying to outdo one another."

Rounding out the starting defense would be Jordan Hancock, who had the versatility to play nickel cornerback against the slot receiver or play a traditional safety role.

Behind that starting 11 were capable players such as linebackers Arvell Reese and Mitchell Melton; defensive linemen Caden Curry, Kenyatta Jackson, Kayden McDonald, and Hero Kanu; and cornerback Jermaine Mathews.

Knowles knew he had all the pieces for a dominant defense. The goal now, he said, was to chase perfection.

15

The Season Arrives

The 2024 season would represent a new era in college football. The College Football Playoff expanded from four to 12 teams. No longer would a single loss potentially be a death knell to a team's national championship hopes. Now, even two losses probably wouldn't be. In the decade of the four-team CFP, no two-loss team ever qualified. The new format gave a little breathing room.

But it also meant a longer season, potentially as many as 17 games if a team lost in its conference championship and then played four playoff games. The minimum would be 16 games—12 in the regular season, a conference title game, and three playoff rounds. That caused Ohio State to take a different approach.

Chip Kelly became known for his ultra-quick-tempo offenses at Oregon, though he'd diversified since then. But Ryan Day wanted to minimize wear and tear on his team as much as possible. In at least half of its games, the Buckeyes would be so superior in talent that the outcome wasn't in much doubt. The fewer the plays, the less risk of injury. Day figured OSU could shave 150-200 snaps over the course of the season on both offense and defense by playing slower. The Buckeyes would occasionally use a quick tempo, but only as a change of pace.

Ohio State seldom huddled in recent years. Now they would. That made sense with Will Howard at quarterback. At least partly because of Michigan's Connor Stalions scandal, the NCAA for the first time allowed coaches to communicate directly with one player on the field on both offense and defense through a microphone in the helmet.

"As we started going with the huddle, we found the players started to like being in the huddle more," Day said. "With Will's personality, it worked well. He was looking guys in the eye. He could carry two plays to the line of scrimmage. We could tag things to remind players, even a young guy like Jeremiah."

TRADITIONALLY, OHIO STATE plays a marquee opponent among its three nonconference games. In 2017, OSU and Washington agreed to a home-and-home series in 2024 and 2025, with the Buckeyes traveling to Seattle for the first game. But with USC and UCLA joining the Big Ten in 2024 and the possibility of a cross-country flight for a conference game, OSU canceled the series in February 2023, paying a $500,000 penalty. A few months later, Washington and Oregon would be invited to join the Big Ten, effective in 2024, as the Pac-12 disintegrated. The Buckeyes replaced Washington with Marshall. College football doesn't have a preseason like the NFL does, but Ohio State's nonconference schedule of Akron, Western Michigan, and Marshall served as a glorified one. The Buckeyes outscored their first three opponents 157–21.

In the opener, Akron took a 3–0 lead and hung in with Ohio State into the second quarter. On the Buckeyes' second snap, Howard threw a wide receiver screen to Jeremiah Smith. The play was well blocked, and Smith had a path to the end zone. But Smith dropped the ball. On the next play, Smith was called for a false start as OSU had a three-and-out. No one on the Ohio State sideline batted an eye. There was no worry that Smith had anything more than momentary freshman jitters. Soon enough, he would show why. He caught passes for OSU's first two touchdowns then caught a 45-yard pass to set up another as the Buckeyes rolled 52–6.

"I could have gotten down on myself and had a bad rest of the game," Smith said. "But I wouldn't let that one drop define who I am. If I drop the ball, I'm going to move on from it. I know I've got more football to play."

Smith didn't drop another pass the rest of the season.

Ohio State's next game against Western Michigan was even more lopsided. The Buckeyes outgained the Broncos 683–99 in a 56–0 rout. Smith caught a 70-yard touchdown pass, and TreVeyon Henderson and Quinshon Judkins each ran for two scores. Julian Sayin capped the scoring with a 55-yard touchdown to tight end Bennett Christian.

The Buckeyes' final nonconference game wasn't much tougher. Ohio State averaged 12.3 yards per play in the first three quarters of a 49–14 blowout of Marshall. The most notable thing about that game occurred when kicker Jayden Fielding hooked three straight kickoffs out of bounds before being benched. What wasn't known at the time was that Fielding had an injured right hip that he tried to fight through. It was diagnosed as a hip flexor, but an MRI after the season revealed that it was instead a torn adductor muscle in his hip.

"I didn't even want to know what was going on with it during the season," Fielding said. "I just wanted to get through the season. I think it was misdiagnosed because it's such a common thing for kickers."

The muscle tear forced Fielding to change his kicking motion. "I had to become a little wider to create the power I had lost from tearing it," he explained. "My approach was a little wider, which caused me to swing across [the ball] sometimes. It took me a couple of weeks to get used to it."

The injury would nag him on and off the rest of the season. Some games, it felt fine. Other games, he said, it felt like he could barely walk.

That Fielding ever made it to Ohio State was the longest of long-shots. He was a soccer player growing up in League City, Texas, as was his older sister, Madison. His introduction to football came when Madison's middle school football team needed a kicker and asked her to join the team. Jayden would tag along to practice. He followed in his sister's footsteps when he got to middle school. Fielding was a talented kicker, but his Clear Creek High School team wasn't a power. He got little attention from recruiters.

At a kicking camp held at the renowned IMG Academy in Florida, Fielding happened to buy a pair of IMG shorts. He was wearing them at another camp when the outgoing IMG kicker saw it. That kicker took a picture and posted it online. Fielding said the IMG special teams coordinator saw the photo and messaged him on Twitter, starting the process that ended with Fielding enrolling there.

IMG travels the country playing games and Fielding's senior year, it came to Ohio for two games. It played infamous Bishop Sycamore, the fraudulent school that somehow bamboozled ESPN into televising its games, and Cincinnati La Salle. Carnell Tate was also at IMG and OSU coaches came to see him at the La Salle game. Fielding boomed several kickoffs through the uprights, which got the attention of the OSU coaches. They eventually invited him to walk on. Scholarship offers out of high school for kickers are rare. Fielding had only one—from Houston Christian, a small school 20 minutes from home. Fielding took the OSU offer. Fielding served as a kickoff specialist his first year and then took over field goals and extra points in 2023. Before that season, Ohio State awarded him a scholarship.

"I got to call my mom and tell her, 'You don't have to pay for my school anymore,'" Fielding recalled. "I could just hear the relief in her voice and my dad's voice. That was a really cool moment for me because coming to a place like this, you're taking a shot. For it to actually come to fruition was really special for me and my parents, especially."

What Fielding couldn't have known was the rollercoaster he'd endure the rest of the season.

OHIO STATE WELCOMED the start of the Big Ten schedule as a way to ramp up the competition. Michigan State was the conference opener and the Buckeyes' first road game. The Spartans were Ohio State's toughest Big Ten competition at the start of the Urban Meyer era, but Mark Dantonio had retired as MSU coach and, after a promising start, the Mel Tucker era crashed and burned. Jonathan Smith was hired from Oregon State to rebuild the program.

Ohio State was a 25-point favorite, and the Buckeyes jumped ahead early. After an OSU field goal, Cody Simon stuffed quarterback Aidan Chiles on fourth-and-1 at the OSU 20. The Buckeyes capitalized by scoring on a fourth-and-goal pass from the 3 from Howard to Gee Scott Jr. to make it 10–0.

Michigan State threatened on its next drive. Jack Velling caught a pass and ran past the OSU 20 before Jordan Hancock stripped the ball free for a turnover. MSU got the ball back on an ill-advised pass by Howard into double-coverage that was intercepted and returned to the Buckeyes' 12. The Spartans scored on the next play.

Ohio State didn't require much time to answer. TreVeyon Henderson ran for 37 yards on first-and-20 to set up a 19-yard end-around by Jeremiah Smith for a touchdown. Michigan State's ensuing drive ended with another fumble inside the red zone, this one caused by Lathan Ransom on Chiles. Smith's touchdown run was just an appetizer for what he did two drives later. He leaped to make a one-handed catch in double coverage near the sideline, holding onto the ball while the defender grabbed his face mask. Howard took a hard shot on the play. After throwing an incomplete pass on second down, he had to leave the game briefly. "I just got the wind knocked out of me, but in the moment, I thought I cracked a rib or something," Howard said.

Devin Brown came in and threw again to Smith. "We told Devin if you have one-on-one on the outside, take it," Ryan Day said. "But that was actually Cover 2."

Smith was well-covered, but he reached out with one hand and snagged it for a ridiculous touchdown. “I didn’t think the ball was going to come to me because of the way the DB was playing,” Smith said, “but Devin threw it, so I just stuck one hand out and caught it.”

Even his coach couldn’t believe it. “On the sideline, I think I grabbed my head, like, ‘What is going on right now?’” Day said. “But that’s the thing—just get the ball to Jeremiah.”

That made it 24–7 right before halftime, and the Buckeyes cruised to a 38–7 win.

By the end, most of the remaining fans were OSU ones. “At the end of the game, there’s a bunch of scarlet still in the stadium doing the O-H I-O,” Howard said. “I’m like, ‘This is different. This is something I’ve never seen before.’ Buckeye fans are pretty different. As we went through the season, it became more and more real, like this is a different level of pressure, and everything is heightened.”

The game was athletics director Ross Bjork’s first on the road. He left the press box to spend the final minutes on the sideline with the team. He was standing with Sawyer and J.T. Tuimoloau while backups played. Sawyer asked Bjork if he’d been on the sideline the whole game. Bjork pointed to the press box and told Sawyer that’s where he’d been.

“He said, ‘Do they have cold beer?’” Bjork recalled with a laugh.

Bjork told him beer was available but that he didn’t have one. “He said, ‘That’d be really cool just to drink a beer and watch a game. I can’t wait to do that.’ Just a cool moment as you get to know these players.”

NEXT UP WAS Iowa. A game against the Hawkeyes is usually like a trip to the dentist. Iowa is bland offensively but plays disciplined defense that forces opponents to be patient.

“I spent a lot of time in the offseason game-planning them, and trying to share it with Chip,” Day said. “I’ve played against these guys before. You could watch them play the same defense and think, ‘Well, we’re going to move the ball on these guys,' and it's not that easy. They're very, very good at what they do."

Iowa, as usual, didn't have much of a passing game, but the Hawkeyes did have the country's second-leading rusher in running back Kaleb Johnson. A Hamilton, Ohio, native, Johnson made headlines during the week when he said that Ohio State hadn't recruited him, and if it had, he wouldn't have gone there. "I want to beat them," he told reporters. "That's my goal."

The Buckeyes downplayed that comment all week, but they quietly used it as motivation. "I remember hearing all week about how good their O-line is and how good their running back is," Sawyer said. "I think he gave us some bulletin board material about us not wanting him, and he can't wait to show what a mistake that was. We were looking to put a stop to that."

They did. The Buckeyes held Johnson in check in a 35–7 win. He gained only 19 yards in eight first-half carries. A couple of 28-yard runs, the second of which ended OSU's shutout bid in the fourth quarter, padded his stats to 86 yards in 15 carries.

"We'd played Iowa multiple times before," nose guard Ty Hamilton said. "Knowing they're a stretch team—they wanted to get him on the outside and be able to stretch the ball—that was our bread and butter. We were able to play vertical and be violent and go against their offensive linemen and just destroy them."

Ohio State's offense opened with a 14-play, 88-yard touchdown drive capped by a Will Howard pass to Emeka Egbuka. The Buckeyes were held scoreless the rest of the half following turnovers by Jeremiah Smith on a fumble and a Howard interception. But the Buckeyes expanded their 7–0 halftime lead with another one-handed Smith touchdown catch in which he flicked away the defender and a four-yard touchdown run by Howard, which was the first rushing score the Hawkeyes allowed all season. Egbuka had the final two scores on touchdown catches in tight coverage.

The three touchdowns were a career-high for Egbuka, who often flew under-the-radar during his career. Though he was a five-star recruit, Egbuka was overshadowed by Marvin Harrison Jr. in his class. He had to wait his turn behind Chris Olave, Garrett Wilson, and Jaxon Smith-Njigba, all first-round picks. But Egbuka had a presence and maturity from the start.

"He chose Ohio State because he knew, or at least he hoped, that it was the best odds of him being the best version of himself," Brian Hartline said. "These guys in this room know nothing is given. They know everything is earned and there are no promises. These guys are coming here to be challenged every day to try to be the best versions of themselves. That's a hard thing to find more and more these day—to choose hard instead of choosing the easiest route to the field."

Egbuka had only nine catches as a freshman but blossomed with 74 catches for 1,151 yards and 10 touchdowns as a sophomore. He was on track for similar success as a junior until a high ankle sprain suffered against Maryland in early October. Egbuka missed a month after having "tightrope" surgery in which a braided cord is used to stabilize the ankle and wasn't quite the same player in 2023 after he returned. But he earned respect for gutting it out.

"A warrior," Day said. "During his time, he did a lot of dirty work. Extremely intelligent. More mature than most people in the entire building. There's not much he could not do. He's just that type of person. He could probably run for office and win, too."

Brian Hartline said Egbuka embodies what he seeks as an Ohio State coach. Egbuka is fast but not the fastest Buckeye receiver. At 6'1" and 205 pounds, he is big and strong but not the biggest or the strongest. "But the way he plays the game—the manipulation of DBs, the art of playing the position—Emeka embodies it," Hartline said. "He has the ultimate mental makeup of a pro athlete. His expectations and the accountability he has for himself are off the chart."

That rubbed off on others in the wide receivers unit. "That room went based on Emeka Egbuka," Hartline said.

THE UNIT THAT might have shined the most against Iowa was the offensive line, which had been the team's biggest question mark entering the season. The Buckeyes ran for 203 yards against a Hawkeyes defense that had yielded only 62 per game, fourth-best in the country.

"They were playing great football," Howard said of OSU's linemen. "We were running the ball well. We were pass-protecting well. We had dudes. Seth was really settling in and being that guy, the mouthpiece for the room. Jimmy was playing really good football. We were rolling at that point."

"Jimmy" was left tackle Josh Simmons. The Buckeyes gave Simmons that nickname to avoid confusion with right tackle Josh Fryar. Simmons had an up-and-down first season in Columbus in 2023 after transferring from San Diego State and switching from right tackle. But after an offseason of diligent work, he had become a dominating player.

"His transformation was immense," left guard Donovan Jackson said. "Even in practice, we joked that we didn't have to worry about anything coming off the edge on the left side because we knew that Josh Simmons was going to block it. We would draw protections in meetings and joke like we don't have to worry about anything over there because he was going to lock that down. His athletic ability and his power to move guys off the ball was very eye-opening."

Jackson was the established star of the line and was playing like it at left guard. McLaughlin had become everything Ohio State had hoped at center. Right guard Tegra Tshabola played well enough against Iowa that he said Hawkeye coaches stopped him on the field to say he impressed them.

Then there was Fryar. More than anyone on the team, Fryar understood the toll football can take. His father, Jeff, played at Indiana in the 1980s and was a part of IU teams that beat Ohio State 31–10 and 41–7. But the Fryar family believes he has chronic traumatic encephalopathy from the head injuries he endured. (CTE can only be definitively diagnosed post-mortem.) Because of his condition, Jeff can be forgetful and prone to mood swings. "He's an unbelievable guy," Josh said of his dad. "I love my dad to death. [But] the family issues were difficult because he wouldn't remember things."

His father's health issues didn't keep Fryar from falling in love with football. He was a three-star recruit, one of the lowest-ranked in OSU's 2020 class. But he worked his way up to being the line's top backup in 2022 and a starter the next year. "I kind of look at myself as an underdog," Fryar said. "It's an underdog mentality, and underdogs just are hungrier for anything and everything they want in life."

He was old school in many ways. If Fryar felt a freshman needed it, he'd bust his chops to make him understand he had to improve.

"Josh Fryar is a dawg, man," Jackson said. "People have been doubting him since he's been here, and he's done nothing but put his head down and work. And he's a very vocal guy, not just in the O-line room but on the team. He's a guy that people need to have in their locker room because he makes everyone laugh and brings everyone together."

Fryar, like the rest of the offensive line, was feeling good after the Iowa game. There was no way to know the adversity the line would face the rest of the season.

16

Disappointment at Autzen

Denzel Burke's choice of colleges came down to Ohio State and Oregon. Imagine how pumped he was to play the Ducks in the Buckeyes' first major test of the season. "I was," he said. "I really was."

Instead, it turned into a nightmare for Burke. In hindsight, it was a bit predictable. He missed a couple of practices that week with a hamstring injury, which he and the Buckeyes understandably didn't divulge. Oregon was one of the few teams in the country with comparable speed as Ohio State, particularly at wide receiver. But Denzel is a confident player, and that self-belief is what enabled him to have early success as a Buckeye. He ranked 17th among OSU's 23 recruits in its 2021 recruiting class, behind several players who washed out. But Burke arrived on campus carrying himself like a veteran. He wasn't the biggest or the fastest cornerback, but he drew praise in spring practice with his competitiveness and maturity. In training camp, he became the first in his class to lose his black helmet stripe, which signifies full-fledged status on the team. "You can't tell he's a freshman," Ryan Day said at the time. When a couple of veteran cornerbacks were injured for the opener against Minnesota, Burke became the rare true freshman to start his first game. He graded as a "champion" that game and went on to have a terrific season and was named to several freshman All-American teams.

If his first season was pretty much smooth sailing, he hit choppy waters in 2022. He admits to some complacency as a sophomore and then battled injuries—to his shoulder, ankle, and finger—starting in training camp. Burke missed a week and a half of training camp as the Buckeyes were learning Jim Knowles' scheme. "I really didn't have a foundation going into the season," he said.

His play reflected it. Burke didn't play poorly enough to get benched, but it was a definite step back. That made him determined to bounce back in 2023, and he did. He was named first-team All-Big Ten and second-team All-American. He was off to a terrific start in 2024 with interceptions against Akron and Michigan State. Even with the hamstring issue, he had no reason to expect what happened against Oregon, which was ranked No. 3 and a 3½-point underdog.

"Definitely the nerves were pumping because this is a big-time game, the top two teams in the conference, so we just had to go out there and perform at a high level," Burke said.

OREGON JOINED THE Big Ten in 2024 after the breakup of the traditional Pac-12, but the Ducks and Buckeyes have a history against each other. They first played in the 1958 Rose Bowl, a 10–7 OSU win. The Buckeyes defeated the Ducks six times in the regular season in the next decades before beating Chip Kelly's Oregon team 26–17 in the 2010 Rose Bowl. OSU beat Oregon and its Heisman Trophy–winning quarterback Marcus Mariota 42–20 to cap their improbable 2014 national title. But in 2021, the Ducks came to Columbus and exposed OSU's defense in a humbling 35–28 upset. Ohio State's veteran players remembered.

This would be the Buckeyes' first trip to Eugene since 1967, the year Autzen Stadium opened. It was billed as the biggest home game in Oregon history, and it felt like it. More than an hour before kickoff, the student section was packed and loud with "Fuck Ohio" chants. A few Buckeye players ran up the ramp after pregame warmups to the locker room with their own rallying cry: "Fuck the Ducks." Autzen's sound reverberates thanks to an overhang atop the south side of the stadium's bowl. The noise from the record crowd of 60,129 was almost deafening. Ohio State running backs coach Carlos Locklyn knew Autzen well, and he said he'd never heard it that loud. "You could hear the ground vibrating," he said.

Added Kelly, "It was as loud as any game I coached there."

Ohio State came close to silencing the crowd early. The Buckeyes scored on their opening drive. The touchdown was set up by a 32-yard pass to tight end Will Kacmarek that should have been ruled an incompletion or even interception instead of a catch. Oregon linebacker Jeffrey Bassa ended up with the ball after Kacmarek bobbled it as they tumbled to the turf. Kacmarek broke his clavicle on the play and missed the next three games.

After a defensive stop, Ohio State got the ball back. Then Oregon defensive tackle Derrick Harmon made the Ducks' first big play. He beat Donovan Jackson and wrested the ball from Quinshon Judkins as he made the tackle. What wasn't known at the time was that Judkins was playing with an injured thumb that required surgery, which he had after the team returned to Columbus. "It was a strange play because he was falling down with the ball as [Harmon] was grabbing onto it," Day said.

Day said Locklyn now teaches ball-carriers to fall to the ground instead of fighting for yardage if they feel a defensive lineman trying to pull the ball free like Harmon did.

Oregon needed only two plays to score, though the Ducks' holder mishandled the snap on the extra point. Ohio State believed it could run on Oregon, and TreVeyon Henderson followed a 17-yard run with a 53-yarder to set up a Judkins one-yard touchdown carry to make it 14–6.

Then Burke's bad day started. Receiver Evan Stewart got behind Burke for a 69-yard gain, with Stewart dragging Burke about 15 yards after making the catch. Stewart then caught a 10-yard touchdown pass with Burke in tight coverage in the corner of the end zone. "Denzel was all over the guy," Ohio State cornerbacks coach Tim Walton said. "A good throw, a good catch. That's part of the game."

Jordan Hancock was called for a face-mask penalty on the touchdown, allowing Oregon to kick off from midfield. Ducks coach Dan Lanning opted to take advantage by attempting an onside kick. Ohio State had Caleb Downs at the 40 in preparation, but the line-drive kick boomed off him before he could get out of the way. Oregon recovered and would kick a field goal for the first of the game's seven lead changes. On that drive, cornerback Davison Igbinosun's feistiness got the best of receiver Traeshon Holden. Igbinosun said he'd noticed Holden trying to stare down the Buckeyes during the National Anthem. "So from the jump, he was talking trash to me first," he said. "He was being fake tough. You know how that goes."

On a play during that drive, Igbinosun drove Holden to the sideline, adding a few choice words. In response, Holden spat on him. An official saw it and ejected the receiver. "I was talking a little trash, and he got upset," Igbinosun said. "I guess he couldn't handle it anymore, so he took the easy way out."

On Ohio State's next drive, left tackle Josh Simmons would be lost for the season. While pass-protecting, his left knee buckled. He'd torn the patellar tendon. "I felt a little pop," Simmons said at the NFL combine. "I thought somebody hit the back of my knee at first—until I tried to get up."

Simmons needed a cart to leave the field.

"Obviously, you feel horrible because Josh is an amazing guy," Jackson said, "and he was really on track to have one of the greatest seasons as a tackle I personally think ever."

An offensive line that had turned from preseason question to strength had to adapt immediately. Simmons wasn't the only injured lineman. Right guard Tegra Tshabola sprained his lower back in practice that week and was trying to play through it. "That was the first hurdle of my college career because I hadn't really ever been hurt to the point where it was questioned whether I could play or not," Tshabola said. "I had just gotten this role and didn't want to give it up. I was doing whatever I could to get on the field."

But as the game went on, the pain became unbearable. "It was the worst pain I had ever been through," Tshabola said. "It felt like a shock going through my legs every time I tried to move or bend." He gave way to Austin Siereveld but returned later in the game. "I have no idea [how]," Tshabola said.

Despite the patchwork offensive line, Ohio State scored on the drive and was able to move the ball all day against the Ducks. But the Buckeyes' defense kept faltering. On Oregon's next drive, quarterback Dillon Gabriel threw to speedy Tez Johnson, who got behind Burke for a 48-yard touchdown and a 22–21 halftime lead.

The Buckeyes regained the lead on a Howard pass to Jeremiah Smith and then got a goal-line stand. But Oregon scored on a 27-yard keeper by Gabriel after J.T. Tuimoloau bit on a fake and Lathan Ransom and Igbinosun couldn't make touchdown-saving tackles.

With six minutes left, Jayden Fielding drilled a 40-yard field goal to put OSU back ahead 31–29. Once again, though, the Buckeyes' defense couldn't get a quick stop. A 26-yard pass to tight end Terrance Ferguson and pass interference call on Hancock moved the ball to the OSU 9. Ohio State kept Oregon out of the end zone, but the Ducks were able to bleed the clock before Atticus Sappington's 19-yard field goal for a 32–31 lead with 1:47 left.

The Buckeyes' final possession would haunt them for weeks, or at least until January 1. Howard threw to Egbuka for a 26-yard gain to the Oregon 28 with 28 seconds left. Two plays later, Howard threw to Smith for a completion to the 21, but a flag was thrown. Smith had gotten separation from Nikko Reed after extending his arms on the defensive back, and that drew an offensive pass interference penalty. "My route was a curl," Smith said. "The DB took an inside release. He was putting his hands on me, so I tried to clear his hands. I caught the ball, and as soon as I got tackled, I see a flag come. I thought I was just being physical, but they said I pushed off. I felt definitely that was a bad call."

In Day's mind, Smith and other OSU receivers had been manhandled all day without getting calls. "If they weren't going to call the defensive pass interference on some of those that they were hanging all over them," Day said, "and then they call the offensive one on him, those are tough calls. But that's why we always said, 'Leave no doubt.' Don't leave to one call because that's what's going to happen to the Buckeyes. It's just the way it goes. I told the guys that in the regular season, so when it happened, I don't think you heard us complain all that much because we know that when it comes to one call, we ain't going to get it."

Day said that following the Oregon game, he talked to referees to explain to them that Smith wasn't a typical receiver. "It's almost like you need to referee this guy different because he's that big and that strong," he said. "Guys will bounce off him. Guys are going to hang all over him. [Reed] is 5-10½ and 180 pounds. Against Jeremiah, he's going to get thrown sometimes because he's going to bounce off him, and I think that's what happened on that play."

The 15-yard penalty moved the ball back to the 43 with 13 seconds left. Oregon then got a five-yard penalty for having 12 men on the field, which Ducks coach Dan Lanning coyly admitted was intentional to bleed the clock and safeguard against a big play. It would be a decision that Chip Kelly would remember and use as motivation down the road. But after the penalty, only six seconds remained. Howard dropped back, couldn't immediately find a receiver and took off running. He got to the 26 before sliding to kill the play and hopefully get a timeout. The clock showed 1 second left when Howard slid. But officials ruled that time expired. "I was right there calling timeout on the sideline," Day said. "I was right next to the referee."

Day later sent a screenshot of Howard sliding with time remaining to Bill Carollo, the Big Ten's head of officiating. "They felt like by the time he went down, and I called it and in the time [it took] to blow the whistle, the game was over," Day said. "My argument was he should have been [ruled] down when he started the slide."

Oregon fans stormed the field immediately after the play, which Ohio State believes contributed to the finality of the call. The officials would have had to clear the field, which might have made for an ugly situation. "I don't know if that happened or not, but it certainly felt that way down there," Day said.

Kelly blamed himself for putting Howard in a difficult spot. He had called for a flood route to the short side of the field, with one receiver going five yards, another 15 and a third 25, all to the sideline so whoever caught it could get out of bounds.

"He had Brandon [Inniss], but Brandon would have been short of the field goal [distance]," Kelly said. "They did a good job defending the sideline. I should have called a better play to put Will in a better situation. I know Will beat himself up, but I take 100 percent responsibility. It's our job as coaches to put them in positions to make plays, and I didn't do that."

In the postgame locker room, the Buckeyes were frustrated and upset. Howard went around the locker room hugging his teammates and was gratified to see each of them reassured him that the loss was not his fault. "In that moment, I knew we had something special," Howard said. "Our brotherhood was strong. As tough as that moment was, it made it better."

The loss was hard to accept, but it wasn't devastating. In a 12-team College Football Playoff, one loss wouldn't end their national championship hopes. Nor would it even end their hopes of a Big Ten title. The Buckeyes fully expected to meet the Ducks again, maybe more than once. But Ohio State knew they couldn't play like that again against an elite team. "It's going to be who gets better faster," Day told his players. "We have to identify what we did wrong here and get it fixed."

There was plenty that went wrong, especially on defense. The Buckeyes entered the game yielding only 6.8 points per game. Oregon gained 496 yards and averaged 7.6 yards per play. Denzel Burke bore the brunt of the criticism. Honest to the core, he owned up to his struggles. "Oh, it was dog shit," he said. "It wasn't good at all."

But the problems went beyond Burke. Cornerbacks coach Tim Walton said the lack of a pass rush—the Buckeyes didn't sack Gabriel—left him out to dry at times. Nick Saban, now a TV commentator, called Ohio State's reliance on a four-man pass rush "antiquated."

"Yeah, that was a tough statement," defensive line coach Larry Johnson said. "But when you can't affect the quarterback in man coverage, it's going to be a long day in the secondary. If the ball is coming out fast, you can't affect it. Sometimes with a four-man rush, you have to add a fifth guy. But no doubt [criticism like Saban's] affects you because that's your job. You're trying to find ways to get those guys to the quarterback, so you have to look at it from all eyes. You can't just say, 'I'm not going to change.'"

What was clear was that the Buckeye defense's dominance in the first five games was partly a product of inferior competition. Oregon exposed that. The Ducks often caught the Buckeyes flat-footed because they snapped the ball before Jim Knowles could call in the plays. Knowles acknowledged that he tried too often to get the perfect matchup and alignment. On some key plays, the Buckeyes were scrambling to get set.

"The tempo at times got us," Knowles conceded. "I don't think I did a good job of getting the guys prepared for that. There's definitely a feeling that you let the players down, you let the program down, you let the fans down. You feel all those things. It was certainly a wakeup call."

17

Close Call in a Clunker

The Buckeyes didn't play the Saturday after the Oregon loss, but it was no off week for the coaches. They had to figure out how a defense that allowed less than a touchdown per game in the first five games got torched by the Ducks. "Anytime you have a game that's subpar, as a coordinator, I don't care what level you're at, you've got to answer for that," Knowles said. "At Ohio State, it just becomes more glaring, more scrutiny."

Everything was put under the microscope in what would be described as a "reengineering" of the defense. The discussions didn't result in a dramatic change of scheme. The Buckeyes didn't suddenly change from a 4–3 to a 3–4 defense. But there were tweaks. They adjusted how nose guard Ty Hamilton lined up against the center and changed some fits in the run game. They pared down the defensive playbook significantly from about 25 defensive looks to about 12-15, Denzel Burke said. "I felt like there were a lot of checks that made you think too much while you're on the field," Hamilton said. "When you're on the field, you want to be locked in."

One change was an insistence that Knowles get the play calls in sooner and not have a repeat of the Oregon game when players weren't ready at the snap.

"I give the coaches a lot of credit," Jack Sawyer said. "We just said, look, we've got the best guys in the country on this side of the football, and we're going to let them play fast. Stop with all the thinking and stop with the extra checks trying to get to the perfect call. At some point, we're going to have to line up and play man to man."

They also made a point of getting safety Caleb Downs more involved. He'd come to Ohio State eager to play in a different scheme, but in the first half of the season, he hadn't made the impact he'd hoped. That wasn't Downs' fault. He'd been playing as a traditional safety most of the time, and teams generally avoided going in his direction. He acknowledged frustration with not always being in the center of the action. "It was a tough pill to swallow for me because I wasn't used to it," Downs said. "At Bama, I had 107 tackles. I had to get used to the ball not coming to me as much. It wasn't an easy thing for me because it was a new defense. It was a new scheme."

After the Oregon game, coaches frequently moved Downs closer to the line of scrimmage, often having Jordan Hancock play more of a traditional safety role instead of always lining up against the slot receiver. "I was very thankful for the coaches for putting me around the ball," Downs said. "I felt I really had to be around the ball to have a chance to make a play, and they did that, so I appreciate them."

Hancock's versatility made that adjustment possible. Day called him and Ty Hamilton the unsung heroes of the defense. Hancock's first love growing up in suburban Atlanta was basketball. He could dunk in the eighth grade despite being only about 5'7". Hancock thought hoops would be his path until Mel Tucker, then Georgia's defensive coordinator before going to Michigan State, came to a spring practice in Hancock's freshman year at North Gwinnett High School high school. He told

Hancock's coaches that he saw immense potential in Hancock in football. That convinced Hancock to put most of his energy into that sport.

He weighed only 165 pounds when he enrolled after spring practice in 2021. Usually, players who arrive that late see little or no playing time as a freshman because they're so far behind. But Hancock impressed enough that he played in seven games. He expected to compete for a bigger role as a sophomore, but on the third day of training camp, he fully tore his hamstring while covering Jaxon Smith-Njigba on a crossing route. The injury was so painful that he couldn't put on his socks. Hancock missed the first half of the season and played the second half at less than full strength only because the secondary was ravaged by injuries. Fully healthy as a junior, Hancock blossomed as a nickel cornerback. But he also had the size, toughness, and intelligence to play safety.

"I don't think there's a better nickel safety in college football than him this year," Sawyer said. "The way he can cover, how athletic he is. He's bigger than people think he is, and just a such a smart and cerebral guy, too."

OHIO STATE'S GAME against Nebraska was expected to be a cakewalk. The Cornhuskers have never been the contender in the Big Ten that their rich history would have indicated. A series of coaches have failed to turn around Nebraska's fortunes. Matt Rhule is the latest to try. He and Day coached together at Temple. Day has much respect for him. Nebraska was 5–1 heading into its game at undefeated Indiana while the Buckeyes were off. It was a chance for the Huskers to show they'd turned the corner. Instead, they got bludgeoned, 56–7. It was no surprise that Ohio State was a 25-point favorite when Nebraska came to Columbus on October 26.

But Day was wary. He believed the Huskers' performance against Indiana was an aberration. "It was just a strange game," he said. "It's like everything that could go wrong for Nebraska went wrong."

Day sensed that Nebraska would play with desperation against the Buckeyes. He worried that his players would underestimate the Huskers because of the IU blowout despite his warning that Nebraska was dangerous. He was wary of the effect the week off might have in terms of getting back into game rhythm.

Day was right to be concerned. The Huskers played like imposters against Indiana, but they came to play against Ohio State. The Buckeyes, meanwhile, were flat. Their defense played well early, though quarterback Dylan Raiola, a one-time Buckeye commitment, had some success on scrambles.

OSU took a 14–3 lead midway through the second quarter on long touchdown passes from Will Howard to Carnell Tate and Jeremiah Smith, but then the offense went into a long slumber. The offensive line struggled as it felt the effects of losing left tackle Josh Simmons. Replacement Zen Michalski had a dismal game, allowing two sacks and four pressures, according to *Pro Football Focus*, which gave him a pass-blocking grade of only 14.2.

"They had a good D-line," Chip Kelly said of Nebraska. "A couple of those kids got drafted. They were tough, hard-nosed physical guys."

After Jayden Fielding pushed a 42-yard field goal wide right, Nebraska kicked a 54-yard field goal to make it 14–6 at halftime.

A third-down pass-interference call on Davison Igbinosun—a recurring problem in 2024—allowed the Huskers to get into range to kick another field goal. Howard threw an interception that Malcolm Hartzog Jr. returned 34 yards to the Buckeyes' 7. But the Buckeyes' defense answered the call. On fourth down at the 2, Cody Simon and Igbinosun tackled Dante Dowdell short of the goal line. It would be a short-lived reprieve. Nebraska went 75 yards in nine plays for a touchdown and converted a two-point conversion to take a 17–14 lead with less than 11 minutes left.

The offense had done nothing for almost two quarters. It was a moment of truth. "We're struggling to run the ball and now we've got to start pushing the ball down the field," Day said. "Will's confidence is a little shook coming off that [interception], but if we just sit there and just sit on the runs, it's not going to go well. We've got to be able to throw the ball down the field."

So they did. Howard threw to Carnell Tate for a 37-yard completion to the Nebraska 38. Emeka Egbuka caught a pass on fourth-and-1 to keep the drive alive. Howard then threw to Quinshon Judkins for a nine-yard touchdown to put the Buckeyes back ahead with six minutes left.

The OSU defense closed it out. It got a three-and-out, and after Ohio State's offense did the same, Nebraska got possession at its 24 with 3½ minutes left. Ohio State looked to have sealed the game when linebacker Arvell Reese knocked the ball free from receiver Jahmal Brown and OSU recovered. But on replay review, officials deemed that Reese was guilty of targeting, overturning the turnover and giving Nebraska a first down at its own 46. (Ohio State successfully appealed to the Big Ten to have the Reese ejection reversed, and he didn't have to sit out the first half against Penn State the following week.)

But Ohio State didn't let Nebraska get any closer. After a false start by the Huskers, Simon read a screen pass and made a tackle for a three-yard loss. On third-and-19, Raiola threw over the middle into the arms of Hancock for a game-clinching interception. Ohio State had survived, but it was hardly a confidence-inspiring win, especially with a trip to State College against undefeated Penn State next.

"We were just off a little bit," Kelly said. "Sometimes, there are things you can't explain. It just wasn't clicking. It was just one of those days. But you know when you have a really, really good football team, you win those games. Things aren't going your way, but you just find a way."

18

New-Look Line Delivers

During training camp, offensive line coach Justin Frye approached Donovan Jackson with a suggestion that baffled him. Jackson was a two-time first-team All-Big Ten left guard, but Frye wanted him to take some reps at left tackle. "I was like, 'Why would I ever do this? This makes no sense,'" Jackson recalled.

But Frye had a good reason. Football is a game of injuries. Linemen are in hand-to-hand combat on every play. Coaches must prepare for worst-case scenarios. And now the Buckeyes had one. Zen Michalski struggled badly against Nebraska, then injured his left hip late in the fourth quarter. "I looked to the sideline, and I saw coach Frye pointing at me and telling me to move out [to tackle]," Jackson said. "I was like, 'No way that I'm about to play tackle at Ohio State.'"

Yes, way. Jackson finished out the Nebraska game at left tackle. But that was just a few plays. He figured that would be a one-time emergency thing. It would not be. Ohio State simply didn't have any other viable options. Coaches asked him if he would play tackle against Penn State. "Initially, I was very apprehensive," Jackson said. "I was like, 'Why do I have to do it?' We had other tackles on the team, but they had no playing experience. Coach Frye said, 'I believe you can do it. Coach Day believes you can do it. We wouldn't be having this conversation if we thought you couldn't do it. We just need you to go out there and play as hard as you can.'"

Jackson said he wrestled with it for a day or two and then agreed to move to tackle. Whatever apprehension he had was outweighed by wanting to help the team. Jackson has always been selfless. When he was a toddler, he saw a boy push older sister Rachel off the swing at a playground. Jackson ran over and shoved the boy. "He was like a bouncer, even at three years old," Melanie Jackson said with a laugh about her son.

As he entered high school, Jackson had already shown he was an elite athlete. When he had to decide whether to be an offensive or defensive lineman, Jackson chose offense because he preferred being a protector. Jackson also shined in the classroom. His mom and grandmothers were teachers. Good grades were nonnegotiable in the Jackson family. Jackson had a grade point average above 3.7 at OSU, where he became a starter as a sophomore. After excelling at left guard for 2½ years, he now decided to accept his biggest test. He would line up against Penn State defensive end Abdul Carter, who'd be the third pick in the 2025 NFL draft.

Jackson took a crash course in learning to play left tackle, which he had last played in high school. He studied video of Josh Simmons and NFL tackles. Ohio State's pass-rushers stayed after practice to run drills with him and give tips. Moving from guard to tackle is not a simple switch, especially in pass protection. A tackle lines up farther away from a defensive end than a guard does against a defensive tackle. That allows the rusher more space to gain speed.

The key for a tackle, Jackson said, is "setting to the spot." That's the spot around the line of scrimmage where the pass-rusher and tackle engage. If the blocker gets there first, he has the advantage. If the defensive end does, he could have a clear path to the quarterback's blind side.

Consistently beating the lightning-quick Carter to the spot would be quite a challenge.

Jackson also knew that Ohio State would likely have to use a silent count because of the crowd noise. Beaver Stadium is one of the loudest in the country, even if Ohio State wasn't the Nittany Lions' designated "White Out" opponent in 2024. Jackson would have to turn his head toward the ball to see when it was snapped instead of being able to hear Howard yell for the snap. If Jackson was slow getting his head back and reacting to the snap, Carter would probably blow by him. "I was solely focused on getting out of my stance as best as possible," Jackson said. "In the locker room before warmups, I was very nervous. When I got to the field, I had a sense of calm, like I'll be fine. I'm realistic. He's probably going to get his because he's a great rusher. But I was going to fight with all I have, and I'm going to be all right in the end."

Jackson's move to left tackle meant that Ohio State had to replace him at left guard. Austin Siereveld started the first two games of the season when Jackson was out with a hamstring injury. But Day and the coaches decided to start Carson Hinzman against Penn State because he had more experience.

HINZMAN HAD ALMOST been a forgotten man the first half of the season. He'd taken over as the center in 2023 as a redshirt freshman after Luke Wypler entered the NFL draft and was taken in the sixth round by the Cleveland Browns. "I was trying to convince myself, 'Oh yeah, I'm ready for this role,'" Hinzman said, "and realizing in hindsight I had no idea what I was getting myself into."

He struggled to the point coaches benched him for the Cotton Bowl loss against Missouri. Then coaches pursued McLaughlin. Transferring crossed Hinzman's mind, but he decided he loved Ohio State too much to leave. Besides, as much as he wanted to dislike McLaughlin, he couldn't. "I definitely hated how likeable he was," Hinzman said with a laugh. "He's such a good dude. He's very funny, very witty. He taught me so much. I'm super grateful for him. But I definitely had to look at the long term rather than the short term for a while."

Mickey Marotti has seen players react to adversity in every conceivable way in his decades as a strength coach. He admires the way Hinzman did. "He got beat out," Mickey Marotti said. "He could have gone in the tank. But he never wavered. He never gave up, never had a bad day, never put his head down. He just got better and better and better."

Hinzman credits much of his attitude to growing up on his family's farm in Wisconsin. He understood what hard work was. "I'm used to getting up early and getting back at night, and no one ever complained," Hinzman said. "It's just literally what we do. That's why I didn't understand people that didn't want to be in the weight room or be on the field with each other and do all the hard stuff. Obviously, it's not the most fun in the world. But I would way rather be doing this than waking up at 4:00 AM and milking a cow."

But Hinzman hadn't taken any snaps at left guard, even in practice. He hadn't taken any game snaps since the Iowa game. "I was nervous, but I also felt I was ready," he said. "That was the biggest thing for me."

FOR WILL HOWARD, this was a game he'd craved playing since transferring to Ohio State. He hadn't forgotten how Penn State, his home-state school, had stopped recruiting him after he was injured as a high school junior. In his press conference after the Nebraska game, he said he was still salty about it.

"I didn't even really know what I was saying," Howard said. "I was pissed off we didn't play great against Nebraska and said that, like, 'Hey, I want to prove that I'm good enough.' I knew that one was big. I really wanted that one. No matter what happened or how big I was making it, we were going to win that game. Just the look in everybody's eyes in the locker, I knew we had them."

McLaughlin, in particular, was pumped up for the game. The criticism the offensive line got for its performance against Nebraska and the concerns about having to move Jackson to tackle had festered in McLaughlin all week. In the cramped visitors' locker room at Beaver Stadium, he spoke up. "I was pissed off at the way people talked about our offensive line," McLaughlin said. "It was the first time I stepped up as a verbal leader on the team in a pregame speech, pumping everybody up. I think it got a lot of people going. That was definitely an attitude game for me because I was going against a couple of good players on the inside, and I wanted everybody to feed off my energy. I thought I'd earned respect from my teammates by that point in the season as a player and a leader, so I thought it was my time to step up."

Ohio State had reason to be confident against the Nittany Lions. The Buckeyes had won 11 of their last 12 games against them. James Franklin's only victory over OSU came in 2016 thanks to a blocked punt and a blocked field goal returned for a touchdown. Though undefeated Penn State was ranked No. 3 and Ohio State No. 4, Las Vegas made the visiting Buckeyes a 3½-point favorite. Oddsmakers factored in Franklin's 1–13 record against top-5 teams. But Ohio State had much to prove as well. Another loss would give OSU no margin for error in terms of making the CFP. And Day's 3–6 record against top-5 teams was hardly stellar, either.

THE GAME COULDN'T have started worse for Ohio State. Penn State took the opening kickoff and drove for a field goal, chewing eight minutes off the clock. When the Buckeyes finally got the ball, it turned disastrous. Howard misread a coverage on a pass to Smith. Penn State's Zion Tracy jumped the route, intercepted the pass, and ran 31 yards for a touchdown. Ten minutes into the game, the Buckeyes trailed 10–0.

"It feels damn near like the world could start crumbling around you," Howard said. "But in that moment, nobody said anything to me. They all knew I was going to be fine because shit like that doesn't faze me. I've seen a lot. I've done a lot. It is what it is."

Chip Kelly said the play was less about a bad throw by Howard and more a terrific one by Tracy. "The DB fooled Will, but when I saw the play starting to develop, he fooled us up in the box, too," he said. "Sometimes, you've got to tip your cap. That was a helluva play by the defensive back."

The Buckeyes knew they had to right the ship quickly, and they did. Ohio State went 74 yards and scored on a 25-yard pass from Howard to Egbuka. A 21-yard touchdown pass to Brandon Inniss on their next drive gave the Buckeyes the lead. Ohio State then appeared to have taken firm control of the game when Howard got free on a scramble toward the end zone. But right before he crossed the goal line, Penn State safety Zakee Wheatley knocked the ball from Howard's grip. The ball went out of bounds through the end zone for a touchback.

Penn State looked like it had regained the lead just before halftime. Cornerback Davison Igbinosun was beaten (and called for interference) on a completion to the OSU 3. On the next play, Penn State targeted Igbinosun again. Drew Allar threw a fade pattern to Trey Wallace, who appeared to have caught the pass on the sideline for a touchdown. Officials ruled it that way on the field before it was reviewed. But Igbinosun had wrested the ball from Wallace before the receiver could establish possession for a huge interception.

In those two plays, the worst and best of Igbinosun was on display. He could be overly aggressive. He committed 19 penalties, mostly pass interference, during the 2024 season. The rest of the OSU defense was flagged only 25 times. "It definitely was frustrating to deal with," Igbinosun said. "But I take full accountability for those. I probably could do a lot better getting my head around and tracking the football. I would also say the refs don't cut me any slack. If they see it's close to me, they're throwing it."

To keep himself from being too handsy, he began wearing mittens in practice, which he said was his idea. A player that prone to penalties is also prone to being benched, but Igbinosun kept his job. Coaches loved his ultra-competitiveness. That's why they pursued him when he entered the transfer portal after his freshman season at Ole Miss. When he arrived at OSU, he made it clear he wasn't going to back down to anyone.

"I think he was the reason our defensive backfield all of a sudden became BIA," said Marotti, referring to the secondary's motto of being the best in America, "because he came in and said, 'I'm taking your job. I'm taking your job. I'm taking your job.' He told Denzel, 'I'm taking your job.' Everybody was like, 'Who's this guy?'"

But Igbinosun earned Iron Buckeye honors in the offseason and won the job opposite Burke. No play he made as a Buckeye was bigger than that interception before halftime.

Jayden Fielding kicked two field goals and Penn State kicked one to make it 20–13 in the fourth quarter. That lead was suddenly in jeopardy when Nittany Lions' All-American tight end Tyler Warren broke free down the left sideline. Burke fought through blockers to push him out of bounds at the OSU 3 with seven minutes left.

Ohio State then came up with its biggest goal-line stand so far in 2024. Tyleik Williams had just injured his ankle, so the Buckeyes added lineman Kayden McDonald and Hero Kanu to join Ty Hamilton, Jack Sawyer, and J.T. Tuimoloau up front. McDonald lined up against the center. The linemen's job was to prevent Penn State's linemen from getting any push. "That's the goal," defensive line coach Larry Johnson said. "Keep the pads down and create knockback. Get your feet to where the ball is and make sure you play on the other side of the ball."

That's exactly what the Buckeyes did. Kaytron Allen, Penn State's 220-pound running back, was stuffed on first down. And on second. And on third as Penn State fans booed Franklin's conservative play calls. "I was surprised they ran it the second time," Johnson said. "We got a great play from K-Mac. The center got knocked all the way back in the backfield."

On fourth down from the 1, the Buckeyes figured Penn State would try something different, most likely a play for Warren. But Lathan Ransom had Warren covered so Allar threw toward tight end Khalil Dinkins, who was surrounded by Buckeyes, and the pass fell incomplete.

A brilliant defensive call perfectly executed? Well…

"On that last play, we were all messed up," Sonny Styles said. "A lot of us were covering the wrong guys, but we ended up making a play anyway. We were laughing about it—me, Cody, and the safeties. It was like we were playing backyard defensive football. 'You've got him. I've got him.' Just on the fly. It ended up working out pretty well, but it was definitely a crazy play."

The goal-line stand became a defining moment for a defense that had to regroup after the Oregon game. "My memory of it is the guys up front kicking ass," Jim Knowles said. "We just controlled the line of scrimmage. It was great to see from a physical standpoint because I had always preached, 'Give us an inch,' and the defense would say, 'We'll defend it.' It was a mantra for us, and it played out in that goal-line stand."

The Buckeyes hadn't clinched the game yet. Pinned at its own 1, Ohio State still had more than five minutes on the clock to kill. They would do just that. On first down, Howard used his 235-pound frame and a strong push from the offensive line to gain four yards. The way it felt, it might as well have been 40. "After that, we knew we could roll these guys off the ball," McLaughlin said. "For lack of a better term, we had to drop our nuts."

Howard's sneak was followed by runs of nine, six, and 15 yards by Quinshon Judkins. Howard then converted consecutive third downs with runs. After the second, which clinched the victory, he slid and signaled a triumphant first down. "It was probably the first time since I've been at Ohio State where coach Day just looked at us and was like, 'I'm giving the game to you guys,'" right guard Tegra Tshabola said. "It was a really proud moment for the offensive line."

It was an especially triumphant moment for Jackson and Hinzman. Jackson yielded two sacks to Carter, once when Carter used his speed to beat him and the other when he pushed Carter past Howard before Carter tracked him down after the quarterback began to scramble. Other than those, he kept Carter at bay.

Hinzman played as if guard was his natural position. "I had so much fun in that game because I was back playing with my friends," Hinzman said. "Playing hard and playing in an environment like that was really fun. To go out there and show out like that was important for us, especially because we needed a statement after the Oregon game."

It was a statement, but this was still a team that wasn't playing to its vast potential. "I think that game shouldn't have been that close," Kelly said. "We gave them seven [with the pick-six]. We had seven that we took away [with the fumble at the goal line]. That's a 14-point difference, and it shouldn't have been that close."

Coordinator Jim Knowles—architect of what became the nation's top-ranked defense—addresses the media during a press conference prior to the start of the 2024 season.

Alabama transfer Seth McLaughlin (56) block against Penn State on November 2, 2024. An Achilles tear ended his season two weeks later, McLaughlin still won t Rimington Trophy as th nation's top center.

Michigan beat the Buckeyes in Columbus on November 30, then planted "M" flags in the Block O at midfield—spawning fights but kickstarting a turnaround for Ohio State's season.

ensive linemen Carson Hinzman (75) and Tegra Tshabola (77) pray before the playoff game with nessee. Faith was a key element of the close bonds formed by the 2024 team.

Jeremiah Smith heads downfield after a reception against Tennessee. The freshman wide receiver revealed himself as a transcendent talent from the time he arrived at Ohio State.

TreVeyon Henderson ran for 80 yards and two touchdowns against Tennessee. He ended the season with 1,016 rushing yards and later was drafted in the second round by the Patriots.

Gee Scott Jr. evades a tackle against Oregon in the Rose Bowl. The senior tight end leaned on his newfou religious faith to resu what had been a disappointing Ohio S career.

Safety Caleb Downs tackles Oregon's Noah Whittington during the Rose Bowl. The Alabama transfer used the 2024 season to confirm his reputation as one of the nation's top defenders.

r linebacker Cody Simon sacks Oregon quarterback Dillon Gabriel during the Rose Bowl.
ı was later drafted in the fourth round by the Arizona Cardinals.

Buckeyes' football is a family endeavor for head coach Ryan Day. Here he celebrates the Rose Bowl victory with his wife, Nina (wearing white), and daughters, Grace and Nia.

Quinshon Judkins' one-yard touchdown opened the scoring in the hard-fought semifinal win over Texas. In his one season at Ohio State, the running back rushed for 1,060 yards and 14 TDs.

Wide receiver Emek Egbuka looks for roo to turn upfield agai Texas. The future fi round NFL draft pi finished the semifin victory with 51 rece yards on five catches

Safety Sonny Styles (6) and cornerback Denzel Burke pursue Texas receiver Ryan Wingo during the playoff semifinal. The Buckeyes boasted the nation's No. 3 passing defense in 2024–2025.

Ohio State defensive end J.T. Tuimoloau battles Outland Trophy–winner and future first-round pick Kelvin Banks Jr. during the semifinal against Texas.

After sacking quarterback Quinn Ewers and forcing a fumble, Buckeyes linebacker Jack Sawyer took advantage of a fortuitous bounce, scored an 83-yard touchdown, and sealed the win over Texas.

Offensive coordinator Chip Kelly (shown before the championship) was a late and unlikely addition to the 2024 staff. Head coach Ryan Day had previously played for and served as an assistant to Kelly.

Kicker Jayden Fielding lines up for an extra point against Notre Dame. His flawless championsh performance was redemption for a season marred by injury and missed field goals against Michig

Quarterback Will Howard quickly transitioned from transfer to the Buckeyes' key leader on offen His play against Notre Dame earned him the offensive MVP award in the championship game.

ries robbed the Ohio State offensive line of two key starters in 2024 but by season's end the unit regained its footing and dominated Notre Dame during the championship game.

keyes players celebrate after Ohio State defeated Notre Dame 34–23 in the CFP National mpionship Game in Dallas on January 20, 2025, completing an unlikely run to the title.

19

Putting IU in Its Place

Before Ohio State had its next showdown game, it played two Big Ten bottom-dwellers. Purdue went winless in the conference; Northwestern finished 2–7.

The 45–0 rout of the Boilermakers was devoid of much drama. Ohio State got its first shutout of a Big Ten opponent since blanking Rutgers in 2017. Purdue gained only 206 yards while Will Howard completed 21 of 26 passes for 260 yards and three touchdowns. The Northwestern game was interesting mainly because of the venue. The Wildcats' home stadium in Evanston, Ryan Field, was in the midst of a major rebuild, so the game was moved to Wrigley Field, home of the Chicago Cubs.

"Honestly, that was a cool experience," Jack Sawyer said. "My grandpa, who played in the minors for the Pittsburgh Pirates, always talked about Wrigley as one of the fields he wanted to watch a game at."

It was a Northwestern home game in name only. The overwhelming majority of spectators wore scarlet. The Buckeyes started slowly. After Sawyer forced a fumble recovered by Davison Igbinosun at the OSU 16, an apparent touchdown catch by Jeremiah Smith was ruled an incompletion on replay review and the Buckeyes came up empty. Northwestern then drove 92 yards to take a 7–0 lead early in the second quarter. The Wildcats outgained Ohio State 118–30 to that point.

After that, though, the Buckeyes seized control. Howard converted a fourth-and-3 on a completion to Smith, and Carnell Tate made a diving 14-yard catch in tight coverage to set up a one-yard touchdown run by Quinshon Judkins. Ohio State took the lead after Northwestern punter Hunter Renner couldn't catch a bad snap; Dave Adolph blocked the kick after Renner retrieved the ball. The Buckeyes got the ball at the 1, and Judkins punched it in.

After a three-and-out by the defense, Ohio State made it 21–7 at halftime on a 25-yard touchdown catch by Tate, who caught another touchdown pass in the third quarter as the Buckeyes pulled away for a 31–7 win. For Tate, a Chicago native, it was an emotional day. His mother, Ashley Griggs, was killed in July 2023 when a drive-by shooter fired into a crowd leaving an event on the city's West Side. "She was full of life, very passionate about her son," Brian Hartline said. "She always traveled on his recruiting visits and was always here. She was full of energy and would always tell you what was on her mind. She was just a joy to be around."

When Griggs was killed, Hartline acknowledged he didn't know how to handle it. "I didn't want to even talk about it and make it real," he said. "I just didn't do a good job with it, in my mind. It was a dark day. It will always be a dark day. I still have trouble with it."

After his mom's death, Tate simply went back to work. "It was eerie because the day after it happened, he was back at workouts," Mickey Marotti said. "I grabbed him and said, 'Carnell, you don't need to be here right now, bro. Take one day, three days, a week, two weeks.' He said, 'I'm good, coach.'

"I can't remember exactly when it happened, but there was a break maybe a month and a half down the road, and I think he went back [to Chicago], and I think that's when it all kind of hit him."

Tate was overshadowed in 2024 by Smith and Emeka Egbuka, but the sophomore caught 52 passes for 733 yards and four touchdowns. "He's a very mature player, a very willing blocker," Hartline said. "He is a very reliable, sure-handed, high-execution guy that just seems to always make the play."

Tate left Chicago as a sophomore in high school to attend IMG Academy in Florida, so his relatives and friends hadn't seen him play in years. He asked teammates for their unused tickets and hosted more than 30 people at Wrigley. He also insisted on the team having Italian subs as their post-game meal. "It was very special being back home," Tate said. "That was my first time playing back there since high school, so it meant a lot to me being in Chicago and also being there for my family. It was a blessing for me, definitely."

Said Day, "We all tried to do the best we could to help him and put our arms around him and tried to make that game as special as we could for him. He's just not a very outspoken guy or creates a lot of drama. He's a great teammate."

THE PRELIMS WERE now over for Ohio State. Every game from now on would be a big one. Up next was undefeated Indiana, followed by The Game against Michigan, then presumably the Big Ten championship game before the College Football Playoff.

That Indiana would be considered a big game for Ohio State took some getting used to. The Hoosiers are the losingest program in college football history. Though they'd given the Buckeyes a few scares over the years, IU hadn't beaten Ohio State since 1988. But this was a different Hoosiers team. First-year coach Curt Cignetti brought a swagger—and a lot of his former James Madison players—to Bloomington. Shortly after he was hired, he was introduced at an IU basketball game at Assembly Hall. "Purdue sucks," he told the crowd, referring to the Hoosiers' hated in-state rival, "but so do Michigan and Ohio State." IU fans roared. To skeptics who questioned whether Cignetti could turn IU into a winner, he had a quick answer, "I win. Google me."

Cignetti then backed up the talk. Indiana shocked the college football world by winning its first 10 games for the first time. The Hoosiers rose to No. 5 in the CFP rankings. Only in their previous game, a 20–15 win over Michigan, had IU won by fewer than 14 points.

"It was the first big-time home matchup of the year, another top-5 team coming in," Seth McLaughlin said. "The weather just started getting cold. It was going to be a cold, wet, tough game. It was going to be like the first Big Ten weather experience in my career, and I was really looking forward to it."

That made what happened on a play early in Tuesday's practice even harder to swallow. McLaughlin snapped the ball and stepped to his right on a zone-read play when he felt what he thought was a thud to the back of his leg or foot by left guard Carson Hinzman. McLaughlin fell to the turf but oddly felt no pain.

"I jumped up ready to get mad at Carson for stepping on my foot, and I turned around and he was three yards upfield, nowhere near me," McLaughlin recalled. "I went to take a step back to the line, and my foot was just dangling. I turned around, and coach Day was standing right there. I'm like, 'Coach, I just tore my Achilles,' and his face went white, like he saw ghosts."

McLaughlin threw his helmet across the field in anger. His season and college career, he knew, were over. "I saw his helmet rolling," Hinzman said. "My heart sank right through my whole body."

But football stops for no man and no injury. The Buckeyes resumed practice with Hinzman back at center, the position he played in 2023. Howard saw how heartbroken everyone was. He and McLaughlin had become close friends. McLaughlin had a longtime girlfriend, Sarah Skoglund, whom he met, coincidentally enough, when Alabama played Ohio State in the 2021 CFP championship in Florida. Sarah thought her sister, Skyler, might be compatible with Howard. Sarah was right. Howard and Skyler became friends and then a couple. That made Howard's friendship with McLaughlin even closer. But now he had to put that aside.

"It was not easy," Howard said. "The friend in me and the human in me wanted to freaking curl up into a ball for the guy. I just hurt for him. He'd had such a great season and was making such a revenge story for himself. I hated that it had to end that way. But in the moment, I knew he wouldn't want to stop practicing. Everyone in practice damn near—coaches and staff—went silent when that happened. I just had to keep the shit moving. I took it upon myself to be that guy to rally the troops because my boy was hurting, and everybody's hurting with him."

Howard went to each of the offensive linemen and told them that they'd be all right, that they'd figure out a way to overcome the injury. "Will's leadership that day, his leadership that week, was just tremendous," Day said. "The worse the situation was, he just became more positive. I'd never really quite experienced somebody in that moment like the way he did, and everybody fed off of it, coaches included."

But all the leadership in the world couldn't erase the fact that the Buckeyes had lost two of their best linemen for the season. Despite the injury, McLaughlin would win the Rimington Trophy as the country's top center. The loss of him and left tackle Josh Simmons looked insurmountable, especially factoring in that Donovan Jackson was still adjusting to playing a new position. Ohio State's national championship hopes looked doomed. "Yeah, I mean you couldn't help but think that," Day said.

McLaughlin immediately went into coaching mode. Doctors wanted him to have surgery that Friday. He refused. He wanted to tutor his linemates that week, so he delayed the surgery for three days. Though he knew he wasn't to blame for the injury, he felt he'd let the team down by getting hurt. "It was a very emotional week for me because I had worked so hard and put so much energy into it," McLaughlin said. "I loved all these guys on the team. The offensive line was playing really well, just catching their stride."

Sitting on his scooter, he gave the team's pregame speech. "I forget what I said, but it was just rallying the fellas," he said.

WITH HINZMAN MOVING to center, Austin Siereveld took over at left guard. To his teammates and coaches, he was known as "Piggy." That was his gamer tag on Xbox, which he said was his dad's originally. "He told me that was his nickname, too, back in college and high school," Siereveld said.

Teammates joked that Siereveld had no calves, that they were just as big as thighs. "There's no difference from his hips to his quads to his calves," Hinzman said. "He's just a block of meat. We call him Piggy for a reason."

Siereveld said that finding clothes that fit is a constant challenge. "I got my first pair of jeans this year for Christmas, so that was cool," he said. "I couldn't find a pair of jeans that would fit me correctly. It was like that with sweatpants. I would always squeeze in sweatpants or dress pants. It was a nightmare."

Siereveld grew up north of Cincinnati as a big Buckeyes fan. Like Jack Sawyer and so many native Ohioans, he remembers watching Ohio State's 2014 national championship and dreamed of being on a team one like it. After redshirting as a freshman in 2023, Siereveld entered the season hoping to be a top backup. He caught a break when he was one of the few linemen not to contract hand, foot, and mouth disease in training camp. That allowed him to get valuable reps. He started the season's first two games when Jackson missed the first two games with a hamstring injury. Siereveld admits he was disappointed when coaches chose Hinzman to play left guard instead of him after Jackson moved to left tackle after Josh Simmons' injury. Now, because of another season-ending injury, he would get another chance. "Yeah, that [injury] was a shock during practice," Siereveld said. "Then my whole mindset just flipped. I knew everyone was relying on me, and I knew I couldn't mess up."

INDIANA MIGHT HAVE been college football's darling, but Ohio State was intent on showing that nothing had changed between the programs. Cignetti's comment that "Ohio State sucks" along with Purdue and Michigan were shown all week in the Woody.

"The feeling going into that game," Jack Sawyer said, "was you want to run your mouth all you want, but you've got to eventually put the pads on, step in the Shoe in the middle of Columbus late in the season where it's going to be snowing and cold out, against the damn Buckeyes. All week, we had this pissed off mentality that we've given teams the ability to feel like they can come into our house and take it over. And so for us, we're like it's time to set these guys back a little bit here, let them know that you're not going to run through the Big Ten. You're not going to run through us. And we took it personal."

Day had some concerns heading into the Indiana game, especially with the reshuffled offensive line. IU's linemen shifted a lot before the snap, and Day worried whether his blockers could adjust. But overall, he was confident. In his view, Indiana didn't have a lot of NFL-caliber players. "You've got to play the game, but we felt like we liked our match-ups," Day said.

Indiana started the game, however, like it had against its previous 10 opponents. After Ohio State received the opening kickoff, the Hoosiers forced a three-and-out and drove 70 yards, aided by two more Davison Igbinosun pass-interference penalties, for a touchdown. On the Buckeyes' next possession, they overcame a third-and-35 to get a first down on passes of 25 and 24 yards to Tate, only to have Quinshon Judkins stuffed on fourth down at the IU 9.

The offense finally cashed in on its next drive when OSU's defense gave it a short field. Emeka Egbuka caught an 11-yard pass that grazed the hand of the Indiana defender to tie the game. The Buckeyes appeared poised to take the lead when Cody Simon drilled Indiana quarterback Kurtis Rourke from the blind side, forcing a fumble recovered by Ty Hamilton at the IU 18. But the Buckeyes couldn't capitalize. Howard threw to Jelani Thurman, but the ball deflected off the tight end's hands and Indiana intercepted it.

It seemed the game would go to halftime tied, but with less than two minutes left, OSU's defense forced a punt. The snap was fine, but the slick ball went through IU punter James Evans's hands. Evans retrieved the ball but was immediately tackled by Caden Curry at the 7. Three plays later, TreVeyon Henderson scored from the 4 to give OSU a 14–7 halftime lead.

Another punt play early in the third quarter would spark Ohio State's second-half rout. Buckeyes coaches had been seeking to take advantage of Caleb Downs' athleticism. He was so gifted that in the spring OSU coaches toyed with the idea of giving him snaps as a running back, which he played in high school, but nothing came of that. But starting against Nebraska, they began using him as a punt returner.

Downs anticipated that Evans would try to kick it to his left, but it went to his right. Downs couldn't catch it in the air, and the ball bounced twice before it came to him at the 21. Denzel Burke and Lorenzo Styles Jr. made blocks on the IU gunners to give Downs a chance to head upfield. Downs made a nifty spin move at the 24 to avoid Indiana long-snapper Mark Langston and raced down the OSU sideline. "I was like, 'OK, I might have a chance here,'" Downs recalled.

He got a block from C.J. Hicks and cut toward the middle of the field to daylight. No Hoosier came close to chasing him down as he ran to the end zone for a 79-yard score. It was Ohio State's first punt return for a touchdown since Jalin Marshall did it 10 years earlier, also against Indiana, in 2014. After that, Ohio State rolled. OSU added two touchdowns to lead 31–7. The Buckeyes' defense dominated. After IU's touchdown on its opening drive, the Hoosiers gained a total of five yards in their next six possessions. The Buckeyes sacked Rourke eight times. (After the season, the quarterback revealed he'd played all season with a torn ACL.)

Indiana finally scored again with just under two minutes left. Cignetti then went for a two-point conversion, which IU made, and an onside kick, which it didn't. Ohio State took possession, and Henderson broke free on a handoff. He could have scored but slid down at the 1, which would have allowed OSU to run out the clock. Instead of taking a knee, however, Ohio State punched it into the end zone for a final touchdown to make the final 38–15 and all but ensure a berth in the College Football Playoff.

"They wanted to keep playing, and that's fine," Day said of Cignetti going for two and attempting the onside kick. "So if they want to keep playing, we'll keep playing. We told [our offense] it was 'down time,' which meant if you got a first down, you can get what you can get and then get down."

But the offense wanted to make a final statement, Day said. "The guys came over before the drive and they really wanted to score," he said. "They took offense to some of the things that were said."

Yes, they did. "If you're going to take a big game, you've got to back it up," right tackle Josh Fryar said. "If you're going to rub it in other people's faces, then we're going to rub it in your face. When we were in the huddle [at the 1-yard line, we were like, 'We're scoring this.' I wanted to score just knowing it was Indiana, and I wanted to run it up on my dad just one more time. We talk a lot of shit because he always says, 'We beat Ohio State 31–10 in the Horseshoe.' And I was like, 'Guess what, I'm 5–0 against Indiana, so fuck you,' and we start laughing about it. It's all in good fun."

For Ohio State's reshuffled (again) offensive line, the IU game was a mixed bag. Howard wasn't sacked, but OSU struggled in the run game. Before Henderson's final 39-yard run, the Buckeyes managed only 76 yards in 26 carries. "I don't think we played very well on offense that day," Day said. "I don't think we blocked them particularly well."

In hindsight, it was a harbinger of what was to come the next week.

20

The Michigan Debacle

Nobody saw it coming.

Ohio State was sure it would end its three-game losing streak to Michigan. So was the rest of the world. The Buckeyes were a three-touchdown favorite, and with good reason. After winning the national championship, Michigan hit the skids. Jim Harbaugh left to coach the Los Angeles Chargers. Months later, the NCAA levied a one-year suspension and four-year show-cause penalty against Harbaugh after it concluded he "violated recruiting and inducement rules, engaged in unethical conduct, failed to promote an atmosphere of compliance, and violated head coach responsibility obligations."

The core of Michigan's team, including quarterback J.J. McCarthy, running back Blake Corum, defensive tackle Kris Jenkins, and defensive back Mike Sainristil, was in the NFL. The loss of McCarthy was particularly devastating because Michigan didn't have an adequate replacement. Davis Warren was an inspirational story after overcoming leukemia in high school and winning the job as a former walk-on. But his passing was inconsistent at best. He threw more interceptions (nine) than touchdowns (seven). With a feeble passing game, Michigan under new coach Sherrone Moore had to rely on running backs Donovan Edwards and Kalel Mullings and its stout defense, particularly defensive tackles Mason Graham and Kenneth Grant. Graham would become the fifth pick of the 2025 draft. Grant was the 13th.

It often wasn't enough. Texas rolled over the Wolverines 31–12 the second week of the season in Ann Arbor. Michigan also lost to Washington and Illinois in addition to its loss to Indiana. A 50–6 thrashing of Northwestern the week before the Ohio State game gave Michigan some optimism, but almost nobody thought Michigan could pull off an upset over the Buckeyes. The Wolverines' chances seemed even bleaker when two of their biggest stars—cornerback Will Johnson and tight end Colston Loveland—couldn't play because of injuries.

"We were pretty confident going into the game," Day said. "We were concerned about our matchups on the inside [against Graham and Grant] for sure. Watching them on defense, they were better than people gave them credit for. They were very good up front. They could stop the run with six [players]."

THE TEMPERATURE FOR the noon kickoff was 27 degrees with sunny skies and a moderate wind that increased throughout the afternoon. The game started well enough for the Buckeyes. They held Michigan to one first down on its game-opening drive and then drove 58 yards before settling for a 29-yard field goal by Jayden Fielding. Michigan followed with its best drive of the half, but Ohio State stuffed Mullings on fourth-and-1 at the OSU 3.

Then came the turning point. Two Ohio State run plays went nowhere, so Day and Chip Kelly decided to be aggressive. Howard threw to the right on a short sideline pass toward Carnell Tate. But the pass wasn't far enough outside. Michigan cornerback Aamir Hall jumped the route, caught the ball at the 13 and returned it to the 2. "I missed my spot a little bit," Howard said. "In that situation, I've got to put the ball high and away and make sure that only my receiver can get it. That one hurt. That was not good."

Mullings scored two plays later to give Michigan a 7–3 lead. Throughout the stadium, the feeling of here-we-go-again was almost palpable. Did Day feel that? "I tried not to," Day said. "You could probably feel it in the stadium that there was that feeling. I tried to continually [emphasize] that has nothing to do with what's going on here. We've just got to keep playing every play."

It would get worse for the Buckeyes. On their next drive, Howard tried to run for a first down on third-and-3 but got drilled high by Michigan safety Makari Paige short of the first-down marker. Howard was slow to get up and went to the medical tent. The nature and extent of Howard's injury were never announced. One Ohio State official described it later as a neck and shoulder issue.

Months later, Howard revealed the truth...mostly. "It wasn't neck and shoulder," Howard said. "It was upper extremities—not my arm." That would leave his head as the only remaining body part. "Yeah, my head was a little banged up," Howard said. "I definitely felt it in my head."

Howard said he was examined for a possible concussion. "They tested me," he said. "Nothing was diagnosed, though. They said I was good enough to go back in." Certainly, Howard was hell-bent on returning. "They weren't taking me out of that game, man," Howard said. "Only God himself could have taken me out of that thing, like I was *not* coming out."

Howard missed only one play, a Devin Brown handoff to Quinshon Judkins for a first down. But the drive stalled after that. Consecutive run plays lost a yard, and Howard threw a third-down incompletion. Fielding came in to kick a 38-yard field goal, but he missed it wide right. The teams then traded three-and-outs, though Michigan flipped the field with a 68-yard punt that went over the head of Caleb Downs. Joe McGuire's punt for OSU went only 31 yards, giving the Wolverines the ball on the Buckeyes' 39. When Michigan gained only three yards on its possession, it appeared Ohio State would escape unscathed. But Dominic Zvada's

54-yard field goal with the wind at his back was good, giving Michigan a 10–3 lead with 2:15 left before halftime.

Ohio State's offense finally came alive on its two-minute drill. Howard threw to Emeka Egbuka for 18 yards and to Tate for 11. A pass to the end zone to Jeremiah Smith drew an interference call. On the next play, Howard connected with Smith, who was wide open in the back of the end zone for a touchdown and a 10–10 halftime tie.

OHIO STATE HOPED that touchdown would spark the Buckeyes in the second half. It didn't. The second half was mostly a stalemate. It began with another special-teams mistake. TreVeyon Henderson misjudged the kickoff into the wind and had to fall on the ball at the 6. Henderson gained 24 yards on a screen pass to move the ball to the Michigan 41, but the drive ended when Howard threw behind Egbuka on third down. On Ohio State's next possession, the Buckeyes drove to the Michigan 16, but Howard again was off target on a pass to Egbuka and Paige intercepted it.

Howard completed only 7 of 15 passes for 56 yards in the third and fourth quarters, clearly feeling the effects of the first-half hit. Michigan geared its pass defense toward Jeremiah Smith and made him a nonfactor in the second half. The freshman was targeted twice and caught one of them for only three yards.

"I wasn't 100 percent," Howard said. "I'll say that. Nothing was diagnosed, and I didn't have too many problems afterward, but I definitely didn't feel like myself. I wasn't clicking on all cylinders like I normally do, and I wasn't as sharp as I normally am. But the competitor in me was going to leave all of everything I had for that game. I wasn't coming out. I wanted to give everything I had to this university, and that game means so much."

Coaches banked on Howard's resilience and leadership compensating for the injury. "In hindsight, as you go through it, I don't think he was 100 percent," Kelly said. "But he's such a tough dude that even Will not at 100 percent, you feel you've got a shot to win."

With the passing game struggling, Day leaned on the run game. But the makeshift line lost the battle in the trenches to Michigan, particularly Graham and Grant. It didn't help that both Ohio State guards were playing through injuries sustained in the game. Left guard Austin Siereveld, like Howard, was dealing with a head injury. It happened early in the second half, but he didn't tell anyone and gutted it out. "I don't remember much because I did suffer a concussion during that game," Siereveld. "I kept playing, which was probably not the smartest idea."

Linemen pride themselves on toughness, and Siereveld thought he could persevere. But by the end of the game, his vision was so affected that he couldn't read the scoreboard. He would spend the rest of that day and the next day at home on the couch in darkness because of the concussion-caused light sensitivity before he finally went to the Woody and had his concussion diagnosed.

Right guard Tegra Tshabola, who'd been dealing with the back issue since the Oregon game, injured an AC shoulder joint in the third quarter. With Tshabola and Siereveld hurting and the line as a whole struggling, the crowd got restless the more Ohio State ran into the teeth of the Wolverines' defense. "Looking back, we didn't do a good enough job of getting the ball in space on the perimeter to our skill guys," Day said. "We should have been able to block better. We still should have been able to run better than we did, but we also should have done a better job of getting the ball on the perimeter."

But Michigan's offense had similar futility against Ohio State's defense. The Buckeyes got what looked to be a huge turnover when Downs intercepted a pass at the Michigan 16. Again, the Buckeyes went nowhere. But with a chance to take the lead, Fielding missed wide left on a 34-yard field goal.

The nagging adductor injury Fielding suffered against Marshall in September flared up against Michigan. He had good days and bad days with it. This was one of the bad ones, and the cold and wind didn't help. "It wasn't feeling very good that day," Fielding said. "You try to battle through things as a competitor, but I had no idea it was going to be a bad day. It just went that way on me."

On the missed 38-yarder in the first half, Fielding said the wind pushed the ball right of the uprights. On the 34-yarder, he said he over-corrected and pulled it too far left.

Michigan took possession and finally got some traction. The Wolverines drove to the Ohio State 3 after a pass-interference penalty on Denzel Burke with eight minutes left in the game. Then Jack Sawyer made what would have been an iconic play if the Buckeyes had won. Warren dropped back and had tight end Hogan Hansen wide open in the end zone. But Warren underthrew the ball. Sawyer read the play and made a leaping interception.

"We were in a Bear front on the goal line thinking they're going to run the ball," Sawyer said. "I remember engaging with the tackle. At first, it looked like the ball was going away [from me]. I was going to chase it from the back [side]." Then Sawyer realized Warren still had the ball. "Honestly, I can't even tell you what took over me, what made me drop," he said. "Coach J [Larry Johnson] said, 'The only reason you dropped is God wanted you to be in position to catch that ball,' and I really believe that. He threw it right to me. I don't think he saw me."

But the Buckeyes couldn't capitalize. On second down, Carnell Tate dropped what would have been a first down. It was only his second drop of the season. Ohio State had to punt, and Michigan took over at its 40 with 6:13 left. The Wolverines got a first down but then faced a third-and-6 at the OSU 44.

Then came the biggest play of the game. Warren handed the ball to Mullings, who seemingly had nowhere to go. Ty Hamilton had his arms around the running back, but Mullings shed that tackle. Sawyer was right behind Hamilton, but Michigan right tackle Evan Link bear-hugged him from behind, preventing him from making the tackle (or drawing the first holding call by an opponent since the Marshall game). Mullings squirted free and ran 27 yards to the Ohio State 17 with 2½ minutes left.

"We had a stunt, and I ended up getting free," Hamilton said. "I had him. I thought he was down, so I kind of let go, and then as soon as I looked up, he's still running. I think Jack was supposed to be outside, and he ended up going inside, so the outside was wide open. I thought we were both together and made the tackle, but he ended up staying on his feet and running through it. It was devastating because no matter how the offense was playing, if we had stopped them, we could have won that game."

It got worse. On third-and-2, the Buckeyes were penalized for an illegal substitution after having the wrong personnel group on the field. Day noticed the error and called timeout, but it was disallowed because the Buckeyes called time on the previous play and consecutive timeouts without a snap are prohibited. That gave Michigan a first down and allowed them to bleed the clock. Zvada kicked a 21-yard field goal with 45 seconds left.

Ohio State had one last chance, but the Buckeyes couldn't even get a first down. Howard's fourth-and-9 pass under pressure fell incomplete. Game over: Michigan 13, Ohio State 10.

"You put so much time into it that it just becomes surreal," Day said of The Game. "That was nothing that any of us expected was going to happen in that game. You're almost in shock. How did this happen? What's about to come? It's obviously not something you want to go through."

THE BUCKEYES TRUDGED toward the south stands of the Horseshoe to sing "Carmen Ohio" while Michigan celebrated. Then the Wolverines took their flag and planted it inside the Block O at midfield. Ohio State players reacted predictably. Several Buckeyes, including Lathan Ransom, J.T. Tuimoloau, and tight end Bennett Christian, confronted Michigan players. A Wolverine body-slammed Lorenzo Styles Jr. to the turf. Wave after wave of skirmishes broke out. Finally, Jack Sawyer grabbed the Michigan flag from a Wolverine and threw it to the ground.

Sawyer had been about to sing "Carmen Ohio" when he heard the commotion at midfield. "I turned back and saw the flag in the air going toward our 50 and I was like, 'Yeah, this shit ain't happening this time,'" Sawyer said. "The chaos ensued and I'm trying to get over there. Thankfully, a few of my teammates picked me up off the ground. They were trying to hold me back and I was finally able to break through. By the time I got there, the cops were spraying mace, and it was kind of crazy. I couldn't really get in the middle of it.

"Then I see the flag come back out again. I was raised to where you don't let that shit fly. You can take your win and get the hell off our field. You're not going to sit there and do that to us. That's why I pulled it down, and I'd do it again, too."

After Sawyer threw the flag, Davison Igbinosun picked it up and ripped a piece of it as someone from Michigan grabbed it back. "I had a feeling that the guys weren't going to just let that happen," Day said. "At that point, you're really in a no-win situation. If you run over there and get in the middle of it, it's a disaster. The whole thing is a mess."

OSU athletics director Ross Bjork was standing near Day during "Carmen Ohio" when he heard boos. He thought fans were booing Ohio State players until he turned around and saw the Michigan players at midfield. He understood why Sawyer reacted the way he did.

"In the heat of the moment, you're not going to blame him because he's defending our turf, our stadium, if you will," Bjork said. "I think the passion, his love for the Buckeyes, the emotion of losing that game, all of those things came out. But in my mind, I wish some [Michigan] adult would have said, 'Hey guys, we're just going to stay down here and celebrate.' The moment both flags were brought to the middle of our field, there was going to be a reaction, and it was not going to be pretty.

"It escalated when they were allowed by their folks to bring flags to the middle of our field. That's where sportsmanship should come into play. We got accused of being poor losers. That's not what happened. They could have celebrated in a way different manner, and they chose not to, and so it escalated because of that."

Bjork said a University of Michigan police officer was the first to use the pepper spray. "Honestly, our officers and our security people did a great job by not allowing it to escalate to a whole other level where people could have gotten seriously hurt," he said.

Michigan, or at least Sherrone Moore, clearly didn't have much regret about the Wolverines' actions. A week later, at a home men's basketball game, Moore made a flag-planting gesture when he was shown on the video board.

Not everyone got involved in the fight. Some players, including Gee Scott Jr. and TreVeyon Henderson, took a knee and prayed. Will Howard was torn about what he should do. "The competitor in me wanted to run in there and freaking start throwing haymakers, but I had to keep my head on straight a little bit and be the better man, I guess," he said.

Eventually, things calmed down on the field and the players went to their locker rooms. "I was infuriated and humiliated," Igbinosun said. "Just disappointed. We put a good season together, and we still couldn't beat the team up north. It was demoralizing."

Ohio State's locker room was understandably tense. There was disbelief. There was anger. "We had guys in there praying over each other," Seth McLaughlin said. "We had guys in there throwing pads and throwing helmets and breaking chairs. It was just every single range of emotions that you could see. It was like a war movie."

Some of the players had gotten hit by pepper spray. Sonny Styles said he went into a pile of players after seeing a teammate get hit. Styles was rescuing him when he got sprayed. When he got to the locker room, he was in the shower for about 20 minutes rinsing his eyes. "The sensation is like your whole face is burning," he said.

THE GAME STARTED at noon, so players had all day to contemplate what had happened and replay in their mind every mistake they thought contributed to the loss. Almost every player spent it the same way. They went home and tuned out the world. They mostly ignored any family or friends that were there. They just stared into space and wondered how they'd lost to Michigan yet again.

"I don't think I ate for two days," Josh Fryar said. "I said, 'I'm good' to my mom because they were worried about me after about two hours of me just sitting there and not talking. I didn't greet them. I just went and sat on the couch."

This was the last chance for Ohio State's seniors to beat Michigan. For two decades, the Buckeyes dominated the rivalry. None of the 2024 Ohio State players could say they'd beaten Michigan. Gone also was a chance for a Big Ten championship. Penn State would play Oregon for that. "We didn't do what we needed to do, and I felt like I let all of Buckeye Nation down," linebacker Cody Simon said. "I felt like I let all of Ohio down. At that point, I wasn't thinking of a championship game. I wasn't thinking of the playoff. It was like everything's gone.

"The person that made me think that we still have the playoff to play was my mom. She was like, 'Enough with the sulking. You guys have got games to play.' She even texted coach Day a message about that, like there's more to accomplish here."

But the playoff was three weeks away. It would be a very long, very hard three weeks.

21
The Fallout

The game wasn't even over when the vitriol began. Nina Day was watching the game in her suite early in the fourth quarter when she started receiving nasty text messages. "Just alluding to the fact that if we lost this game, we wouldn't make it out alive," she said. "Just stupid stuff."

She didn't want to risk getting caught in the middle of an angry crowd at the end of the game, so she and her daughters took a back way to Ohio State's locker room and sat in her husband's private area there. RJ was on the field, as was customary. When the game ended and Ryan finally made it to the locker room, Grace and Nia were crying. Two years earlier, when Michigan stunned Ohio State 45–23 in Columbus, Nina said Ryan was so upset that he dropped to his knees and said he was sorry. This time, she said, he just hugged her and the girls and said things would be okay and the family would get through this.

"I think he was just numb," Nina said. "I don't think he knew how to react. I was just staring at the wall. I was just trying to keep it together because my kids were so upset."

Day said it felt like he was in a funeral home. "When you lose that game, this is what you've got to deal with," he said. "It's a bad feeling."

They drove home together mostly in silence, calling ahead to make sure security was in place. One security officer was stationed at the front of the driveway and two others, for a time, roamed the property. Ryan repeatedly told the kids what he said in the locker room, that things would be okay. Nina had a lot of anxiety. She knew what the next days and weeks would be like for the family. She said nobody slept that night. When Ryan took his shower early the next morning and got ready to leave for work, Nina was in bed in the fetal position.

"He just looked down at me and said, 'I'm going to fight my way out of this. It's the only thing I can do,'" Nina said. "He left and I just cried and thought, 'Well, he's said that to me before, and he's done it,' so I just had to believe he was going to find a way out of this again."

That morning, Ross Bjork called OSU president Ted Carter. Bjork was on the field at the end of the Michigan game. He heard fans yelling, "Fix it!" to him. Ohio State fans might have wanted Day fired on the spot, but Bjork's faith in Day was firm. Bjork rebuffed questions on game day from reporters who wanted to ask about Day's future. When Bjork and Carter talked, they concluded that Ohio State needed to provide public support for the players and for Day. A *Columbus Dispatch* reporter texted Bjork at noon. Six hours later, Bjork responded. He said he had faith in Day's leadership, that the foundation and culture of the program were strong. Bjork said the Michigan game was obviously disappointing and that failure would be addressed, but the focus needed to be on the College Football Playoff starting in three weeks.

"If the theme of the season was, 'Leave no doubt,' to me I wanted to leave no doubt in the moment to say we've got the right guy, we've got the right team," Bjork said. "We don't know what's going to happen in the playoff, but let's go make a run."

Day appreciated the support from Bjork. Day also had a long conversation with Carter, who was a Navy vice admiral before entering academia. Carter shared stories of military victories that followed difficult struggles. "He said to me, 'I think you're right on the brink of greatness,'" Day recalled.

Day was determined to achieve just that. He would work crazy hours during Ohio State's playoff run.

"Ridiculous," Nina said. "He became maniacal. It was every second of every day. Even in the middle of the night, he would be up typing notes."

Only in the preparation for the Clemson game in the CFP semifinals in 2020 the year after losing that heartbreaker to the Tigers had Nina seen her husband work as hard. "He was like that for that game," she said. "But he was like this for six straight weeks during this run. It was insane. He was running on adrenaline and anger and a lot of things, I guess. I think what got him up every day was the work and making things right for the program, for the players, for his family. The only time he felt peace during that time was when he was working, so I just let him go."

Ohio State was on winter break, so players could devote themselves to nothing but football without worrying about academics. (The Buckeyes excelled in classroom in the fall, posting a cumulative 3.3 grade point average for the semester.) Ohio State had more walk-through practices and put to good use the extra time.

With plenty of time until the College Football Playoff started, Day could spend more time working with Chip Kelly and Jim Knowles in game-planning. "We found a really good rhythm with that," Day said. "It was early mornings. It was late nights. We just tried to do everything we possibly could do to put our guys in the best position to be successful."

The only off time was the day of the Big Ten championship game. Knowles had something special planned. He flew to Oklahoma and proposed to his girlfriend, Andi Fudickar, who accepted. Knowles was supposed to fly back that Saturday night, but the flight was canceled. A coaches meeting was scheduled for Sunday morning, and Knowles knew he couldn't miss it. He rented a car and drove 13 hours overnight to Columbus.

DAY COULD TAKE refuge in his work, but for his family, there was no respite. Someone had leaked Nina's cell and the Days' address on social media. Some of them suggested Ryan do what his father did. Her parents and twin sister, Kelly, pleaded with her not to read the text messages because it was affecting her mental health. "They were using our mental health stuff against us—his vulnerability of coming out and saying his dad died of suicide," Nina said. "It was really sick that people were telling him to follow in his dad's footsteps and take his own life. It was disgusting stuff."

Three days after the game, Nina got more bad news. Her father, Stan Spirou, was diagnosed with cancer. "That kind of broke me," she said.

Meanwhile, the threats and insults continued. The Days held their kids out of school for days. RJ, a sophomore in high school, said he got about 10 death threats. Not wanting to add to his parents' burden, RJ kept them to himself. "People were attacking me for something I had no part of," he said. "As a 16-year-old kid, it feels like the world's caving in on you. There were a lot of lessons to be learned in that moment. The biggest lesson I learned is when life gets hard—I'm talking really hard—you lean on the people close to you and your support staff, and you just hang on."

Even Ryan's brother Chris, who still lives in New Hampshire, got a taste of it. "A moving company came to my house to try to kick me out of my house," Chris said. "Fucking crazy." The two trucks had Michigan license plates, he said.

The Days did have a small but strong support system. Nina's sister and parents stayed in Columbus. Her closest friends in town provided invaluable support. Administrators and teachers at the kids' schools did what they could to protect them. Ryan would personally thank them at the end of the season.

But it felt like the rest of the world, especially the Ohio State fan base, was against them. The Days had conversations with their kids about where they might want to move. Nina didn't want to leave Columbus before the College Football Playoff started because she didn't want Ryan to be alone. But staying beyond that seemed untenable. Nina started taking down family photos and decluttering the house. After all the moves the Days had to make during Ryan's coaching career, she was an expert at that.

"At that point, I wanted to leave," she said. "I felt in that moment that it was so negative and the things my kids and I and Ryan were dealing with were just not healthy or normal. We're mental-health advocates, yet we're putting our kids in a situation where it's just not healthy, and it's detrimental to their mental health."

Nina talked to a therapist and took anti-anxiety medication. But she had no appetite. From the Michigan game until the CFP opener against Tennessee, she lost 20 pounds. RJ, who had craved stability when the family arrived in 2017, was ready for a change. "I wanted to get out of Columbus," he said.

For Ryan Day, seeing his family suffer because of a football defeat was excruciating. "There are times where you become numb to it, and there are times when you say to yourself, 'What are we doing with our lives?'" he said. "I didn't kill anybody. There are so many bad things going on in the world to treat people that way. That's hard to take because we are good people. My family cares about that game more than anybody in the world. Nobody has more to lose than my family, so to get treated like that is hard to wrap your mind around sometimes.

"There are people who don't have any character. There are people who break the law. There are people who cheat on their wives. There are people who do awful things on a daily basis, yet the hate we received during that time was just ridiculous.

"You look at your kids and you're like, well, they certainly didn't do anything wrong. As a dad and a man, you're like, I'm putting these kids and my wife in a bad situation. Where did it turn like this in my life? But it doesn't do you any good to sit around and think about it. The only thing to do is get it fixed and get some solutions and move forward."

Day didn't share much of what he and his family experienced, but Kelly, his friend as well as colleague, knew. "I was aware of it all, and it was awful," he said. "That's the part that can bother you because it's not supposed to be that way, whether you win or whether you lose. But you also know, and they know, that if you're going to be at Ohio State, heavy is the head that wears the crown. It all comes with the territory, and I thought he did an amazing job of navigating all of that."

AS MUCH AS he loved his players, his family comes first to Day. He knew what it was like not to have a father. He was determined to be a good one for his kids, even with all the demands on his time. "That's his best quality," Nina said. "He connects with those three kids like I've never seen, and they idolize him."

Said RJ, "My dad is a good man. He's very disciplined, very family-based, and he tries to instill very good morals in his kids. He's always done things the right way, no matter how hard times have gotten."

Nina said her husband knows all their kids' friends and their teachers' names. He genuinely listens as RJ, Grace, and Nia share their adolescent drama from school. "They tell him everything," Nina said. "I think because he lost that opportunity to have a dad, he takes it so seriously. If you ask my kids, they'll start crying about how much they love their dad."

That doesn't mean they don't feel the way most teenagers do about a mid-40s dad. "If you ask my kids what his personality is on a day-to-day basis, they'd say, 'Cringy,' because he has a lot of stupid dad jokes and tries to talk like young kids," Nina said with a laugh. "He does it constantly in front of their boyfriends and girlfriends. On a day-to-day basis, one of my kids is calling him the cringiest person in the world."

If the kids tell him that he's embarrassing them, it only encourages Day to do it more. Day's relationship with RJ is obviously close because he's a son who plays quarterback and has hung around the Woody with him and OSU players since the Days came to Columbus. He considers the players to be like older brothers, and they treat him as a younger brother. RJ had a particularly close friendship with Dwayne Haskins Jr. They would even go to high school games on Friday nights together.

RJ described having a father who's the head coach at Ohio State as a blessing and a curse. "People live and die on certain things, and that makes it challenging because people take out their frustrations [they have for] him on us," he said. "You've got to mature a little bit quicker because you've got to deal with situations that kids don't typically have to deal with, which is the sad part about it. But there are always great parts. You get to be on the stage with him, and he's done a good job of embracing that it's a family act to get him where he is now. He's never forgotten where he came from, and he's always appreciative of everything we do for him."

As close as Ryan and RJ are, Nina said her husband is as close with Grace and Nia. "He's a really great girl dad," she said. "He's really taught them to be fighters and have resilience and a lot of different things. One of the things I admire most about Ryan is the way he handles our girls."

But there is one way in which Day has never cut anyone in his family any slack. If there's a competition of any kind, he can't accept losing. When the kids were little and they'd play a game, he wouldn't let them win. When he and Nina played miniature golf when they were dating, he had to win.

"I always felt that when you get used to losing, you get used to losing," Day said in his defense. "It's just a mindset. I've never believed in letting somebody win because then when they beat you, it's not really an accomplishment. Let's say we're playing one-on-one in basketball, I'd rather spot someone seven or eight and then try to beat them as opposed to not trying. It just doesn't make sense to me."

RJ said that no matter the competition, it usually ends with an argument or someone storming off in anger. On the rare occasions when Ryan loses, he does not handle it well. Nina, the former college basketball player, beat him in a game of "Pig" a few years ago. "He didn't talk to me for like a week," Nina said. "He's such a baby. I just tell him, 'Grow up.' But I kept trash-talking him, too, which didn't help."

A couple of years ago, RJ beat his dad in a game of one-on-one for the first time. It was one of those games when everything he shot went in. When RJ sank the winning basket, he ran screaming gleefully into the house.

What did Ryan do? "I'm pretty sure he just went on a walk and then came back 35 minutes later," RJ said, "and we didn't talk for a day or two."

RJ admitted that it was hard for him when he was young to have a father who never let him win. Now he appreciates it. "I have this competitive nature that I try to bring to my teammates and my athletic career that I wouldn't have had if I wasn't raised around him," RJ said.

After RJ broke his high school's passing record in 2024, he said his dad told him he was a better quarterback than he ever was. "Since then, he's tried to take it back, but I won't let him," RJ said.

At times, the competitiveness between them borders on the absurd. Nina used to measure RJ's height regularly. That became a problem when RJ grew as tall as Ryan. "They make me bring the measuring tape and it's just one big fight, so I stopped doing it," she said.

Nina said RJ and Ryan sometimes act like brothers. They annoy each other. They steal each other's clothes and sneakers. Nina thought it was hilarious that one day RJ parked in his father's spot at the Woody. "I'm just crying laughing," she said. "They just do stuff to piss each other off."

22
The Turning Point

After evaluating the film from the Michigan game, Day and the players on the leadership committee decided to meet on the Monday following the game. "What's funny is that I didn't even know we were having it because I had my phone off for two straight days," Jack Sawyer said.

He only found out because J.T. Tuimoloau showed up at his house. Otherwise, he probably would have missed it. "It was a tough, tough time to be in the Woody and be in Columbus at that moment," Sawyer said. "I remember at that meeting coach Day promising us we're going to do what it takes to fix this because we're going to get in the playoff and we're going to have a shot to win it all."

Day and the committee agreed that they should have a meeting with all the players the next day. Day knew his players remained upset and confused about what happened against Michigan. Social media criticism about the Buckeyes' performance was unrelenting. "They're trying to sort through it," Day said. "They're repeating some things I'm sure they saw online or that their family had said. Some of it was accurate and some of it not accurate. It was all of our jobs, and certainly my job, to recognize, okay, here are the things that that caused us to lose."

THAT TEAM MEETING might have been the most pivotal moment of the season. Day sat in a chair in the front of the team room where Ohio State holds its press conferences. Day was the only non-player in the room. Sawyer was the first player who spoke.

"I just told them why we're all doing this," Sawyer said. "I was like, 'Look, whatever you guys have on your chest, whatever you think is going to hold you back from not giving everything you've got in this playoff, say it now. Don't feel bad. No one's going to hold this against you. This is the time to get together and realize what we can do and talk about the things we need to change.'"

TreVeyon Henderson and Emeka Egbuka then asked if anyone had questions. Mitchell Melton was the first to speak up. Melton was a respected backup fifth-year senior defensive end who'd overcome two ACL tears that cost him the 2021 and 2022 seasons. He, like all the other veterans, desperately wanted a victory over Michigan. Melton asked a pointed question to Day.

"I raised my hand and asked coach Day, 'These past two years losing the way we had, what did you learn?'" Melton said.

He said Day began his answer by talking about scheme. That didn't satisfy Melton. He said Day talked before the game about the need to establish a run game because the winner of the OSU-Michigan game tends to be whichever has more rushing yardage. But that can be an effect rather than cause. Teams run more when they're ahead. Melton, and probably others, believed that coaches knew Michigan was a ground-based offense and stubbornly wanted to beat the Wolverines at their own game.

"I realized soon after the game that was very prideful in our own right, and it cost us a Big Ten championship," Melton said. "What I wanted out of that meeting was to be very honest with ourselves and clear on what happened and why it happened, so that it would never happen again."

That got the ball rolling for what became a contentious meeting. Other players challenged Day when he gave answers they deemed unsatisfactory.

"I forget who said it," Seth McLaughlin said, "but someone was like, 'You know, Coach Day, when you go on about stuff like this, I'm not going to lie, people hate you when you act like this.'"

Cody Simon said there was a lot of frustration expressed. Players raised their voices at each other at times. "A lot of it was not actually directed at coach Day, but he's obviously the head coach of the team," Simon said. "They wanted to ask him, 'What happened? Why didn't we do this? Why didn't we do that?' and he gave his answers."

But this wasn't just a bitch-fest to allow gripes to be vented. The goal was accountability and finding solutions. Day agreed with the criticism that coaches failed to call plays to get the ball in playmakers' hands more often. He promised that the Buckeyes would be more aggressive in the playoff.

Day also challenged the players. He said coaches can only do so much. If Howard hadn't thrown two interceptions, if the Buckeyes hadn't squandered critical field position by failing to field two kicks properly, if Jayden Fielding hadn't missed two field goals, the outcome would have been different, he told them.

"Ultimately, we all have to take accountability," Day said. "There was a lot of challenging between [position] groups, but it was also my responsibility to make sure those guys understand that you have to do your job. If you don't, we're going to lose the game. We don't need to overthink it. It's not some mystical game. It's just the bottom line."

The interior of the offensive line took much of the criticism. They had failed to open holes against Mason Graham and Kenneth Grant and the rest of the Michigan run defense even though the Wolverines' defensive focus was on containing Ohio State's explosive passing game.

Carson Hinzman owned up to it on behalf of the linemen. "I said, 'Look, if we're going to be real, it was our fault,'" he said. "Regardless of the scheme, or what we tried to do, we had to execute when it matters."

But Donovan Jackson explained that the line before the injuries to Josh Simmons and Seth McLaughlin excelled at zone blocking. But now the Buckeyes were using a patchwork line that seemed to change game by game. "We just couldn't find that rhythm again," Jackson said. "Different guys sub in and out, and you lose your timing. You're losing your chemistry. Going into The Game, they gave us five- and six-man boxes. They were playing cloud coverage on the wideouts, bracketing our receivers, so it's not like we could throw deep bombs on them. The corners were playing off [the receivers], basically telling us to run the ball, and we weren't able to. I was explaining that we're trying to find out who we are as an offensive line right now. It's five guys trying to do the job as one. If one guy messes up, the whole thing doesn't work."

Day told the linemen that they go against Ty Hamilton and Tyleik Williams every day in practice. That should prepare them for anyone they face. "We can block anybody in the country, and that has to be our mentality," Day said he told them. "And I think moving forward, that was our mentality."

AS THE MEETING progressed, the mood began to shift. Just the fact Day was willing to face the music from players earned him more respect. McLaughlin and Caleb Downs couldn't imagine their former coach Nick Saban allowing himself to be that vulnerable. "Sitting in a team meeting with coach Saban and saying these things to Saban would not have been received well on his end," McLaughlin said. "Coach Day is not that type of leader. He's a big boy. He's open to change. He's open to criticism. He'll do whatever it takes to win football games. It takes a lot of balls for a dude to sit in front of 100 angry kids and listen to that and guide the conversation and listen and let people speak when they felt they needed to be heard."

Day hadn't shared with his players the nastiness he and his family had been subjected to since the loss. But players knew that if they faced heat, their coach must have gotten it worse.

"It was just about every single emotion that you could have in the span of about an hour and a half, every single emotion that you could have,"

Tegra Tshabola said. "We had every single leader stand up and talk. Coach Day was about as vulnerable as I've ever seen him. We all were so hurt by the things that he was going through, the things that his own community was putting them through, and his own fan base was putting them through. The way he looked, it broke all of us. There were a lot of tears in that meeting. A lot of emotions poured by a lot of older guys that may not statistically stand out as much but had put in their work and wanted it more than anything."

Nothing was off-limits. Some criticized the players who kneeled in prayer while the Michigan flag-planting unfolded. Gee Scott Jr. addressed that. He explained he was no longer the hothead who committed the costly head-butting penalty in 2022. He no longer believed violence was justified unless it was necessary to protect his family or his own life.

Lathan Ransom told his teammates that they must learn from their mistakes, so they never again feel the way they did in that meeting. "It got heated, but I almost looked at it like if you have siblings or family members, you argue and sometimes you say that you stuff that you maybe don't want to hear, but you need to hear," he said. "I feel like that's what we did. We're a brotherhood, and we just talked like brothers and family members in that meeting."

Cornerback Davison Igbinosun, ever the fiery competitor, bristled when someone said he tried to succeed against Michigan. "I stood up and said, 'That's our problem right there,'" Igbinosun said. "On the football field, my mindset is not, I'm going to *try* to do this. My mindset is I'm going to do this and I'm going to get it done. There are no ifs, ands, or buts about it. I said let's hold each other accountable, and it starts in practice."

Will Howard waited until later in the meeting to speak. "All I really said was that we've got to have an identity and be about what we are," he said. "We want to be an inside zone [blocking] team. We want to be a team that runs the pro-style [offense]. We've got to stick to it. We've got to be really good at what we do. My biggest message was that we've still got so much to play for. In previous years [without the new 12-team playoff], we'd be sitting here with our thumbs in our ass, not knowing what to do with ourselves. But this year we've got a freaking chance to do something special and right this wrong."

Some players said nothing. Fielding was among those who stayed silent. No single player probably got more abuse than he did after the Michigan game. Kickers are unique in that success is defined in black and white. The kick is either good or it isn't. He described the Michigan game as the worst day of his life. He felt he let down his teammates in the biggest game of all. Like what happened to Nina Day, someone leaked Fielding's cell phone and address, and the texts were beyond nasty. A few fans even confronted Fielding when he arrived home, "Just telling me to get off the team and kill myself," he said. "It was a pretty rough time."

He estimated that about half of those besieging him were bettors upset they'd lost money on the game. "They said, 'I lost this amount of money. You better pay me this, or I'm going to come and kill you,'" Fielding said.

Fielding turned off his phone. His mom had flown from Texas for the game and decided to stay with him when it was clear how bad things had gotten. Fielding needed a police escort just to walk to class the next week. He considered transferring right away but decided he liked Ohio State and Day enough to stay. In the team meeting, he didn't take it personally when players addressed him. "They said, 'You've got to make your kicks, but we all believe in you,'" Fielding said. "Caleb, Jack, J.T., Lathan—those guys had my back the whole time. They saw it on my face. They knew what I had been going through. I had talked to a couple guys about it."

After all the players said what they wanted to Day, he left. The players talked for a few more minutes. Scott then led the team in prayer. Players locked arms in solidarity. Scott can't remember his exact words, but he asked God to remind the players how much they loved each other and not to let the heated emotions of that moment prevent them from fulfilling

God's plans for them. "I actually saw guys crying as a result of the intimacy of that moment," he said.

The pain of the Michigan loss didn't suddenly evaporate because of the meeting. The sting for those players probably will never entirely go away, regardless of the playoff run that would start soon. An 0-fer against Michigan is intolerable. But the meeting was cathartic. They had aired their grievances. That could have split the team permanently. Instead, it galvanized it.

"It was a complete shift if you would look at the mood of the team before that meeting and the mood of the team after that meeting," Melton said. "It was like two different teams had been in that room."

"I've never been a part of anything like that," Donovan Jackson said. "I've never been part of anything player-led where guys speak their mind truthfully and we try to come together at the end of it. It was a unique experience, for sure."

It was as stern an off-field test as the Buckeyes' brotherhood would face. "As a family, how you handle conflict will make you stronger or it'll make you weaker," Tuimoloau said. "We can't call ourselves a brotherhood if we can't hold each other accountable. That really was the game change for us doing what we needed to do in the playoff."

The Buckeyes had considered themselves a close team all along. That meeting forged them even closer. The blame game was over. Quinshon Judkins said the players never spoke about the Michigan game again. "We truly had each other's back," he said. "That point is we all meshed together as one team—transfers, freshmen, seniors. No matter who you were, you were then a part of the brotherhood. That made us one."

23

"No One Was Beating Us"

With no Big Ten championship to play for, Ohio State waited until the following Sunday to find out their CFP matchup. The Buckeyes fell from No. 2 to No. 6 in the selection committee rankings because of the loss to Michigan. When Oregon defeated Penn State 45–37 in the Big Ten title game, some speculated that the Buckeyes would finish ahead of the Nittany Lions in the final CFP ranking. After all, Ohio State had beaten Penn State in State College and had a stronger overall resume because of victories when factoring in the win over Indiana. Penn State's only win over a ranked team was a 21–7 win at home against No. 19 Illinois. The Nittany Lions didn't play Michigan or Indiana. Even their loss to Oregon was a bit misleading. Penn State fell behind 28–10 and never got closer than seven points after halftime. The Nittany Lions trailed 45–30 before scoring with less than four minutes left.

But the next day when the CFP committee released its bracket, it had Penn State No. 4 behind Oregon, Georgia, and Texas and ahead of Notre Dame and Ohio State. Because the CFP gave first-round byes to four conference champions—Boise State got the No. 3 seed and Arizona State the No. 4 seed—Ohio State was dropped to No. 8 spot in the bracket. The Buckeyes would play host to Tennessee, which was ranked seventh but dropped to ninth in the bracket, in the first-ever playoff game at Ohio Stadium. The winner would play undefeated Oregon in the Rose Bowl.

Day said the Buckeyes' seeding provided extra motivation. "We saw those teams," Day said. "We watched them play, and we knew we were better than them."

But the Buckeyes also recognized they put themselves at risk for recency bias because of their performance against Michigan. "I felt we didn't have any right to bitch about it," Day said, "because we lost that game. We made our bed, and we've got to live with it. Me being angry, pissed off, edgy, it was like, 'We deserve to have the hardest road, so let's go and make it as hard as it can be.'"

Day was looking at a bracket that had the Buckeyes facing the No. 3 team in the SEC, a game at the Rose Bowl on the West Coast against Oregon, potentially a semifinal game against Texas in Dallas and a title game against Georgia in Atlanta. It was the hardest path possible. "But now you get a chance to write one of the best stories in the history of Ohio State and college football," Day said he told his team. "We had no momentum, so we knew it was a mountain and a half to climb. But if you did it, it was going to be unbelievable."

THE BUCKEYES ANTICIPATED playing Tennessee even before the bracket was announced, so coaches got a head start in game-planning for the Volunteers. Discussion among coaches and the players' meeting with Day prompted some changes, particularly with the offensive line. Coaches decided to open the competition at the guard spots. Sophomore Luke Montgomery had failed to earn a starting job in the spring, but now he'd get his chance to prove he was ready. In practice before the Tennessee game, he took advantage. Coaches instituted a rotation system with Montgomery, Austin Siereveld, and Tegra Tshabola. Montgomery would play left guard and Tshabola would stay at right guard, and Siereveld would be the swingman. That would enable all three to get breaks and solve any issues by reviewing plays on iPads on the sideline, which became legal in 2024.

Coaches also decided to shift more to a gap blocking scheme from the normal zone blocking scheme. In laymen's terms, linemen were now responsible for blocking an area to create seams rather than trying to overpower defensive linemen. That made sense considering that Tennessee's interior defensive linemen Omari Thomas and Bryson Eason weighed a combined 637 pounds.

"Instead of lining up and saying that our five were physically better than yours, running fuck-you football like we were the previous 11 games, we started running some misdirection and a bunch of motion to confuse the linebackers," Seth McLaughlin said.

With all the changes on the offensive line, Donovan Jackson said, it was hard for all five linemen to get consistent timing with their blocks in a zone scheme. "Gap schemes are good because you literally stay in your gap," he said. "If there's a guy in your gap, you block your gap. If there's a guy not in your gap, you double-team up to your gap."

For Montgomery, a chance for meaningful playing time in the playoff was a reward after a frustrating start to his Buckeye career. Montgomery was a four-star recruit from Findlay, Ohio, who saw some action as a freshman. When he didn't win a starting job in the spring and other linemen got their chance before he did, he began contemplating whether he'd have a future at Ohio State. "That was the last thing I wanted to do because I'm an Ohio kid," Montgomery said. "I wanted to continue to fight. I was trusting the Lord's timing and continued to pray and talk to my parents. Once I got my [chance], I wasn't going to let that opportunity slip away from me."

Practices before the Tennessee game were intense. The Buckeyes knew the 12-team playoff gave them a chance for redemption. They were determined not to squander it. Everyone was on edge. "[Practices] were filled with a lot of hard work and not a lot of joy," Howard said. "It was grinding. We knew we had one chance to make this thing right."

Jayden Fielding was grateful for the support he'd gotten from his teammates, but that didn't mean his job was secure. He had to fend off backup kicker Austin Snyder, who was making a push to take over the starting role. The competition between the two kickers came down to the final days before the start of the playoff. At a practice outside in freezing weather, each kicker got 10 field-goal attempts. Teammates were in their faces to add to the pressure.

"You've got Jack Sawyer, a big dude, breathing down your neck, yelling at you, trying to make you mess up," Fielding said.

After one successful kick by Fielding, Day tried to rattle him by saying there had been a false-start penalty and he had to kick again from five yards farther. Fielding didn't flinch. Snyder made 8 of 10 kicks, he said. Fielding made all 10. He kept his job.

"Coach Day was like, 'If you can do it then, you can do it anytime,'" Fielding said.

OHIO STATE WAS a seven-point favorite over the Volunteers, but there was a feeling of foreboding among many OSU fans as the game approached. Which team would show up—the one supposed to be a national championship contender, or the one that laid the egg against Michigan? Many OSU fans put their tickets up for sale. Tennessee fans gobbled them up. Volunteer fans predicted that they could turn the Horseshoe into Neyland Stadium North. Buckeye players took note.

"Another team saying they're going to come in our house in Columbus, Ohio, in December from the South and you're going to walk in the Shoe and take it over, it added more fuel and more fire to us," Sawyer said. "I remember that game week being cranked up like I've never seen it. Guys were watching more film and being more intense than I've ever seen it, myself included, because we knew this was our last shot ever to put this uniform on in the Shoe.

"The intensity level, you could almost feel it within the Shoe. It wasn't nervous. It wasn't being worried. It was confident as shit. We're about to play Buckeye football again and make people scared to play the Buckeyes again."

When game day arrived, Tennessee fans had indeed descended on campus. It seemed there was as much orange as scarlet on campus. During Day's morning appearance on ESPN's GameDay pregame show with the stadium as a backdrop, one person—it was impossible to tell if it was a Buckeye or Vols fan—held a sign that read, "Ryan's Last Day." At the normally packed Skull Session at St. John Arena in which the OSU marching band (The Best Damn Band in the Land) play and players and coaches give a pep talk, the upper level was largely empty. The Buckeyes' traditional walk from St. John Arena to the stadium was unlike any they'd experienced because of how loud the visiting fans were.

"They were singing 'Rocky Top' in our faces," Cody Simon said. "I'm kind of in shock, like this is a completely different ballgame. It's going to be 50-50 with fans here and we've got to shut everybody out."

Buckeye players joked about having to use a silent count in their own stadium. Visiting fans tend to get to the stadium earlier because they want to leave time for logistical issues, and soon after the gates opened, it looked like a Tennessee home crowd. When Ohio State players came out for warmups, they heard boos. Most were presumably from Volunteers fans, but some probably came from Buckeye fans who might have come to see what they hoped was the end of the Ryan Day era. By kickoff, the stadium was about one-third orange, a far bigger number of visiting fans than ever could be recalled at the Horseshoe.

"At that point, we're like, 'Fuck it,'" Sawyer said. "It doesn't matter. It's the Woody against the world. We felt that. Obviously, we love our fans and need our fans. But at the time, it was so chaotic and so toxic between a lot of the fan base that we were like, 'It's our brothers in arms right now versus everybody.' I remember running out of that tunnel, and I felt it."

After three weeks of hell, Nina Day arrived at the stadium unsure whether that would be her last game at the Horseshoe. She texted Ryan before the game saying that she didn't care if he got fired. All she wanted was for him to swing as hard as he could. If that wasn't enough, the Days would be ready to leave. As she settled into her suite, the sight of so much orange disturbed her. "I just felt that there was a portion of our fan base that just gave up and sold their tickets," she said. "I was angry, and our players were angry."

The players' emotions were further inflamed when a bunch of Tennessee linemen ran into the field shirtless for warmups with temperatures in the mid-20s. To the Buckeyes, it didn't show toughness. They took it as false bravado, and it added to their confidence. "I saw them with their shirts off and was like, 'Dude, that's just being stupid,'" Josh Fryar said.

Said Denzel Burke, "We knew we were going to beat their ass as soon as they came out for warmups."

Ohio State players also believed they were playing for Day's job, no matter the public support the OSU administration had given him. "Absolutely, I did," Sawyer said. "I felt it, and I think a lot of guys did, too. I think that made us want it that bad. It doesn't matter what we have to do. We're going to get it done tonight."

AFTER THREE WEEKS of anger, grief, and resolve, the moment had finally arrived for the Buckeyes to play football again. Tennessee won the coin flip and elected to defer. It's easy to remember the game as a blowout from start to finish, and it was. But the game turned on the third snap. On third-and-2, Bryson Eason beat Tshabola and sacked Howard but grabbed the quarterback's face mask as he did it. That gave the Buckeyes a first down. A 21-yard pass on a wheel route to TreVeyon Henderson moved the ball to the Tennessee 37. On the next play, Howard threw deep to Jeremiah Smith, who got a step on cornerback Rickey Gibson III and caught the perfectly thrown pass for a touchdown.

After the Michigan game, coaches vowed to be more aggressive, which included finding ways to get Smith the ball. They didn't want a repeat of the Michigan game when he was a nonfactor. Smith himself went to

Brian Hartline and told him to push Smith to his limits by being intensely critical if he made any mistakes. "The reason I asked him that was because it's playoff time," Smith said. "It's time to go."

He wouldn't stop until the end of the playoff.

Now it was the defense's turn. Tennessee's offense revolved around running back Dylan Sampson, who'd run for almost 1,500 yards and 22 touchdowns. But he was nursing a hamstring injury entering the game, which the Volunteers kept quiet. "More than people know," Sampson said at the NFL combine when asked how injured he was.

Tennessee's quarterback was redshirt freshman Nico Iamaleava, a five-star recruit who showed promise but was not close to a finished product. (He would transfer to UCLA after the season following a dispute about NIL.) Jim Knowles said the defensive game plan was to confuse Iamaleava and not to let him get clean looks where he could isolate on a receiver and go for big plays. Tennessee's receivers lined up closer to the sideline than any OSU opponent had. That would put more pressure on Ohio State's cornerbacks to play effective man coverage.

The Buckeyes set the tone on the first Tennessee series. On third-and-4, the defense forced Iamaleava to scramble. Cody Simon hit the quarterback short of the first-down market so hard that Iamaleava's helmet cracked. After a Tennessee punt, the Buckeyes sliced through the Volunteers again. Howard hit Emeka Egbuka for a 40-yard gain on a deep ball down the seam, and Quinshon Judkins scored two plays later from the 1, running behind a three-tight-end formation.

The Buckeyes smelled blood. They forced another three-and-out on Tennessee's next possession. Tyleik Williams and J.T. Tuimoloau combined for a tackle for loss on first down and a sack on second down. Sawyer tipped a third-down pass for an incompletion.

Tuimoloau credited the changes implemented after the Oregon loss to simplify the defense. "It was really just playing free and letting players go," he said. "Understanding the game plan, but not having it complicated to the point we're thinking out there. Just put the ball down and play football. Take the chains off and the collar off and let the dogs roam."

The offense made it 21–0 on its next possession. The Buckeyes moved the ball to the Tennessee 27 and after a two-yard loss called for a counter to Henderson. He took the handoff and paused to allow a hole to open. Boy, did it. Donovan Jackson blocked a linebacker, and Montgomery at left guard moved to his right and pancaked defensive tackle Jaxson Moi as Henderson used his vision and speed to score. It was the kind of block they show in coaching clinics.

Montgomery said it was two years of frustration being unleashed. "After that play, I was celebrating, but I looked at coach Frye and probably said some explicit things," he said with a laugh. "Just some hyped-up stuff, telling him, 'That's what I do. That's what I'm here to do.' There was a little bit of amped-up anger for not being able to play all year, but also excitement."

Even his fellow linemen were taken aback, not just by that play but his overall rising to the occasion. "The biggest surprise of the year was to have Luke Montgomery coming to the Tennessee game and throwing people around, playing with strength, playing with confidence, which was something he didn't do in practice," Seth McLaughlin said. "Luke played 10 times better than he ever had in practice."

The Buckeyes led 21–0 after one quarter, but it already felt like the game was over. Ohio State had outgained Tennessee 205–16. During the break between quarters, Buckeye offensive linemen waved their arms to the crowd in triumph as the crowd roared.

Tennessee did threaten to make it a game at the end of the first half. A Buckeye drive was thwarted when a pass to Smith was deflected and intercepted in the back of the end zone. An Igbinosun pick on the ensuing Tennessee drive was nullified by a questionable roughing-the-passer penalty against Kenyatta Jackson. The Vols kicked a field goal and then went on a 16-play drive to score a touchdown with 20 seconds left in the half to make it 21–10.

"They were a really good offense," Knowles said of Tennessee. "They made some plays, and we didn't, but overall, I felt we had control of the game. There wasn't much need to make too many adjustments because our offense was doing well."

Tennessee got the ball to start the second half with a chance to make it a one-possession game. The Vols didn't come close to scoring. After one first down, Lathan Ransom diagnosed an option pitch and made a tackle for a five-yard loss on third down.

Then, just as it had in the first half, the Ohio State offense scored touchdowns on its first three possessions of the second half to make it 42–10. It started with a 22-yard pass to Smith in the end zone that was similar to his first score. On the next score, Judkins powered in from the 1 aided by the blocking of four tight ends—Will Kacmarek, Jelani Thurman, Bennett Christian, and Patrick Gurd. Henderson capped OSU's scoring with a nifty 24-yard run in which he appeared hemmed in behind the line of scrimmage before finding a crease and dashing through it. In the final minutes, OSU fans derisively shouted, "S-E-C!" and the stadium loudspeakers played "Rocky Top" mockingly.

It was a dominating performance. Ohio State outgained Tennessee 473–256, and 73 of the Volunteers' yards came on a garbage-time touchdown drive against OSU backups that made it a 42–17 final score. Dylan Sampson's hamstring allowed him to get only two carries for six yards. Iamaleava completed just 14 of 31 passes for 104 yards. The Buckeyes sacked him four times, including two by Tuimoloau and 1½ by Sawyer. Cody Simon had 12 tackles. Howard was 24 of 29 for 311 yards. Ohio State's reshuffled offensive line was nearly flawless. It didn't allow a sack and paved the way for 156 rushing yards.

"It didn't matter who we were playing against in the Shoe that day," Sawyer said. "I don't care if it was one of the best teams ever assembled in college football. No one was beating us that night."

But the celebration was muted. The Buckeyes had won convincingly to avoid a doomsday scenario. But this was just the start of the playoff. They knew they had much more work to do.

24

Dominant Redemption

For generations, the Rose Bowl was the ultimate destination for Ohio State. Until the 1970s, it was the only bowl a Big Ten team could play in. To mention Pasadena to an Ohioan was to conjure images of sun-splashed California, the magnificent sunset against the San Gabriel Mountains, and a New Year's game against a Pac-12 opponent. Oregon, of course, was now Big Ten brethren, and the Ducks' win in October added a layer to the teams' rematch in the 2025 Rose Bowl. Oregon was the No. 1 seed and the country's only undefeated team. But Ohio State wasn't there to enjoy the pageantry of Pasadena. The Buckeyes viewed this as a College Football Playoff quarterfinal that would either end their season or leave them two victories from a national title.

As Ohio State craved redemption for the October loss, another Buckeye who'd found long-sought redemption accompanied the team on the trip. More than two decades earlier, Maurice Clarett helped Ohio State win the 2002 national championship. He was the offensive star of that team, a brash freshman running back from Warren, Ohio, who took college football by storm with his powerful running. He scored the winning touchdown in the upset victory over Miami in double overtime. But his biggest play in the game was stripping the ball from Sean Taylor after the star safety intercepted a pass.

That game would be the last for Clarett in a Buckeye uniform. His life fell apart after that. Clarett was suspended from the team and unsuccessfully challenged the NFL to let him enter the 2004 draft. The next year, he failed to make the NFL as a third-round draft pick. Clarett eventually was imprisoned for his part in an armed robbery at a Columbus dance club and an incident in which he was charged with carrying a concealed weapon without a permit. He served 3½ years in prison. Clarett turned his life around after that. He credited reading, primarily books about behavior and self-help, as well as sobriety with the aid of medicine. Clarett became a successful businessman and in demand as a speaker. He also served as a consultant for the UConn men's basketball team.

But Clarett remained estranged from the Ohio State program. After the 2023 loss to Michigan, he posted on X, "Ryan Day...Love you bro but gotta go. This is why you're paid millions. Cant (sic) get paid 9'ms and lose 3 straight." In a conversation with Jim Tressel, the former coach encouraged Day to reach out to Clarett. Day reluctantly did and arranged a meeting in his office. They had a long conversation and surprised each other by hitting it off. "We had a lot in common," Day said. "I knew there was something pretty special about him."

Day invited Clarett to be around the team, believing he could be a positive influence and resource. Clarett started coming to the Woody regularly on Tuesdays and developed relationships with players. They were too young to remember—or not even born—during Clarett's brief star turn with the Buckeyes. But he connected with them, an example of the brotherhood transcending a generation.

"He was a person that you can go to that wasn't a coach that you can still trust," Austin Siereveld said. "He's been through it, and you can rely on him. If you needed to talk to him, he was there."

Clarett didn't have an official title, but he thought of himself as a "mentality" coach. "It's just teaching guys," he said, "that you don't have to be loud and angry and pompous and brash, but you do have to be serious about kicking somebody's ass, prepare like you're going to kick somebody's ass, practice like you're going to kick somebody's ass, and then going out there and kicking somebody's ass. And when shit gets hard, be a fucking man and push through all of the pain. That's the mentality."

Having been in trouble, Clarett knew how to avoid it. When the fight broke out after the Michigan game, he was standing near Jeremiah Smith. He grabbed the receiver and walked with him up the tunnel to the locker room "just to make sure he wasn't caught up in that shit."

After the Tennessee game, Day invited Clarett to accompany the team to the Rose Bowl. It was his first road trip with the Buckeyes since the trip to Arizona to win the national title in 2003. "I was a man on a mission," Clarett said. "I hung out with players. I'm with the players in the players' lounge. I'm with the players in the elevator. I'm with the players at practice.

"I would get to the point where I would pace the locker room and have a serious look on my face as if I was playing. I would see the kids look at me and see where my mind was at, and I could see it affected them. It was like, 'Hey man. This is where your head, your mind, your eyes, your spirit, and your energy needs to be because we're about to go play.' I would really have it in my heart like I'm about to compete."

AS OHIO STATE prepared for the rematch against Oregon, the Buckeyes buzzed with confidence, even if they didn't broadcast it publicly. Round 2 of Bucks vs. Ducks, Day told his players, didn't have to be close. He knew his Buckeye team was different than it was in October, and now it had the momentum from the blowout of Tennessee. "When you look back at that game, we were still trying to figure ourselves out in a lot of areas," Day said.

Still fresh in his mind was the memory that Ohio State essentially gifted Oregon two scores. Ohio State was in control early at Autzen until

Quinshon Judkins, playing with an injured thumb, had the ball stripped from him to set up the Ducks' first touchdown. Another Oregon score was set up by the line-drive kickoff that bounced off Caleb Downs when the Ducks kicked from midfield because of a penalty. Ohio State's defense was caught flat-footed for much of that game because the signals were slow to get called in, an issue that was fixed after that loss.

"Defensively, I think our guys were embarrassed by how we didn't get aligned in that game," Day said. "We were playing much better in terms of getting aligned and getting our cleats in the ground."

Ohio State's offense gained 467 yards in the October game, and there was no reason it couldn't do it again, even if Oregon would have star defensive end Jordan Burch available unlike in October. Day was confident that if Ohio State didn't hurt itself, "It could be very, very much a different game."

The hard work after the Michigan loss followed by the convincing victory over Tennessee had the Buckeyes brimming with confidence. "Everything about [the preparation] was in synergy with each other," Day said. "The guys were just so prepared. That built us some momentum and some confidence. The week before the Oregon game, we really started to peak."

For Jim Knowles, the defensive game plan was simple: Prevent the explosive plays from quarterback Dillon Gabriel, Oregon's speedy receivers, and running back Jordan James. "You had the quarterback who was great at making plays post-snap and running around," Knowles said. "We had to be able to counter that with different things we did for the rush. It was all about not giving up those explosive plays and isolations on our secondary."

Knowles said the strategy was to flush the left-handed Gabriel to his right with the pass rush to make him throw across his body or limit the amount of the field he could throw to. He employed Cody Simon as a spy on Gabriel.

OSU's offensive players noticed that offensive coordinator Chip Kelly was almost giddy about the prospect of another matchup against his former school. "The one thing that got us all excited and hyped up was how excited coach Kelly was to see those guys again," Tegra Tshabola said. "It seemed like he knew them like the back of his hand, and he was so excited to tell us the game plan that it got us all excited. I forget exactly what he said, but it was something along the lines of, 'We're gonna carve them up.' He was extremely confident in that. When a coach like coach Kelly radiates that much confidence, it pours into the team fast."

Kelly's confidence was rooted in part by how the October Oregon game ended, specifically the play on Ohio State's last drive when Ducks coach Dan Lanning deliberately used 12 players. "It meant a lot to me that you gave me your cards, and you told us you had to play 12 guys to stop us," Kelly said. "You've already told us that you can't stop us, so that's the way I felt going into that game. If that's the mindset you're going to give us, then guess what? You're not going to be able to put 12 guys on the field in the Rose Bowl."

Will Howard, whose stellar game against the Ducks in October was largely overshadowed by the second-too-late slide on the game's final play, liked the matchup against the Ducks' defense. "They ran a very match-based coverage, so I felt we had a lot of opportunities for one-on-one," Howard said.

He said Oregon tried to show a deep two-safety look, but he knew that was mostly a disguise. Ohio State's outside receivers—Jeremiah Smith and Carnell Tate—would face a lot of man coverage. "We had a lot of different ways to exploit them," he said.

Nina Day said she had never seen her husband more confident before a big game. "He just saw the look in the players' eyes," she said. "It was the least nervous he's ever been before a game. He just knew they were going to show up."

Right tackle Josh Fryar noticed that after Oregon's pregame warmups, some of the Ducks walked very deliberately back off the field while staring at the Buckeyes. Much like Ohio State scoffed at Tennessee's players coming out shirtless for pregame before the CFP first-round game, Fryar thought Oregon was showing false confidence. "Just the arrogance they had walking off the field and trying to stare us down, I thought it was over from that point," he said.

NOBODY EXPECTED THE Buckeyes to blow Oregon off the field the way they did. Ohio State got the ball to start the game, and the domination started from the first snap. The Buckeyes had previously used a wide screen with tight end Gee Scott Jr. put in motion to block. Kelly knew Oregon would recognize the look. Yet instead of passing to Quinshon Judkins on the perimeter, Will Howard faked a throw to the running back while Scott slipped past defenders and was wide open along the sideline. Howard threw to Scott, who ran for a 30-yard completion.

"This is the beauty of having a couple of extra days," Day said. "We have that play, but what if we pump [fake] it and then throw the pump screen off of it?" Day said. "Chip felt that was a good way to start the game. We were going to be aggressive."

The message was clear. "We're not here to play around," Howard said. "We're coming out guns-a-blazing, and we're taking the fight to them. We wanted to put the pressure on them, and I think we did a really good job of that. It fired me up. I knew we were in attack mode."

Two plays later, Ohio State ran a run-pass option play based off misdirection. Donovan Jackson and left guard Austin Siereveld pulled to the right, drawing Oregon defenders with them to the short side of the field. That left Smith wide open for a little flip pass from Howard. Smith caught the pass at the Oregon 48 and turned upfield. Scott plowed a Duck defender at least five yards from the left hashmark, and Carnell Tate tied up his man. Smith ran through both Ducks at the Ohio State 30 for an easy touchdown. Exactly one minute into the game, the Buckeyes had already made a statement.

Now it was the defense's turn. Oregon running back Jordan James had a big game against the Buckeyes in October, and the Ducks gave him the ball on a sweep to the right on their first snap. Simon diagnosed the play, shot the gap, and tackled James for a loss. "When I look back on it, that was one of my favorite plays of the season just because it was somewhat of a tone-setter," Simon said. "We weren't going to go back to how it was earlier in the season. I wanted to start off strong, and we knew if they got big plays on offense, it'd be a tough game for us, a long game for us, because they're a good offense and a good team."

Simon and Jordan Hancock combined for a third-down tackle a yard short of a first down, forcing an Oregon punt. The Buckeyes couldn't cash in after Smith made a leaping 29-yard catch in double coverage on their next possession, but the OSU defense forced another three-and-out on Oregon's next series.

The Buckeyes needed only three plays to make it 14–0. After one first down, Howard threw a laser to Egbuka streaking down the middle with a step on his man. Egbuka caught it for a 42-yard touchdown.

Howard said the Buckeyes waited until the play clock was under 15 seconds to line up to prevent Oregon from reacting to the alignment. (The communication from coach to the designated defensive player cuts off at 15 seconds.) They liked the matchup against Brandon Johnson, a 5'10", 185-pound safety the Buckeyes considered Oregon's weakest defensive back. "I knew if his back's turned, Emeka is wide open, so I just put the ball over the top and let 'Mek go run for it," Howard said. "We've thrown that ball a zillion times."

Smith set up a Fielding 46-yard field goal with a 32-yard catch to make it 17–0. At that point, Ohio State had outgained Oregon 228–37. The Ducks had only two first downs. It would get worse for them. On the second play of OSU's next possession, the Buckeyes went deep to Smith again. Howard recognized that the weakside cornerback was playing close to the line of scrimmage and that Gee Scott would run a pattern that would occupy another defensive back.

"My eyes were already big before that play even started," Howard said.

Oregon didn't try to jam Smith at the line of scrimmage. The only defender even in the vicinity of Smith was a safety. It was a mismatch.

Smith sprinted downfield, made a quick movement like he was going left, which caused the safety to turn, and then went right. Nobody was within 10 yards of Smith when he made the catch and jogged into the end zone.

After another three-and-out by the Ohio State defense, the Buckeyes needed only one play to make it 31–0 with just less than nine minutes left in the second quarter. TreVeyon Henderson took a handoff, headed right, got a block from Donovan Jackson, and broke the tackle of safety Koby Savage. After that, Henderson only had daylight for a 66-yard touchdown. Kelly said the play call was the same one used on the first touchdown to Smith—an RPO in which Howard had to decide whether to pass or hand off based on the defense's reaction. Oregon linebacker Jeff Bassa recognized the play and chased the receiver—Tate instead of Smith on this play—and Howard read it and handed off to Henderson. The Buckeyes had scored four touchdowns. None of them required more than three plays.

"It was a little surreal, but I wouldn't say we were overly surprised," Day said. "There was a confidence going into that game that we had a chance to dominate. They're a very good team, but there were things we took out of that Oregon game on the road that we could make improvements on. We were peaking in all three phases. I think once we went out to that lead right there, we all felt this is going to be our national championship to lose."

Ohio State's revamped offensive line showed that its performance against Tennessee wasn't a fluke. Buckeye linemen were manhandling the Ducks up front. "As an offensive lineman, every time you block somebody, it's kind of a car crash," Jackson said. "You can tell when the other side is starting to give a little bit, and we could feel the other side starting to give. Once you feel that, you keep that foot on the gas, and you know you have them where you want them."

Ohio State tacked on another Fielding field goal before Oregon finally got some offensive traction. The Ducks scored at the end of the half on a 75-yard drive and made the two-point conversion to make it 34–8 at halftime.

"Calling plays in that game was easy," Kelly said. "I think anybody could have called plays in that game because of how dialed in our players were."

EVEN AFTER THAT domination, Ohio State was businesslike heading for the locker room. The Buckeyes calmly walked off the field as if this was what they expected to happen. "We felt awesome," Howard said. "Obviously, in our heads we were like the game's not over. We've still got 30 minutes left to play, but they would have to do something pretty drastic for us to be worried."

What Ohio State's defensive players weren't expecting was the greeting Jim Knowles would give them when he came down from the booth to the locker room. Ohio State had yielded only 139 yards to Oregon's high-powered offense, including only 14 yards in 11 carries on the ground. If OSU's defensive players expected pats on the back from Knowles, well…

"We get in the locker room," Jack Sawyer said, "and we're feeling good. All of a sudden, the door slams shut to the coaches' office and here comes Knowles." Sawyer imitated Knowles high-pitched voice. "I mean, c'mon, guys," Sawyer said, reciting Knowles' words. "Don't take your fucking foot off the gas. You guys let up for one second. Why?"

The players were taken aback. "We're sitting there kind of pissed off, like, 'This is how we're going to start this?'" Sawyer said. "He's like, 'You guys are killing them in the run [game]. Can we get to this guy in the pass? Can we get to [Gabriel].'"

Sawyer told him the defense could if Knowles would unleash them in the pass rush. "I said, 'Coach, I promise you we can get to him. Let us go,'" Sawyer said.

Knowles said he would.

"Just go get him then," Sawyer said, still impersonating Knowles. "Get his ass on the ground. I'm tired of seeing him just dinking and diving back there, man."

Sonny Styles said Sawyer's retelling wasn't embellished. "It's super accurate," he said with a laugh.

The second half was a formality. Oregon had the first score of the third quarter to make it 34–15 and stopped Ohio State without a first down on OSU's first possession. But Sawyer and Cody Simon had consecutive sacks for a three-and-out on Oregon's next possession. The Buckeyes went 56 yards for a touchdown to make it 41–15 late in the third quarter to end any doubt. Oregon scored with 10 minutes left in the fourth quarter to cut OSU's lead to 41–21, which ended the scoring. Ohio State's defense swarmed Gabriel as Sawyer promised, sacking the quarterback seven times in the second half. Simon, Sawyer, and J.T. Tuimoloau each had two sacks. Ohio State gained 500 yards and held Oregon to 276. The Buckeyes gave up only one play longer than 27 yards, a 44-yarder in the second quarter.

"We used a lot of bullets in that first half and were in game-management mode in the second half," Howard said. "We did what we had to do. We scored once, but we probably could have put more points up if we really wanted to."

It was a happily quiet game for Denzel Burke. After being burned repeatedly in the October game, Oregon threw at the cornerback only once in the Rose Bowl. That deep ball was overthrown and Burke had good coverage on it. He was closer to the ball than the receiver was. As much as he was happy to have a second crack at the Ducks, he didn't make the game too big. After the game, he clutched a rose between his teeth in celebration. "It wasn't really a revenge thing for me," Burke said. "When you have that mindset going into your game, you can play a little antsy. I was calm, being myself, and having fun."

The game was also a special one for Lathan Ransom. It was at the Rose Bowl three years earlier that he suffered the gruesome broken tibia/fibula injury on a kickoff. He wasn't sure he'd ever be the same player again. He finished with seven tackles, second on the team behind Simon's 11, including a tackle for a loss.

Before the game, Ransom saw Gene Smith, the former athletics director who arranged for a charter flight home for Ransom after he contracted COVID-19 following his surgery. "I hadn't seen the players yet," Smith said. "He's coming down the ramp and he runs over to me and looks me in the eye and says, 'I've come full circle. I'm finally back here.' It was one of those emotional moments for me."

Ransom was just happy to share that moment. "Anytime I see Gene Smith and his wife," he said, "I get a little emotional because he did so much for me and my family when I was hurt. We built a great relationship and still talk to this day. When I needed someone in my life, he was there for me. I can't thank him and his wife enough. Gene Smith, for the rest of his life, if he ever needs anything, I'll be there for him."

For the Buckeyes, it was two down and two to go.

25

"The Best Team We Played"

Of all its opponents in the College Football Playoff, Texas concerned Ohio State the most. The Longhorns are one of the few programs in the country with resources comparable to Ohio State. They would have 12 players taken in the 2025 NFL draft, only two fewer than the Buckeyes. Coach Steve Sarkisian is known as one of the most gifted play callers in college football. Unlike Oregon and Notre Dame, the Buckeyes had not played the Longhorns in years. Unlike Tennessee, Texas had an experienced quarterback.

Quinn Ewers was the No. 1 prospect in the 2022 recruiting class, given a perfect score in the 247Sports.com composite rankings. The suburban Dallas native committed to Texas in August 2020 before decommitting in October. He explained then that COVID-19 had limited his recruitment, and he wanted to explore his options. Two months later, he committed to Ohio State. After name, image, and likeness rights were granted in July 2021, Ewers decided to reclassify into the 2021 class because Texas didn't allow high school athletes to profit from NIL. On August 15, two weeks after Ohio State opened training camp, Ewers enrolled in Columbus.

"Me and my family had a pretty big opportunity in front of us," Ewers said before the CFP semifinal. "We felt it was a good decision for me to forgo my senior year and enroll early at Ohio State and have the opportunity to have some good money in our pockets as a family."

It worked out financially for Ewers, who signed an endorsement deal with a kombucha company reportedly worth $1.4 million. But in terms of football, the timing was awkward. The Buckeyes were in the midst of a quarterback competition among C.J. Stroud, Jack Miller, and Kyle McCord. "He came in not just as a freshman but a reclassified freshman, behind the 8-ball," Day said. "It was a real challenge for him. I totally understood why they did it as a family, but I did share with the dad that if it were my son, I wouldn't do it. It was hard for him, and I think as time went on, our guys really did a nice job rallying around him."

Jack Sawyer was one player who befriended him. Ewers moved in with Sawyer, tight end Sam Hart, and linebacker Reid Carrico. Sawyer said he and Ewers quickly became close. "He comes from a strong family," Sawyer said. "Great kid, strong in his faith. I've always loved Quinn and always will."

Because he arrived so late, Ewers was never a factor in the quarterback competition. Stroud won the job and established himself as a star. He would be ineligible for the NFL until 2023, so there was no path to significant early playing time for Ewers. His only snaps as an Ohio State quarterback came at the end of a blowout against Michigan State when he handed off twice. On December 3, 2021, Ewers entered the transfer portal. Nine days later, he announced he would become a Longhorn after all. "I remember him always missing home, so for me it was no surprise he was going to go back to Texas," Sawyer said.

It wasn't a shock to Day, either, but he was disappointed. He tried to change Ewers' mind but couldn't. "I really wanted to work with him," Day said. "I really did feel we could develop him into a Heisman Trophy–like quarterback. When he left, I certainly was upset, but I wished him the best. He and his family are good people."

Ewers said he enjoyed his brief time as a Buckeye. "I learned a lot while I was there," he said. "Coach Day and C.J. and that whole room was awesome to be around. I'm super thankful for that time I got to spend there. I don't regret any decision I made on going."

Now he would be a major obstacle in Ohio State's path. But Ewers was no one-man show. Left tackle Kelvin Banks won the Outland and Lombardi awards and became the ninth pick in the NFL draft. Receiver Matthew Golden and Jim Thorpe Award–winning defensive back Jahdae Barron also were first-round picks. The Longhorns had talent and depth at most positions.

"I think that was by far the best team we played," Sonny Styles said. "That's no hit to any other team. We played some other really good teams, but when you look on paper, that was definitely the best team."

THE GAME WAS played at AT&T Stadium, home of the Dallas Cowboys, so the Buckeyes knew it would be a pro-Longhorn crowd, no matter how well OSU fans traveled. Forecasts of a winter storm put a damper on travel for those inclined to go. The Buckeyes decided to use a silent count to snap the ball on offense, which put a premium on concentration. Ohio State expected Texas's defensive strategy to resemble Michigan's more than Oregon's or Tennessee's. Kelly had coached against Texas defensive coordinator Pete Kwiatkowski when Kwiatkowski was at Washington. He expected a conservative game plan. In other words, the Longhorns would do everything they could to keep Jeremiah Smith from beating them. Will Howard likened it to the Iowa game when the Hawkeyes forced OSU to be patient and move methodically down the field.

"They were going to play a big shell over the top and cloud some stuff and bring some simulated pressure," Howard said. "It was going to be a checkdown game. That week of practice, coach Day made us do walk-throughs with checkdowns, just walking through with the running backs. I think we did that twice that week."

Ohio State had no shortage of motivation, but Day called upon a former NFL player and Navy SEAL to add to the fire. Clint Bruce was a middle linebacker and captain for Navy and played for the Baltimore Ravens and New Orleans Saints before becoming a Navy SEAL in 1998. He was deployed in multiple counterterrorism and national security missions around the world. Bruce had spoken to OSU players at a Real Life Wednesday event, which was started under Urban Meyer to help players plan for life after football. Under Day, Bruce has spoken to the Buckeyes several times. He was living in Dallas, so Day asked him to speak before the Texas game. Clint came to the team hotel and told the Buckeyes how the SEALs prepare for a mission, likening it to a football game. They get their bearings, become calibrated, and practice until they are prepared for any contingency.

"They'll go into a place, wreck shit, and then find out what the new mission is," Day said. "The guys really liked that story. There was an ice storm there, and he said, 'People think there's a storm coming, but the storm is going to be in the stadium.'"

OHIO STATE WON the coin toss and deferred, so Texas got the ball first. Jim Knowles had gone against Sarkisian while at Oklahoma State. He knew how adept Sarkisian was at play-calling, particularly on the scripted first drives. "They got me when I was at Oklahoma State," Knowles said. "We were down 14–0 before we knew it. I definitely wanted to start fast and have some different looks, some calls that he wasn't expecting in his opening script because he was so good at it. Throw him off balance early, and it worked."

Texas did drive to the Ohio State 36-yard line, but on fourth-and-3, Knowles had safety Jordan Hancock blitz. He and Sawyer got close enough to Ewers that he had to rush his throw, which was low to DeAndre Moore and fell incomplete with Cody Simon in tight coverage.

The Buckeyes executed the game plan of not forcing anything almost perfectly on their first drive. Twice, Howard converted third downs on passes to Emeka Egbuka. Howard took one shot at getting the ball downfield to Smith, but that fell incomplete into double-coverage. A 14-yard completion to Egbuka gave the Buckeyes a first down at the 9. On first-and-goal, Carnell Tate dropped a pass on a slant pattern in the end zone, but on the next play, Quinshon Judkins ran through a hole created by Tegra Tshabola and Josh Fryar to power for a touchdown.

Two sacks by J.T. Tuimoloau, the second assisted by Ty Hamilton, thwarted Texas on its next drive. Ohio State's ensuing possession started with a three-yard swing pass to Smith, which would be his only official catch of the game. (Another completion was negated by a penalty.) The Buckeyes moved the ball to the Texas 38 before TreVeyon Henderson lost his cool and threw a jab to the helmet of defensive lineman Jermayne Lole after being tackled. The Buckeyes couldn't overcome that 15-yard unsportsmanlike conduct penalty and punted.

Both teams were fortunate on the ensuing punt return. Silas Bolden, who'd returned a punt for a touchdown in the CFP quarterfinal against Arizona State, caught Joe McGuire's punt at the 10 and broke left. He looked to have a path for a touchdown until Caden Curry continued his knack for making special-teams plays. Curry swatted the ball free from Bolden. But the ball bounced right back into Bolden's arms after hitting the turf—a similar thing would happen a second time later on this night—preventing OSU from getting a potential turnover. Texas did nothing in its possession, which ended with a Styles strip sack the Longhorns recovered.

While the defense kept Texas off the scoreboard, the OSU offense kept stymying itself with penalties. Flags on Gee Scott Jr. and Fryar helped kill successive drives, and a sack ended another one. Ohio State's defense finally cracked on Texas' final drive of the half. The more mobile Arch Manning, the highly touted heir apparent to Ewers, converted a fourth-and-1 with an eight-yard run to the OSU 42. Bolden then slipped a tackle by Denzel Burke for a 24-yard reception. Two plays later, running back Jaydon Blue ran a wheel route and got past Styles for a touchdown.

Ewers hit him in stride for the game-tying score with 29 seconds left in the first half.

"I would change that, obviously," Knowles said of his play call. "Sonny's a really good player, but you'd like to avoid those matchups—a linebacker on a running back going deep."

It looked like Texas would have all the momentum heading into halftime. Certainly, Ohio State's players didn't think anything special would come on their first snap after a touchback on the kickoff. The Buckeyes had practiced this play—a screen pass—all year with no success. But it was a play with little risk. Get Henderson the ball in the open field, and who knows?

"When Will called the play," Fryar said, "I remember looking at Donnie [Jackson], and we have this look on our face like, 'This is never going to fucking work.' It never worked in scrimmages against our defense. It never worked on the scout team. It's never going to work."

Howard took the snap and took a deep drop. Fryar didn't expect to have to hold his block that long, and his guy almost got to Howard, who flipped the ball to Henderson just in time.

"At first, I saw the nickel that was blitzing was going to take Tre," Howard said. "I thought he was going to see [Henderson] releasing and he was going to lock onto him. I was ready to dirt the ball, throw it into the ground. But he runs right past Tre, and Tre slips him. I just had to get the ball to Tre. I don't think I've ever backed up that much, but coach Day would always talk about it in screen drilling practice: Get depth, get depth. Just keep backing up. I probably took 12 crossover steps to get back. By the end of it, I was damn near in the end zone. I had no idea he was going to do what he did."

Henderson was just looking for redemption after his bone-headed penalty earlier. He said he went to the sideline and prayed and repented. He knew as Texas rushed, he'd have to bluff making a block so he could slip out of the backfield. He hoped to maybe get a first down and get out of bounds. Instead, Henderson caught the ball at the 19 and headed upfield with no Texas player within 10 yards of him. Tshabola blocked the first potential tackler. Hinzman blocked safety Andrew Mukuba at the 35 as another Texas defender ran into Mukuba. Henderson now had an opening and used his speed to burst into the clear. Tshabola said Henderson was running so fast that he felt a burst of wind as the running back raced by.

"At this point," Tshabola said, "we're almost shocked like, 'Damn, this is about to work.'"

As he watched Henderson take off, Howard noticed a Texas assistant coach's reaction on the sideline. "I saw the Texas coach fall down," Howard said, "and I was like, 'Oh shit. This is good for us.' I think it was their DBs coach that fell down, like face-planted on the ground he was so pissed."

With good reason. No Texas player came close to catching Henderson as he finished the 75-yard score. Henderson had redeemed himself after the penalty earlier, and the Buckeyes had a 14–7 lead.

HENDERSON'S TOUCHDOWN WAS a huge momentum shift, but Ohio State couldn't sustain it when the second half started. Howard tried to throw downfield toward Smith, but he didn't notice linebacker David Gbenda dropping back into coverage, and Gbenda intercepted the pass.

The teams traded punts before Texas took over at its 33 midway through the third quarter. On third-and-10, Sawyer went around Cam Williams and grabbed Ewers around the legs. But a fraction of a second before Ewers' knee hit the ground, he underhanded the ball to Wisner, who gained 14 yards. On the next play, Sawyer got his arms around Ewers' waist as the quarterback completed a short pass.

"I'm like, 'This dude is really going to get the ball out like that, so I can't sack my former roommate,'" Sawyer said. "Just these great plays he made. Since he left, I've always wanted to sack him. We used to joke about that."

At this point, Ohio State's defense started to falter. Tuimoloau had his left ankle rolled up on in the second quarter. He returned but was playing with his left ankle heavily taped. "I think the adrenaline of it all made me go back in," Tuimoloau said.

Simon was back in after injuring his knee on the last play of the previous possession. But Denzel Burke hurt his shoulder in the first half and couldn't play. Jermaine Mathews replaced him. Texas moved the ball to the OSU 26 before facing third-and-7. Knowles brought two blitzers, but Ewers threw the ball before unblocked defensive end Kenyatta Jackson could get to him. Blue caught the short pass with no Buckeye near him. The only player with a chance to tackle him was Lathan Ransom near the goal line, but Blue slipped his tackle for a touchdown to tie the game.

That put the onus on the offense, whose only score since the game-opening drive came on the Henderson screen pass. But again, the Buckeyes shot themselves in the foot. Carnell Tate caught a pass for 15 yards, but that yardage was negated by a personal foul on Austin Siereveld after he ran upfield to block a Texas player just after the whistle blew. A sack on the next play doomed the possession.

After an OSU stop, the Buckeyes took over at their 12-yard line early in the fourth quarter. On third-and-8 from the 29, Texas blitzed. Henderson, who reveled in pass protection, threw his body at Mukuba and knocked him down. That allowed Howard, playing despite a popped blood vessel that caused a golf ball-sized bump on his throwing hand, the time to find Tate for an 18-yard completion. The Buckeyes faced third-and-9 at the Texas 41 when Howard threw a short pass to Gee Scott Jr. Scott was hit at the 39 but maintained his balance to lunge forward for an extra five yards to make it a more manageable fourth-and-2. Texas called timeout before the snap, and OSU called for an RPO, with Howard given the option to run or pass based on the defense.

Day said he trusted Howard to make the right read. "All the confidence in the world," Day said. "I knew he was going to get us into the right play, and he loves quarterback power. He always said that if he was asked what's his favorite run, he'd say quarterback power."

Sure enough, Howard took the snap and found a hole to the right on a hole opened by Tshabola and Fryar. There was no one in front of him as he ran toward the end zone, but he stumbled over his own feet and fell at the Texas 16. "I'm ready to run somebody over to get those two yards, and I get through the line and nobody's there," Howard said. "I'm like, 'Oh shoot, I don't have to actually run anybody over.'" But he said his body was already leaning forward so much in anticipation of having to plow a tackler that he couldn't regain his balance.

But Howard got more than OSU needed. A short pass to Egbuka and a run by Judkins gave the Buckeyes another first down. Judkins scored from the 1 to give Ohio State the lead with seven minutes left.

Texas' offense responded. Ewers threw to tight end Gunnar Helm for 34 yards, though Helm was penalized 15 yards for taunting after pointing to tackler Caleb Downs after the play. On the next play, Ewers completed a 27-yard pass to Golden to the Ohio State 13. On third-and-3, Lathan Ransom was called for interference in the end zone. On the next, Mathews was penalized for the same thing, giving Texas first-and-goal from the 1.

Ohio State's defensive motto all year had been, "Give us an inch and we'll defend it." Now it had to deliver again. On first down, Texas tried a run up the middle. Tuimoloau beat his man and stuffed Jerrick Gibson for no gain. In some ways, that was the key play of the sequence.

"One of the things we talk about all the time is you're playing against your opponent, but you're also playing against your next opponent," Day said.

In other words, Ohio State knew its previous goal-line stands, most notably against Penn State, would factor into Texas' play-calling. The Buckeyes knew Texas probably wouldn't try another run up the middle. Student of the game that he is, Downs had an idea what was coming. Ewers pitched the ball to Wisner, who ran to the left behind the line of scrimmage, scanning for a hole. Downs diagnosed the play immediately and shot the gap. Wisner slipped his tackle, but Ransom and Davison Igbinosun pursued to drop him for a seven-yard loss.

"I've seen that play a couple of times," Downs said. "Georgia ran it on us last year in the SEC championship, so it was a play I was familiar with.... It kind of made me mad I didn't tackle him myself."

Igbinosun also knew the perimeter run was coming. "If I'm being completely honest, I heard them say, 'Stretch,'" he said. "I heard the wide receivers tell each other, "Stretch." But I'm thinking I'm a corner, so I'm going to play the pass first. Then he actually ran a stretch, so I just thought, "Go make a play.'"

That forced Texas into a passing situation on third down at the 8. Even as a sophomore, Downs earned a reputation for being a coach on the field. He was on the next play. He said Knowles called for a coverage Ohio State had practiced but never used in a game. When Texas ran motion to bunch three receivers to the right, Downs took it upon himself to make a change.

"We were supposed play the bunch a certain way," he said. "But we hadn't played the coverage in the game before, so I was like, 'I don't want to put anybody in a position they don't want to be in. Let me just call something everybody knows.' There has to be communication on the field, and someone has to make the call. Whoever's the most confident pretty much has to make the call, and that was me in this case."

Ewers glanced briefly to his right after getting the snap and then looked to the lone receiver, Ryan Wingo, to the left. But Ewers had to rush his throw because Sawyer beat the right guard and pressured him up the middle. Ewers' pass fluttered harmlessly short of Wingo, who was well-covered by Igbinosun. Sawyer had come so close again to getting that elusive sack on Ewers. Fourth down was next. He'd get one more chance.

26
Scoop and Sawyer

Jack Sawyer said the play call was "Florida." Jim Knowles said it was "Disney."

The play on fourth-and-goal from the 8 called for a linebacker to serve as a spy to protect against Ewers scrambling. That meant Sawyer was free to rush without worrying about anything but getting to the quarterback. Cody Simon was the spy. He stepped toward the line of scrimmage across from the Texas right guard. That prevented the guard from double-teaming Sawyer with right tackle Cameron Williams.

"I'm thinking I'm going to get off the ball as fast as I can and see where the tackle is at by my second step," Sawyer said. "If he's slow off the ball, I'm going to try to continue outside. If he jumps quick, I'm going to go inside because we've got the freedom to do so in this defense."

Williams, who missed the CFP quarterfinals with a sprained knee, was slow out of his stance, so Sawyer went to the outside. He swiped at Williams' hands, causing Williams to lose his balance and lunge forward. Sawyer had a clear path to Ewers, who never saw him coming. Sawyer hit the quarterback, jarring the ball free.

"It's funny when you're playing," Sawyer said, "and you have these subconscious thoughts constantly. In this moment, I'm thinking, 'Man, I hope his arm wasn't going forward so it's incomplete, but I'm going to pick it up and run.' I'm just trying to locate the ball."

The ball floated to the turf and serendipitously bounced right back to Sawyer at the 17-yard line. He took off running down the Ohio State sideline, with Ryan Day and others sprinting along gleefully. Texas running back Quintrevion Wisner reacted quickly and was only five yards behind Sawyer when he picked up the ball. But Sonny Styles, gifted both physically and mentally, made an overlooked play. Styles had been covering Wisner and was four yards behind him when Sawyer scooped up the ball. But Styles sprinted past Wisner, got in front of him, and then slowed down to serve as a shield.

"I'd say I'm a pretty fast dude, but there's a little bit of an urgency when those plays happen," Styles said. "It's like when someone breaks a tackle and hits another gear. That was almost like one of those, where you just hit another gear and find a way to make it happen."

Styles said all of OSU's players, defensive as well as offensive, are coached to simply get in the way of a potential tackler in that situation rather than risk being flagged for a crackback block.

"It's just cutting someone off," Styles said. "The whole point is to show the ref, 'Hey, I'm not blindside blocking him. I'm not holding him.' It's really just trying to avoid a penalty. The guy trying to tackle him is not in a position to make a play, so there's no need to block him. You've just got to get in his way, so he doesn't catch him."

Williams was the only other pursuer, and he wasn't going to catch Sawyer, who by then had a convoy of Simon, J.T. Tuimoloau, and Jordan Hancock as well as Styles as he ran 83 yards through the heart of Texas to the end zone.

As Sawyer ran, he had a flashback of Will Howard and the stumble he had on the fourth-down conversion. "I was thinking, 'Don't fall, don't get caught from behind, and if I do get caught, tuck that ball up and don't give it back," he said.

"I was telling myself the whole way that someone's coming to knock it out. Someone is going to try to punch this ball out. As I'm looking, I see coach Hartline pointing. My favorite memory as a Buckeye, besides winning the national championship, is when I look back and all I see is Cody, J.T., Jordan, and Sonny all running with their hands up. It was a feeling I'm never going to forget."

When he scored, an exhausted Sawyer dropped the ball to the ground. He had no memory of what he did with the ball. "At that point, it was such a blur," Sawyer said. "It was a blackout moment."

He got to the sideline and all he wanted was something to drink. "I got as much water as I could," Sawyer said.

He barely had time to drink it. Larry Johnson gave him a big hug and sprayed him with water. The play and the adrenaline from it wiped Sawyer out. "I've never felt my heart beat that fast or be so out of breath as I was after that play," he said.

In the moment, Sawyer didn't realize what an iconic play he'd made. "I was just thankful God put me in position to help the team," he said. "It didn't really sink in to me until afterwards. Obviously, my parents and my sister and everyone had a mix of emotions—so happy for the team and for myself. It was such a great experience. The ball bounced right to me. My teammates blocked their asses off the whole way. It was one of the most special moments I've ever had."

Simon retrieved the ball in the end zone and gave it to a coach who saved it for Sawyer. He gave it to his parents for safe keeping. "It's probably locked up somewhere," he said. "I hope so."

Michelle Sawyer, his mom, said months later that it was just sitting on their kitchen counter. Jack had even tossed it around on his visits home from training for the NFL draft.

THE PLAY BECAME instantly iconic. Months later, those on the Ohio State side remembered the play as if it had just happened. Here are their recollections:

Ryan Day

In your mind, you're saying to yourself, "Are they going to go for it here or not?" They do. So now I'm thinking, "If we got the stop here, the ball's going to be inside the 10-yard line. What do we do? What do we have for runs coming out?" Or they score a touchdown and now we've got to go down and kick a field goal to win the game. You're going through all the scenarios in your head.

[Jim Knowles] called a double coverage that really hadn't run much all year. I think it forced Ewers to kind of double-clutch. Then as he got flushed, I saw Jack tracking him. As he made the play, you watched the ball bounce right up into Jack's hands. That's the bounce I feel we hadn't gotten in the past.

Once he scooped it up and ran, Cody Simon and Sonny Styles made great plays to turn that play from a scoop where it gets returned for 20 or 30 yards into a touchdown. When that happened, I knew we were going to win the national championship.

I said to Jack [on the sideline], "You just became a legend." We had talked before the game about how you become a legend. You become your own legacy by leaving something behind. How do you do that? By making a play like that is obviously how you become a legend.

Jim Knowles

We're going to line up in a variety of funky ways with the linebackers up and with the safeties and corners in different positions, so they don't know what we're in.

J.T. comes inside to the left so that if he's going to scramble, you're going to force the quarterback to his left. Cody is actually using up the guard next to Jack. He kind of pretends to rush. I call it a hypnotized technique on the guard, to kind of hypnotize the guard so the guard can't help out with Jack. That let Jack rush out, so if he's going to go to his left, Cody's going to hit the guard, and then eventually if he would have broken out to the left, Cody would have looped around.

It's the culmination of a lot of work. I would say, "Coverage and rush," and the whole defense would say, "Working together." It was the culmination of a lot of work and of that winning edge of, "Okay, if we make the quarterback hold the ball, don't give him any easy throws and show him something he's not expecting, then the rush will be able to deliver."

And then, of course, you've got all those years of work, of Jack and Larry and all those drills and everything that go into it, of him really being perfect—everything he's worked on for four years coming down to one play.

Larry Johnson

Cody walked into the gap, so he got the attention of the tackle. The tackle didn't know where he's coming from or where Jack is coming from. The tackle looked at Cody and then put his eyes back on Jack, but by that time Jack had a great get-off and hit his hands out with what we call a side scissors move. Then he had a burst to finish. You don't get a sack going the same speed. When he got there, the ball was back. He was looking to hit the wrist, hand on ball, to have a chance to get a sack fumble.

And then how lucky that the ball bounced back into his hands. It was just a perfect bounce. That's all God. But it's something Jack has done over and over again [in practice]. It's just repetition. And then you get in the game, and you get one shot, one moment to recall those skills. That's what Jack did, recalling something he's done over and over again. He remembered all those little things to make that play happen. To me, that's what makes it special.

It was a checkmate play. That's when you knew God was with this team. It'll be a play that we will all talk about for the rest of our lives.

Sonny Styles

As soon as he ran through the end zone, it was like, "Oh, my gosh. What did he just do? No way he made that play." It was almost like I was in disbelief, which I'm sure a lot of people across the country were, too. It was a shell-shocking moment for me.

Cody Simon

My only job is to make sure that guard cannot double-team Jack or the defensive tackle, but it's usually the end, so the end can get a free rush. I'm technically a spy. I'm not going to take any credit for the play, but it's 11 guys all doing our job so Jack could make probably the greatest play in Buckeye history. I've got the guard, making sure he can't double and then I'm wrapping around for the quarterback. Once I saw Jack free, I'm like, "Oh my gosh, this is going to be a big play right here."

J.T. Tuimoloau

I got moved down to 3-tech. I did a spin move on the guard and was like, "OK, I think I can get this." And then I see another red jersey. I'm like, "Damn, who is this?" and I see it's Jack. Oh, he got the sack. Then I saw it was a forced fumble and I'm thinking we've got to pick this up. Once it bounced to him, and he was off and running, the last thing we want is for him to get hawked down. He had it happen to him in the Up North game. Once we got to the 50-yard line, I was like, "I'm already here. I might as well run all the way," and I ended up sprinting just out of excitement and passion. Never again will I run that far. That was the dagger of the whole thing. I was like, "This has to be the greatest play in Buckeye history."

Chip Kelly

We were just talking like we normally do at the end of a game about a two-minute plan [to score] or a four-minute plan [to run out the clock]. When the ball bounced out, I was obviously excited about the play, but selfishly, I was like, 'I don't want to deal with a four-minute offense, so I said, "Score!" and he'd only taken like two steps. Keenan [Bailey] looked at me and said, "What?" I said he's going to score. It wasn't like I was cheering him on. I was like, "He has to score. We don't need to go back on the field offensively." Then he got to about the 25-yard line and I was like, 'He actually may score on this thing." I didn't think when he first picked it up that he was going to go the distance. But our guys just took off after him and there was nobody on Texas anywhere near him. I was like, "He actually is going to score. Holy shit." Because it was Jack and everything about Jack is awesome, it was so cool that he could finish off that game that way.

Ross Bjork

At different places I've been when there's been a key play, sometimes I'll just go stand behind the bench and put my head down. I was like, I'm going to go back there and just pray. I put my head down and said, "God, just put us in the best position." I have my head down and I hear the crowd, and I'm thinking we just stopped them on fourth down. I kept my eyes closed and the crowd just starts getting louder and louder. Then I open my eyes and walk toward the sideline, and I see Jack walking into the end zone. President Carter and I jump up and down and grab each other. Carey Hoyt, our deputy AD for football, and I are hugging each other. Logan Hittle was down there. A couple of former players and my son Paxton was there, and I'm like, "What happened? How did he get the ball?" I had no idea he got by his guy, stripped him, and picked it up.

Caleb Downs

On fourth down, they motioned to a stack on the boundary. Somebody had to make a call, and I was like, "Let's play triangle on my side," which is a three-over-two stack on defense. They tried to isolate me. I thought he was going to throw the ball at me. But I covered my guy up pretty well, and then I turn around and see captain Jack make the best play I've seen in my life. That was a crazy moment for me just watching that.

(There's a photo of Downs dropping to his knees in the end zone and praying.)

That was a miracle, and I had to thank God in that moment for that. I'm like, "God, nobody could have foreseen that play happening, so thank you, thank you, thank you."

Mitchell Melton

I was on the sideline. I had seen that move from him countless times. I used to call it his patented move because whenever he would get into the rhythm of the game, he would hit that move. I know that because me and him would watch hours and hours of film in preparation for all those teams that we played. It was like a T.J. Watt sack. I was standing there next to either KJ [Kenyatta Jackson] or Kayden [McDonald]. And I saw him hit the move on No. 56 and I literally said in my head, "Sack." Literally after that, it was a blur. I've never been a part of such pandemonium in my life.

Do you ever just find yourself in a moment where you don't think it's real? And instead of enjoying it, you're just questioning it. I was like, there's no way this is real. There's no way this is happening. And then I see the score and I see him [get a] touchdown and I see the replay, and I'm just shocked. But I couldn't have been happier for him because he was literally the catalyst. He was one of the main motivators that literally rallied this team together after everything that happened. So just to see that for him and to see him accomplish that moment on one of the biggest stages and be immortalized in Buckeye history, it was awesome.

Lathan Ransom

I was in coverage on that play. [Ewers] looked into the boundary, to our way. I think that me, IGB, and Caleb did a great job covering up in the boundary to where he didn't have a quick throw. Then Jack won so fast off the line and made the tackle look silly.

I just remember running behind and just so happy, so excited, so in disbelief. Whenever we needed a big play like that, Jack came through. I was happy to watch from afar because I couldn't catch up to him, I was so tired.

Josh Fryar

I was sitting on the bench right next to Gee Scott and I was holding his hand, and I think I was holding Tegra's hand to the left of me. I was saying to myself, "Please, God. Give us an opportunity. Just give us a chance." He gave us one. Jack came around the edge, double swipe-barred the right tackle, and then the ball popped out and popped right in his hands, and he started running. I just sat there in awe, just watching it happen. As the field goal unit was running out [for the extra-point kick], I was still sitting on the bench. Then I was like, "Oh shit, I've got to go out for field goal," and I started sprinting out there. It was crazy. It felt like a made-up story.

(Fryar blocked against Sawyer often in practice. He gave his perspective on how Sawyer beat Williams on the play.)

He punched with two hands against Jack, and Jack's really good about swiping. He punched so far that he leaned forward where you're imbalanced and your weight is over your toes, so you can't get back into a good body position to push Jack by the quarterback. You want to push him by the quarterback by having your hands out and head out. Then if Jack swipes your hands, you still have your feet to recover against him. But that guy, he had his weight over his toes, and he was leaning so far to where he couldn't recover. And then Jack popped that ball out and scored.

We've gone against each other a shit ton in practice, and he might've gotten me once or twice on that specific move out of hundreds of reps because I know he's a hand swiper.

Donovan Jackson

The offensive line, we were busy drawing up plays because we though we were going to have a four-minute situation where we had to drive down the field and probably score late. So we were drawing up plays, and we look up at the giant Jerry World Jumbotron, and I see Jack dip around the right tackle. I was like, "Oh, that's a sack." I saw the ball bounce right to him. I was like, "Oh my gosh, he's gone." And then we started losing all our minds.

Tegra Tshabola

I probably had the best view to it because I was just a little bit behind them [on the sideline]. I'm watching Jack get in the stance, and I knew exactly what he was going to do. The tackle from Texas ends up reaching and bending at the waist. He hits a chop around the corner and he bends the corner and I'm watching him like he's running towards me. I'm like frozen at this point. Oh, man. He's about to sack him, maybe a sack fumble, and then we've got the ball, and we get to go back in. But he hits him, and the ball hits the ground, and it might've been the most perfect bounce I've ever seen. It bounced right in his hands, almost like a basketball. I'm like, "Okay, he might get some yardage out of this." And then I see Sonny start to get in front of the running back and block him. I'm like, "Wait, he's going to house it?" I was basically frozen watching that whole thing. I didn't jump up and down. I didn't do anything. I was just frozen and looking around me. I was almost caught in shock.

Davison Igbinosun

I had my eyes in the backfield. I saw Jack stripping and I saw Jack pick it up. I'm like, "Thank you, Lord. Thank you, Jesus." I feel like Jack deserved that play because if you remember the game against Team Up North, Jack caught a pick. That was a big-time moment, but because we ended up losing, nobody showed it love, so him doing it against Texas was the culmination.

Carson Hinzman

We're all sitting on the O-line bench and just got cold rags on our heads. [On the first three plays of the goal-line stand] I'm like, "I can't look." Then I was like, "All right, well, maybe I'll look for this last play." Thankfully, I did, because that was pretty cool. I take my wet rag, and I throw it right in the face of someone who's like the closest fan to us. I can't even remember if they were from Texas or not. I was running on the field hugging everybody. It was crazy. I think Hero [Kanu] punched me in the chest so hard. I was like, "Whoa, whoa, whoa." But that was a pretty cool experience.

Mickey Marotti

Fourth-and-8, I'm like, "There's no way they're going to score." I just felt we had 'em. I was standing on the 20, and I'm like, "Oh shit, he's going to sack him." And the ball bounced right back to [Sawyer]. That never happens to us. It always bounces out of bounds or we miss the [critical] field goal or [Jeff] Okudah strips the guy [in the 2019 Clemson game] and it's not [ruled] a fumble. We don't get calls [or breaks] ever. Never! Never! I'm like, "Oh my God, he's got the ball. It's in his hands and he's taking off." I kept looking for a flag because we always get a flag.

Jayden Fielding

I hadn't gone in the game in probably 20 or 30 minutes of real time, so I had my helmet off. I was warming up because it's late in the fourth quarter and I've got to get ready to maybe kick a game-winning field goal. I'm not even looking at the field. Then I just hear this [hush sound] and then the roar of the crowd. I look up and Jack is running down the sideline, and I start running. And then I'm like, "Oh shit, I've got to go in the game" for the extra point. So I had to run all the way back down the sideline, grab my helmet, and run all the way back. I had to catch my breath. I was telling Joe [McGuire, the holder], "We're going to the national championship! We're going to the national championship game." And he's like, "Breathe. You've got to make the extra point."

(Fielding's extra point made it 28–14. Caleb Downs had an interception on Texas' final possession to ice the victory.)

It was a crazy moment. That was the best play on defense that I think I've ever seen.

Luke Montgomery

I think all of us on the offensive line were holding hands on the bench. When we were looking at the big screen and saw the strip sack, we all stood up as fast as any fat guys could stand up and started running down the field with them, us 300-pound big boys.

After the play, I was on the kicking team, and I saw Pat McAfee behind the end zone. Everyone has a picture of me throwing the "Horns down" after that play. I wasn't doing it to the Texas fans. I was actually doing it to Pat McAfee because I know he picked Oregon over us the game before.

RJ Day

I was on the opposite 30-yard line on the sideline looking up at the Jumbotron. I held my breath when they snapped the ball. I saw Jack break, and I saw the ball pop out, and I looked down to see it in real time. I just saw him running, and I started jumping up and down with tears coming down my face because I knew in my heart that Notre Dame wasn't as good as Texas was.

Everything that happened leading up to that point—all the hardships, everything that we had to go through—just came back in that moment as I saw him run into the end zone. I looked for my mom and I just started punching the air, looking at her, and she's crying. And I looked to my dad and he's jumping up and down. It was just a full circle moment for everything that we had gone through.

Nina Day

I'm in the crowd in the first row. When he hit Quinn, I turned around and put my hands in my face. I was sitting with Matt Dufour, who's one of Ryan's best friends from back home, my best friend. His father was my dad's assistant coach for 40-plus years and he's like family to us. I just fell into his arms and didn't see the play at all. Everyone was screaming and I was just asking, "Is there a flag? Is there a flag?" So I never saw it. I could see what was about to happen and I thought, "I can't watch." There's a picture of me in the stands with my back turned and my head down in my hands.

When he got into the end zone, I started jumping up and down. I have a soft spot for Jack. I always have. I remember sitting in the stands at a basketball game with him when he was still in high school, and we were sharing Swedish Fish and just talking. After the natty, he's like, "From now on, you're aunt Nina and he's uncle Ryan." He'll always be family.

Will Howard

I had my head in a Gatorade towel and my head in my hands. As the ball got snapped, I looked up and I see Jack tearing off the side. Quinn slides to the left a little and then I see Jack hit him, and the ball popped out. I immediately jumped up, put my hands in the air, and started screaming. He's carrying the ball down the sideline, and I just started losing my fucking mind. I don't know what noises were coming out of me, but I was screaming bloody murder. I'm going crazy, jumping up and down, yelling, "Run, Jack! Go, Jack!" It was one of the craziest feelings of my life. It was just the adrenaline pumping through me.

When I came over to the sideline and started screaming at him, and that video went viral of me shaking him. I think I said, "Are you fucking kidding? Let's fucking go, man!" I was talking to Jack the other night, and he said he has no memory of what I said. He just knows I was going crazy in his face.

Quinshon Judkins

It was a surreal feeling. It almost felt like it wasn't real. I just remember running down the sideline, screaming at my teammates and all of us were just jumping full of joy. It was a once-in-a-lifetime experience. We're just screaming, like, "We're going to the national championship!" That's just the moment that you dream of, when I revert back to when it was snowing and it's cold and you're sitting in that car with Will Howard [after first transferring] and we were like, "Let's go fucking do this shit." To foreshadow that to where we were at that point, it was like, "Wow, we actually did it." It's crazy. We're at where we want to be and on track and the sky's the limit. To witness that and be a part of it and help contribute to it, it's something I'll always remember.

27
A Terrible Start

Ohio State and Notre Dame are among the most storied programs in the history of college football. The Buckeyes have won the second-most games and the Fighting Irish the fourth-most, though Notre Dame hasn't won a national title since 1988. The teams first met in 1935 in what was billed as the "Game of the Century." The Fighting Irish rallied from down 13–0 to score 18 unanswered points in the fourth quarter. After the Irish won again the following year, the teams didn't play for almost 60 years.

Ohio State won all six games after the rivalry was renewed, including two in the Fiesta Bowl (2006 and 2016) and in 2022 and 2023. The 2023 game was a dramatic one, both for its conclusion and for Ryan Day's comments after it. After falling behind 14–10 midway through the fourth quarter, Ohio State rallied to win on a one-yard touchdown run by Chip Trayanum as time expired, aided by the fact Notre Dame had only 10 defenders on the field. In his postgame television interview, Day lashed out at former Notre Dame coach (and ex-Ohio State assistant) Lou Holtz after Holtz had questioned the Buckeyes' physicality.

"I'd like to know where Lou Holtz is now?" Day said, his voice rising. "What he said about our team, I cannot believe. This is a tough team right here. We're proud to be from Ohio. It's always been Ohio against the world, and it'll continue to be Ohio against the world. But I tell you what. I love those kids. We've got a tough team. Everybody's questioning these kids all the time. We had one bad half the last couple years [the 2022 Michigan game]. That's it. Everybody wants to question these guys. These guys are warriors here."

Day was praised by some for defending his team and mocked by others for responding to an octogenarian former coach. "At some point, you've got to put your foot in the ground," Day explained. "People make a lot of comments and try to run with narratives. When people are putting on [the air] a coach who has the amount of respect he has nationally and his background to be making comments about our program, eventually enough's enough.

"I know some people were upset I said it because he's an older coach. Well, then don't put him on national TV and have him make those comments because at some point we're going to stand up for what we believe in. I just felt like I wanted to defend our team. It was obviously an emotional win and an emotional way to finish the game. It was just a spur-of-the-moment thing I knew I wanted to say. To show the grit and toughness of us to pull out that win speaks to our guys' mental toughness and resilience."

Day said he grew up having a lot of respect for Holtz. Day believed Holtz should know how hard a coach's job is. That's why it particularly bothered him. Day said he heard nothing from Holtz after that game. No apology. No explanation. No congratulations.

Now Day and the Buckeyes would face the Fighting Irish again with everything at stake. James Laurinaitis knew what it felt like to be on the losing side of that. The OSU linebackers coach was an All-American on the 2006 and 2007 Buckeye teams that lost in the Bowl Championship Series title games. Before the game he told players how the pain from that lingers.

"I remember saying to them," Laurinaitis said, "I'm 38 years old and a lot of great stuff has happened in my life. But I will never forget losing in '06 and '07. When you come to Ohio State, you are judged by, 'Did you get a natty or did you not?'"

He told his players that as important as beating Michigan is—he was 4–0 as a player against the Wolverines—nobody talks much about Ohio State teams that don't win national championships. The 2006 team, for instance, beat Michigan in an epic game of No. 1 vs. No. 2 the day after legendary UM coach Bo Schembechler died. But Urban Meyer's Florida team routed OSU in the national title game, 41–14.

"I told them, 'Guys, no one's calling us in 2026 to be like, hey, it's the 20-year reunion of the runner-up,'" Laurinaitis said. "That's real. I said to capitalize on this moment. Otherwise, you don't want to live with that."

For Laurinaitis, the game was emotional also because Notre Dame coach Marcus Freeman is perhaps his closest friend. They bonded at Ohio State in part because Freeman was a die-hard wrestling fan, and Laurinaitis' dad Joe was a famous wrestler known as "Road Warrior Animal." Almost 20 years later, Freeman gave Laurinaitis his first coaching job.

Freeman had already experienced major highs and lows since succeeding Brian Kelly as coach at the end of the 2021 season. He was harshly criticized for having only 10 men on the field on the final play of the 2022 opening-day loss to OSU, and that game was followed by a loss to Marshall before Notre Dame won 10 of their last 11 games. After the Irish inexplicably lost to Northern Illinois early in the 2024 season, Notre Dame found its footing and went undefeated the rest of the regular season. It beat Indiana comfortably in the first round of the CFP and then beat Georgia in the quarterfinals before rallying to edge Penn State in the semifinals.

"I think when they beat Georgia, I texted him and I'm like, 'You know we're going to play each other, right?'" Laurinaitis said. "I just had this odd, eerie feeling that it was going to happen. It was awful and great all in one. You want him to have the experience of winning one as a head coach and bringing one back to Notre Dame. They haven't had one in forever.

"But then you're like, 'Okay, but I don't want them to do it against me.' The competitor in you is that you're always trying to beat your boy. It doesn't matter how much you're friends. If we're competing, I'm trying to win."

Laurinaitis called Freeman before the game, and they met on the Mercedes-Benz field before the game with Jim Tressel, their coach at Ohio State. They marveled that after all these years, they would share the same field for the championship game.

OHIO STATE WAS an 8½-point favorite over Notre Dame. Just as Ohio State plucked Will Howard out of the transfer portal largely because of his experience and leadership, Notre Dame had welcomed former Duke quarterback Riley Leonard as a transfer for the same reason. Though Leonard wasn't a great passer, he was a rugged runner and indefatigable leader.

Neither team would be at full strength, not surprising for teams playing their 16th game. Notre Dame's star cornerback Benjamin Morrison was out with a hip injury. The Irish had linemen on both sides of the ball who would miss the game. Perhaps the most significant was the absence of left tackle Anthonie Knapp because of an ankle sprain suffered against Penn State. Charles Jagusah, who missed the first 13 games because of torn pectoral muscle and played guard against Penn State, would replace him. Workhorse running back Jeremiyah Love, who averaged 7.1 yards per carry, had a knee injury but said he was close to being fully healthy.

Ohio State, of course, was without left tackle Josh Simmons and Seth McLaughlin, and others on both sides of the line were gutting it out. Defensive tackle Tyleik Williams said he played much of the season at 80 percent because of a core muscle injury. Right tackle Josh Fryar battled through high ankle sprains on both ankles and a shoulder injury. He estimated he was playing at 65 percent.

"He was certainly dealing with a lot of stuff," Donovan Jackson said. "To play the way he did was major because we didn't have anybody else. I told Fryar, 'You can be hurt on the 21st. For the 20th, you're going to be just fine.'"

January 20 was Inauguration Day and Martin Luther King Jr. Day. For Ryan Day, it was also the anniversary of his father's death. "When I saw the game was going to be that day, I knew that was going to be a special day for me, a significant day," he said. "The day of, I tried not to give it too much attention because the focus was the game."

Day liked how his team matched up against Notre Dame. The Buckeyes respected the Irish, but they didn't fear them. Day had much admiration for Al Golden, Notre Dame's defensive coordinator. Golden had given Day his first job as a position coach at Temple and was disappointed with the criticism Day had gotten after the Michigan game. "He's a great coach," Golden said. "He's a tremendous father. He's a great husband, and he's a leader of men. I'm happy for him."

The Irish prided themselves on their man-to-man pass coverage. With Smith, Egbuka, and Tate, Ohio State wondered whether Notre Dame would stick with man-to-man or use more zone coverage. Howard said Ohio State was diligent in preparing for both. "Most of our plays for man had built-in alerts for zone," Howard said. "I felt really, really good about our game plan. I knew there wasn't anything they could throw at us to throw us off."

Ohio State also decided to use more zone blocking in the run game. "We liked our matchups of their front compared to ours, especially inside," Jackson said.

On offense, Notre Dame ran the ball well, but the Buckeyes didn't think a one-dimensional attack could beat them. Ohio State had yielded the third-fewest rushing yards per game (89.9) and held opponents to 2.7 yards per carry.

THEN THE GAME began, and it couldn't have started worse for the Buckeyes. Before the game, Day asked Mickey Marotti about the start of the CFP title game against Oregon 10 years earlier. Marotti told him the Ducks used their quick-tempo offense to slice through the OSU defense for a touchdown on their opening drive. Oregon didn't even face a single a third down. "I remember our defensive players coming off the field [huffing and puffing], like, 'Oh God, we're going to get freaking smoked,'" Marotti said. Then the Buckeyes settled in and shut down the Ducks most of the rest of the way in a 42–20 romp.

The first Notre Dame drive felt more like slow-motion torture. The Irish got the opening kickoff and converted twice on third down and twice on fourth down, both on keepers by Leonard. The quarterback finally punched it in from 1 on his ninth carry of the 18-play, 75-yard drive. The possession consumed nine minutes and 45 seconds.

"It was terrible," Jack Sawyer said. "I gave one of the best speeches I ever gave in my life before we ran out there. It was to the defense. I let everyone know this is the last time I get to wear the scarlet and gray with the brothers I love and would die for. What's it going to look like? What are you going to do the last time you put this uniform on for all the marbles?"

It had been a disastrous start, but Sawyer knew the Buckeyes had taken Notre Dame's best punch. He and others on the team didn't believe the Irish could sustain it. Day had an explanation for the first drive. He said that because his defensive linemen were battling injuries, he backed off that week on the physical practices the Buckeyes normally had.

"When you don't practice in pads and hit as much during the week, sometimes it takes a little while to get into the rhythm of the game," Day said. "That's kind of what happened."

But that didn't make Notre Dame's first drive easier to stomach. When Sawyer got to the sideline, Day told him the defense was getting its ass kicked. Day said Sawyer replied that it was only the interior linemen who got pushed around. But when Sawyer looked at the iPad to review the drive, he realized otherwise. "He came back and said, 'Well, damn coach, you're right,'" Day said.

"That drive sucked," Cody Simon said, "but I do think it put us in a spot where we knew that was their best shot. We didn't know it at the time, but the quarterback was hurting."

When Leonard got to the bench, he was gasping for air and threw up. "I don't know how he made it through that first drive because he was getting hit," Sonny Styles said. "He's a super tough kid. I'm a huge fan of him."

For the Buckeyes, it was the first time in the playoff that they trailed. That put the onus on the offense to answer and give the defense time to rest. It did. Jeremiah Smith caught a pass and used his strength to lunge for a first down to avoid an OSU three-and-out, and TreVeyon Henderson broke a 19-yard run. Quinshon Judkins turned a swing pass into a 15-yard gain and Howard ran to convert a third-and-3 on the last play of the first quarter.

On second-and-5 from the Notre Dame 8, Chip Kelly reached into his bag of tricks. Smith lined up alone to the right. Cornerback Christian Gray thought he'd diagnosed what was coming from film study of the Oregon game in the Rose Bowl and frantically started pointing. When Smith went in motion toward the backfield, Gray anticipated that Smith would keep going, and he ran to the other side of the field. But it was a fake. Smith stopped and reversed back to his right. Howard lobbed him the ball and Smith jogged into the end zone for an easy touchdown to tie the score.

"We started to establish the line of scrimmage early on," Day said, "and the third-down pass to Jeremiah [was key]. It was like a deep breath because you don't want guys to start pressing. Because we were able to answer like that and get the offense rolling, everyone's like, 'Okay, we're going to score some points in this game.'"

Now it was the defense's turn. On the sideline after the first Notre Dame drive, Day and Larry Johnson challenged the linemen with a simple message: "Stop being soft." J.T. Tuimoloau said of the message, "Why are we playing soft? This is not Ohio State Silver Bullet level. We got the honest, brutal answer from coach Day and coach J, and we had to fix it. There was no, 'Hey, let's make adjustments and put more people in the box.' No, it was, 'Are you going to be soft? Are you going to be a man?'"

The defense responded. Notre Dame didn't get another first down the rest of the half, gaining a total of three yards in seven plays. Penalties on Notre Dame's second possession doomed that drive. The Buckeyes even got a holding call when Jagusah was flagged for grabbing Tyleik Williams, the first such penalty called on an OSU opponent since September. The next possession was a three-and-out when Notre Dame's snap glanced off tight end Mitchell Evans, who had gone in motion.

"Guys started getting into the flow of the game," Jim Knowles said. "You need a couple stops and now their confidence level is up. They played a little freer. The cream rises to the top, and they start to play like the No. 1 defense in the country."

Meanwhile, Ohio State's offense kept rolling. The Buckeyes went 76 yards in 10 plays to take the lead. Emeka Egbuka broke the OSU record for career catches with 202 when he caught a pass and lowered his shoulder for a first down at the Irish 20. Judkins capped the drive when he fended off a would-be tackler at the line of scrimmage, made a nifty jump-cut and powered into the end zone for a nine-yard score.

"I was just coming downhill. I saw the linebacker," Judkins said. "I was like, 'He can't get me in a one-on-one position.' That's something I'm going to win 100 percent of the time, so I stiff-armed him, bounced it outside, and then I saw the end zone."

Ohio State made it 21–7 at halftime with an 80-yard drive. Howard hung in the pocket under pressure to hit Brandon Inniss for a 19-yard gain on third-and-7 to start the drive. Tate had a 20-yard catch and Smith a 15-yarder. At that point, Howard had completed his first 13 passes. The Buckeyes cashed in on second-and-goal from the 6 when Howard scrambled to buy time and found Judkins open in the end zone with

27 seconds left in the second quarter. That play came against the zone, which the Irish played much of in the first half. Neither zone nor man coverage slowed the Buckeyes. When halftime came after one perfunctory Notre Dame snap, the Buckeyes waved their arms in jubilation as they ran toward their locker room. Victory was within their grasp, and they knew it.

Laurinaitis wanted to make sure it didn't slip away. "You have 30 minutes to be remembered for the rest of your lives, to be linked together for eternity," he told the Buckeyes.

THE WAY THE SECOND HALF started, it looked like there would be little drama for the Buckeyes. On the second snap after the kickoff, Judkins ran through a hole created by Carlos Hinzman and Tshabola for a 70-yard gain before being tackled at the 5.

"That's what you dream of as a kid—to be in that moment," Judkins said. "I saw the linebackers shift over. I took it back door and went through my progressions and reads."

Judkins said he got caught from behind because he'd run a long way on a wheel route on first down. "I was a little tired," he said.

Two plays later, Judkins scored from the 1 for his third score and a 28–7 lead. Ohio State's defense continued its dominance on Notre Dame's next possession. Denzel Burke made a third-down tackle two yards short of the first-down marker on third down. Freeman sent out the punt team, but no one was surprised that the Irish tried a fake. Jordan Faison couldn't make the catch on a low throw and OSU took over at the Notre Dame 33. After a holding call on Fryar, Howard's pass to Tate in the end zone was a tad too far. Jayden Fielding then kicked a 46-yard field goal to make it 31–7 midway through the third quarter.

Notre Dame seemed dead. The Irish had little success running the ball, gaining only 53 yards on the ground all game and only nine yards after the opening drive. Jeremiyah Love had only four carries and gained just three yards. But the Irish would show their grit, aided by some Buckeye mistakes. On third-and-19 after a sack by Sonny Styles, Leonard threw a pass to Evans that drew a pass-interference call on Davison Igbinosun. The Irish capitalized when receiver Jaden Greathouse caught a short pass and broke tackles by Jermaine Mathews and, remarkably, Caleb Downs for a 34-yard touchdown. Until then, Leonard had completed only nine of 15 passes for 63 yards. Notre Dame converted the two-point conversion on a shovel pass to Love to make it a two-possession game at 31–15.

On the first play of the fourth quarter, Howard threw to Egbuka, who weaved into the open field. But Drayk Bowen knocked the ball from his grasp just before the receiver's knee hit the turf. Notre Dame recovered at its 21. It was Ohio State's first lost fumble since Howard's at the goal line of the Penn State game.

"I remember saying to Emeka [between quarters], 'There's only one thing that matters right now: You come back with the ball in your hands,'" Day said. "Sure enough, the ball comes out. It was like the only thing that could happen for us to lose the game right now is for something like this to happen. But we love Emeka, and nobody was more hurt than he was. That's football. We're in the national championship. This isn't going to be that easy."

Leonard connected with Greathouse for a 30-yard catch, and the Irish drove to the OSU 9 before Jordan Hancock broke up a third-down pass with 9½ minutes to go. Freeman then made a curious decision on fourth-and-9. Needing two touchdowns and a pair of two-point conversions, Freeman decided to kick a field goal.

"I was surprised," Day acknowledged.

That questionable decision backfired when Mitch Jeter's 27-yard field goal attempt hooked and doinked off the left upright. But the Irish kept battling. Howard was off target on a third-down pass to Smith, forcing a punt. Evans caught a pass and ran for a 33-yard gain, and Greathouse got behind Hancock for a 30-yard touchdown. The Irish ran a trick play on the two-point conversion, and it worked. Faison took a pitch and then threw to an open Beaux Collins in the end zone after OSU bit on the fake.

"We hadn't played that much man coverage going into that game," Knowles said. "We played some, but going into that game, we certainly felt we had good matchups on the outside. We felt the quarterback wasn't a great thrower. But I give [Leonard] credit. He was just one of those guys who was going to find a way. Tough as hell. Competitive. All of a sudden, he started making these great throws."

And all of a sudden, it was a one-possession game with 4:10 left. A victory that seemed a foregone conclusion a few minutes earlier was no sure thing. But the Buckeyes had one final answer.

28

An Amazing Finish

Ohio State had been in a similar situation against Penn State and ran out the clock with its run game. "We wanted to get a couple of first downs to have them use their timeouts inside the two-minute warning," Ryan Day said. "We obviously knew we had to run the ball, and they loaded up the box."

Quinshon Judkins ran for three yards and Will Howard got a first down on an eight-yard keeper. But two more Howard runs went nowhere. OSU faced third-and-11 with 2:45 left. Would Day be conservative and rely on his defense, or go for the kill shot? He already knew the answer. "We go through all these scenarios, especially when you have 10 days to prepare," Day said.

One of the options was a deep ball to Jeremiah Smith, who was being covered by Christian Gray. "If they're going to play man, with the game on the line, are we willing to do it?" Day said. "And everybody said yes. We said if you can win the national championship by throwing a go ball to Jeremiah, would everybody be on board with it? So when we get the third down, the decision's already been made."

In truth, Day wanted to go deep to Smith two plays earlier. "We'd seen a little stuff on film where they weren't necessarily super worried about getting hit deep over the top on longer-distance third downs," Howard said. "We had that play call in all week, and coach Day wanted to call it on first down."

Smith hadn't touched the ball in the second half. He was ready for this play—Dos Left 073 Grill. "We practiced that I don't know how many times," Smith said. "We repped it over and over against that style of corner, that technique. At first, we couldn't really get it down pat in practice, but then coach Hartline gave me extra little tips on the way he wanted me to align. In Notre Dame's semifinal against Penn State, Gray made a game-clinching interception on a dig route. Coach Hartline said to attack his leverage and bury him inside and then fade back out," Smith said.

Howard's job was to make sure Notre Dame was in the coverage he expected and if so, throw the ball 42 yards. "When that play call comes in, I'm like, 'Oh shit. Let's go,'" Howard said. "I was so turned up to throw that go ball. I see No. 29 [Gray]. His hips are [facing] inside. He's looking at me. He's trying to mess with me and make me think they're in zone, and I'm like, 'Oh, this clown has no idea what's about to hit him.' If they don't put a safety up over top of him, this thing is going up."

Notre Dame left Gray alone on Smith and brought a blitz. TreVeyon Henderson did what he normally did in pass-protection—stop the blitzer cold. The other linemen blocked their men, allowing Howard to get the ball off in rhythm.

The ball seemed to hang in the air forever as Smith ran toward and then past Gray. He caught the ball at the 28-yard line, and Gray couldn't drag him down until Smith was at the 10 for a 56-yard gain. "There was no doubt in my mind he was making that play," Howard said, "and I knew I put it in a good place." Howard had come a long way from spring practice and even well into the season when he often underthrew receivers on deep balls.

For Smith, the play capped a magical season. "My only intention was to catch the ball," Smith said. "I didn't even really care about scoring. It was exciting knowing I'm about to win a national championship as a freshman. It's something you dream of as a kid, something I've been thinking about since I first got here, so it was a blessing."

The championship hadn't been completely secured yet. The Buckeyes milked the clock with run plays until only 28 seconds remained. It would be Jayden Fielding's job to ice it. Notre Dame had blocked six kicks during the season, but Day didn't mention that to Fielding. Day didn't want to put any negative thoughts in his kicker's head.

As Fielding prepared to kick, Day thought of his father and that this was the anniversary of his death. Two years earlier on the same field, Ohio State's semifinal against Georgia came down to a 50-yard field goal by Noah Ruggles. "I remember in the Georgia game when Noah was kicking that, I remember thinking to myself—not asking or saying anything—but just thinking, 'Hey, Dad, give me some help here.'"

Ruggles missed that kick, denying the Buckeyes a chance for a national championship. Now Day thought about his dad again. "It was something that just hit my mind," he said. "Give me a little help here. When you get to these moments where you're like, 'Okay, this is going to make or break my career, our career,' certain things come to your mind. The more you coach, the more you realize when those moments are."

This time, the Buckeyes wouldn't be denied. Long-snapper John Ferlmann's snap was perfect. Holder Joe McGuire caught and placed the ball cleanly. Fielding's kick flirted at first with the right goalpost but hooked through the uprights to make it 34–23. "Oh my God, we just won the national championship," he remembers thinking. "I was going to run over to coach Day and hug him because that's what Jack did after the strip sack. Then I saw Brandon Inniss running toward me, and I just jumped into him. It was crazy."

Day was thrilled for his kicker. He knew how Fielding had suffered after the Michigan loss. He'd put him through the wringer in his pre-CFP battle with Austin Snyder to keep his job. "You've got to go through tough times," Day said. "You've got to go through tough shit. And he did go through that because those two misses in the Up North game crushed him. But we all told him we wouldn't have put him out there if we didn't believe in him. I knew he was going to make it. I felt strongly about it."

After the field goal, Day pulled off his headset and threw it in celebration, though he has only vague memories of doing so. When Nina saw it, she knew what it represented. "When Ryan chucked that headset, it just released all the pressure that had been built up," she said.

During the game's final seconds, Josh Fryar and Carson Hinzman grabbed the Gatorade cooler and dumped the drink on Day. Fryar then gave Day a bear hug, lifting him off the ground. "I said, 'We did it for you and I love you, coach,'" Fryar said.

Notre Dame ran two final plays. After Jordan Hancock tackled Jaden Greathouse at the Irish 40 as time expired, the Buckeyes spilled onto the field to celebrate. "I don't think there's a feeling that compares to that," Tyleik Williams said. "I don't know how to put it into words, but it was just relief. You finally won something for Ohio State, for the state of Ohio. It was just a great feeling. All the guys I came in with, that's the goal we sought after [losing to Georgia in] 2023."

Amid the jubilation, Fielding took a moment to find and console Mitch Jeter, the Notre Dame kicker who missed the 27-yard field goal. "I told him, 'I've been there before, man. It's all right. Things get better,'" Fielding said.

AS THE CONFETTI fell and the stage was set up for the postgame trophy presentation, Day was just trying to process the moment. He had gone through almost indescribable lows and highs in seven weeks. He had worked almost nonstop to give his players a chance for validation and a tangible reward for their work and perseverance. Day was overjoyed for them. He was also relieved for his family.

"I remember going into the game asking God, 'Just give me some peace. Give my family some peace,'" Day said. "Every time you pray, you're either asking for something or you're thanking. In that moment, I was asking because what I really wanted for the family was peace. I knew once that field goal went through, we were going to get a little peace. Not for very long, but at least a little bit."

Nina Day was surprised by the lack of emotion she felt. The weeks since the Michigan game had been brutal. Despite all the faith she had in her husband, it was hard to process that Ohio State had really won the national title. "It took a few days for it to hit me," she said. "I thought I'd be bawling my eyes out. I didn't feel anything. It was an out-of-body experience. I don't remember a lot of it. I wish I felt more, but I was so numb, like I was afraid it was a dream. I remember looking up at the confetti and asking myself, 'Is this real?' Like, 'Am I going to wake up right now?'"

She does remember her husband saying, "We did it," after she said, "You did it."

"It took all of us to stay strong and stay the course and stay steady in the boat," she said, using one of Ryan Day's pet phrases. "He says to this day he probably couldn't have done it if we didn't stay as strong as we did and believe in him."

Ohio State's team leaders assembled on the stage to be interviewed by ESPN's Rece Davis. Howard, who finished 17 of 21 for 231 yards and ran for 57 important yards, was named the offensive player of the game. "I'm just so glad that God gave me a chance to be a Buckeye," he said.

Cody Simon, who had a team-high eight tackles, was named the defensive player of the game. Then it was time for the Buckeyes to finally put their hands on the CFP championship trophy. J.T. Tuimoloau, Lathan Ransom, Emeka Egbuka, Gee Scott Jr., and Day grabbed it and raised it high, with Day yelling in elation. They then passed it around like the Stanley Cup to Jack Sawyer, Jordan Hancock, Tyleik Williams, Donovan Jackson, and others.

Mickey Marotti was one of the few who'd been with Ohio State when the Buckeyes won the 2014 title. What stood out to him the most about the celebration on this night was the emotion of Egbuka. "He hugged me, and he hugged coach Day," Marotti said. "He hugged coach Hartline, bawling his eyes out. It was just exuberance and probably some relief. It was catharsis. He was squeezing and squeezing and squeezing. I can remember it vividly. It was so cool."

James Laurinaitis gave Marcus Freeman a brief hug. Freeman congratulated him. "Happy for you, Jimmy," Freeman told him.

Laurinaitis said few people other than Freeman call him that. "I hate being called Jimmy," he said. "That's why he does it."

After his moment consoling his Notre Dame counterpart, Jayden Fielding found his parents. The emotion poured out of him. "When I saw my mom, I just started crying," he said, "because she was there for me when it was really bad, and so was my dad. They knew how much stress was on me and how much that [Michigan] game took out of me. To bounce back from that and go on the playoff run we did and winning it all—and the way it happened with the [clinching] field goal—it was just the perfect story."

THE NIGHT'S DRAMA wasn't quite over for Ryan Day. He got into the front seat of a golf cart to be taken to the postgame press conference with Will Howard and Cody Simon in the back. A young woman was the driver. She stopped when Day saw Kenny Wilson, the father of former Buckeye star receiver Garrett Wilson, on the field. Day and Kenny Wilson are close, and Day got out of the cart to give him a hug.

"Well, I get back in the cart, and she guns it and just about takes his knee out," Day said. "At that point, I was like, 'Oh my gosh.' It was like a James Bond movie. I felt as we were driving like we were out of control."

When they got to the concourse, the cart stopped briefly. Then the driver tried to make a sharp left turn near the wall. "I was like, 'Oh boy, I don't think we have enough room,' and she hit it flush," Day said.

The impact must have damaged the cart because the driver couldn't put it in reverse. Howard and Simon were laughing hysterically as they got out of the cart to walk to the press conference. Day didn't find it quite as funny. He was freezing because his clothes were still wet and sticky from the Gatorade bath. Now he'd come close to being injured.

"If my foot was outside the cart," he said, "it could have gotten trapped between the cart and the wall, which would have been a bad, bad situation. I just remember thinking to myself, 'This has become the most stressful part of the night.'"

Day went to the locker room, where he held up the gold-painted brick that was the crowning piece of the pyramid they started in training camp. He didn't stay long because the air was thick with cigar smoke. "We were hotboxing that locker room," Seth McLaughlin said.

One Buckeye who didn't partake was Jeremiah Smith. He took a cigar and put it close to his mouth but not in it. "The way I grew up, my parents always told me, 'Don't do that type of thing. It's bad for your health,'" he said.

He wouldn't make an exception even for an occasion as momentous as this. Even before that, Smith wouldn't fully celebrate the championship right away, according to Hartline. On one play during the game, Smith ran the wrong route. When Hartline yelled at him, Smith's head dropped. After the game, Hartline said, Smith was a bit reserved until he saw Chip Kelly and apologized for the missed assignment.

"I was laughing," Kelly said. "I said, 'J.J., I don't even know what you're talking about right now. But congratulations.' I freaking love that kid. He's just wired different in such a good way. But that's what made that whole group so special. They had attention to detail in all the little things that you as a coach want."

It took a while for Ross Bjork to see Day after the game. When they did, Bjork told him how proud he was of that the team had accomplished and how they'd represented the university and how all the adversity was meant to be. Day thanked Bjork for his public support after the Michigan loss.

After leaving the stadium, the celebration continued at the team hotel for Day with family and friends. At one point, Jack Sawyer and his family visited. Jim Knowles also had friends and family in Atlanta, including his 85-year-old high school coach, Jack Branka. Knowles made sure another retired coaching friend, Kip Cramer, was able to attend. "I really tried to share the moment with people who had been close to me throughout my life," Knowles said.

NOBODY GOT MUCH sleep that night. At the next morning's press conference, Day, Howard, and Simon reflected on the journey the Buckeyes had been on. Simon recalled the decision the seniors had made a year earlier to return for a final chance at glory they'd now achieved.

"They came back for the love of the brotherhood and the appreciation for the culture and all their teammates," he said. "I think that story is about determination, resilience, humility, just thankfulness, faithfulness—just everything good that comes out of a team game and a team sport. I think our team has showed it this year."

The team arrived back in Columbus later that day. When the Days got to their house, Day saw one of the security officers who'd been stationed there since the Michigan game. With a national championship won, the hell the family experienced after the Michigan game had been replaced by joy and relief.

"I think you can go home now," Day told the security officer.

29

Celebration and Departures

What no one knew the night of the championship was that it would be Jim Knowles' last game coaching at Ohio State. Rumors had already begun swirling that Knowles had been given lucrative offers. One was reportedly from the University of Oklahoma. On the field after the game, a reporter asked Knowles if there was any truth to the scuttlebutt.

"I am coaching at Ohio State," he said.

At the time, Knowles said months later, he believed he would remain with the Buckeyes. "Of course," he said. "Absolutely."

Knowles said he'd been offered jobs after the 2023 season and wouldn't even consider them because the veteran players had declared they would return, and Knowles didn't want to leave them. "I'm not even interested in talking to anybody," Knowles said of his mindset after that season. "Those guys coming back, it was validation and faith in me that we could do something special. And we did it. I don't know how you get better than that—No. 1 defense and you win the national championship."

Now that he had reached the pinnacle, he decided to at least listen to offers. He was quite in demand. Michigan defensive coordinator Wink

Martindale was the highest-paid defensive coordinator in college football in 2024 with a salary of $2.5 million. Martindale's contract called for him to make $2.75 million in 2025. Ohio State made it known that it was willing to offer Knowles an extension worth more than that. So were other programs.

"I think it was great for the profession, kind of resetting the whole market," Knowles said.

For him, Penn State had a special allure. He grew up in Philadelphia as a Nittany Lions fan, though his family couldn't afford to travel to games. Their coordinator, former Indiana coach Tom Allen, had left for Clemson. Most of Penn State's veterans had decided to return for the 2025 season in hopes of doing what Ohio State had just done. Knowles would turn 60 before the season. If this was his final job, why not try to replicate the success you just had for the team you grew up rooting for?

Ross Bjork said that after Ohio State made Knowles an offer, it didn't hear back from him. Asked if OSU would have matched Penn State's offer of $3.1 million per year, Bjork said, "We never had an opportunity to do that. I don't know if we would have because the opportunity was never presented."

Knowles disputed that. "Yeah, that's not true," he said. "There were discussions. They did make an offer, but it wasn't at the same level of Penn State or some others, to be honest with you, which I'm not going to get into. There were multiple offers at that level. Ohio State was not there and basically said, 'Here's our offer and this is as high as we're going to go.'"

Would Knowles have stayed if Ohio State had matched Penn State's offer? "I can't speculate because it didn't happen," Knowles said, "but it certainly could have changed things."

Knowles' status was in limbo for several days after the title game on Monday. Ohio State had announced it would hold a celebration for the team on Saturday at the Horseshoe. That made for a potentially awkward situation. Ohio State wanted Knowles to decide about his future before the celebration. If he wasn't going to remain with the Buckeyes, Bjork concluded, it would be better if he didn't attend.

"The conversation was, 'Hey, we need to know,'" Bjork said. "If you don't want to be here, that's fine. Everybody has a right to [leave]. Just tell us. I know coach Day, and he had that conversation: Tell us if you're going to be our coach or not. If you're not, then that's fine, [but] you probably shouldn't come to the celebration."

Knowles said he was not given such an ultimatum. "It was more, 'Hey, with all the speculation out there, we think it would be a distraction for you to attend,'" he said. "It was not, 'Hey, make your decision and you can come.'"

On the day of the celebration, Knowles said, he was still trying to decide whether to take the Penn State offer. He had gone to Oklahoma to see his fiancée for a couple of days after the championship game and weigh his options. "I'm debating," he said. "I like it here at Ohio State. I like Columbus. You're debating whether to take less money instead. Really, that's what the debate was."

Knowles abided by Ohio State's request not to come to the celebration. The celebration was for the players, he said, and didn't want to be a distraction. "It certainly is sobering to be like, 'Okay, now I'm not even allowed to go to the celebration,'" Knowles said. "It's tough, but they're doing what they think is best for their program, and I want what's best for the players, so I know that."

The next day, Knowles accepted the Penn State job. Ryan Day said he was disappointed in Knowles' decision but grateful for the job he did in his three years at Ohio State. "When Jim got here, the defense wasn't in a great place, and when he left, it was," Day said. "We had a very experienced defense, and I think they believed in the defense and liked the defense. There's no question that in the last two years he did an excellent job."

After he left, there was speculation about a supposed rift between Knowles and Larry Johnson, something both coaches strongly denied.

"I don't listen to any of that, good or bad," Knowles said. "Of course, I had heard that was out there, but Larry and I never even spoke about it [because] it wasn't the reality. We worked together fine. I have tremendous respect for what he does. He's legendary."

Johnson has always used a four-man front. When Knowles came to Ohio State, he tried using a hybrid defensive end/linebacker known as the "Jack." Knowles tried Jack Sawyer at that spot as a sophomore, and it didn't work. The next two years, Knowles didn't use a jack.

"But that was not anything to do with Larry," Knowles said. "That was more of just me saying, 'You know what, this doesn't work here.' That's not how we're built. That's not how we recruit. I think Larry is great at what he does. He and I always had a good relationship."

Johnson said Knowles sent him a complimentary text message after taking the Penn State job, repeating the legendary comment and saying he enjoyed working with him. "We have great respect for each other," Johnson said. "That has always been the case."

Some also speculated that Knowles took Day's mandate that OSU make defensive changes after the first Oregon game as a slap in the face. Knowles denied that as well. "My ego wasn't bruised," he said. "You have a subpar game, you've got to answer for it. I didn't take it in any way as [having] a bruised ego. I just wanted to get it right. That had nothing to do with [me leaving]."

A WEEK LATER, Ohio State's other coordinator also left. But Chip Kelly's departure did not catch Day off guard. Day said there was always an understanding that Kelly's time in Columbus would be short term.

"I sensed that when I got here last spring," Bjork said. "Not that Chip ever said, 'I'm only going to be here one year.'"

But the fact he'd achieved what he set out to accomplish at Ohio State made it easier to leave. Like Knowles, Kelly didn't attend the stadium celebration, but for a different reason. He left the day before for a week-long trip recruiting quarterbacks. During that trip, he said, he got calls from two NFL teams about coordinator positions. He didn't specify the first team. The other was the Las Vegas Raiders, which had hired Pete Carroll as head coach. He interviewed with the Raiders that Saturday.

"I went into it with very open eyes," Kelly said. "I've always looked at every decision I've made in my life in terms of what is the next step, what does this opportunity present, and is it better than the opportunity I have?

"I know Pete. I coached against him [when Carroll was at USC]. Talking to him about his vision and then having Tom Brady as an owner with Mark Davis was a big deal. It just felt like the right time. I felt like maybe because we won it, I felt I could leave and wouldn't feel like I let somebody down. It was the right opportunity at the right time."

Kelly's previous coaching stints in the NFL didn't end well. He said that's not what drove his decision. It was more that he wanted to compete again at the highest level. There are no gimme games in the NFL, and that appealed to Kelly. He also has family on the West Coast, which contributed to his decision.

"I went to Ohio State and had an amazing experience and loved the people I worked with," he said. "The hardest thing is not to be with Keenan [Bailey] and Hart [Brian Hartline] and those guys. But to me, it's always been about challenges. What's the next challenge so when you wake up every day and you've got a purpose and a challenge that gets your butt going."

Offensive line coach Justin Frye also left for the Arizona Cardinals. He had often faced criticism for failing to sign elite prospects, but the job he did getting a makeshift line to play at a championship level during the playoff silenced much of that. Ohio State started nine different offensive linemen in 2024.

"I think he had kind of an itch for maybe a different lifestyle with family, more balance, [no] recruiting," Bjork said. "He's got [four] younger kids."

Day hired Matt Patricia, who was a part of the New England Patriots' dynasty under Bill Belichick, to replace Knowles as defensive coordinator and promoted cornerbacks coach Tim Walton to co-coordinator. Day promoted Brian Hartline to offensive coordinator. Hartline was expected to be a play caller in 2025 unlike his previous one-year stint as coordinator in 2023. Tyler Bowen was hired away from Virginia Tech to be the offensive line coach.

IN THIS AGE of almost unfettered player movement in college football, it's no surprise that other programs wanted to pluck Ohio State's players. A few left. Devin Brown transferred to Cal. Hero Kanu went to Texas. Mitchell Melton left for Virginia. The biggest prize was uninterested in leaving. After his sensational freshman season, Jeremiah Smith could have broken the bank if he'd decided to consider transferring. Other teams tried to pry him loose.

"I don't really want to get into details, but there were some pretty crazy offers, for sure," Smith said. "A lot of schools were hitting my agent up, trying to get me in the transfer portal. But why would I do that? That's something dumb. We just won a national championship. Why not be able to run it back for another year? It wasn't something that was even on my mind. I'm a Buckeye for life."

Most of Ohio State's departing seniors reunited three times after scattering across the country to train for the NFL draft. Fifteen Buckeyes were invited to the NFL combine in Indianapolis. Ohio State then had its pro day in late March. The final reunion was at the White House on April 14.

"I grew up watching championship teams go to the White House," Day said. "It's been a great tradition for so long, so when we had the opportunity, our leaders wanted to do it and so we were excited about the opportunity to do that."

Day said politics were not an issue. "When you bring a whole team in, there are mixed bags in terms of political beliefs," Day said. "But what everyone did that day was put their politics aside and just enjoy the opportunity to be a part of history."

Groups of players took turns visiting the Oval Office and other rooms in the White House. Day said he was surprised that many who work in the White House are from Ohio. The pastry chef, Susan Morrison, is from Bay Village near Cleveland. Day said she wore Ohio State sneakers. The most famous Ohioan there was Vice President J.D. Vance, and he made headlines when he lifted the national championship trophy, and the base fell to the ground. Fortunately, TreVeyon Henderson was able to grab the trophy itself, so it didn't fall.

"It's funny that a lot of people grab that trophy, they think it's all one [piece]," Day said. "It's a good thing that base didn't fall and break someone's toe because that's a heavy base."

Though in his remarks President Donald Trump referred to Will Howard as the "Tennessee quarterback" and mispronounced the names of TreVeyon Henderson, Emeka Egbuka, and Carson Hinzman, it was a special event for the team. "It was a great experience," Day said. "We were treated very well."

Two weeks later in the NFL draft, 14 Buckeyes were selected, tying the school record set in 2004 when the bulk of the 2002 title team turned pro. Four Buckeyes—Egbuka, Donovan Jackson, Tyleik Williams, and Josh Simmons—were taken in the first round. Egbuka went 19th overall to Tampa Bay, followed by Jackson to Minnesota, Williams to Detroit, and Simmons to Kansas City.

The Cleveland Browns picked Quinshon Judkins early in the second round. TreVeyon Henderson was taken two picks later by New England. The picks fulfilled Carlos Locklyn's preseason prediction that both backs would surpass 1,000 yards rushing (which happened against Notre Dame), win a national championship, and be early round draft choices. J.T. Tuimoloau also went in the second round to Indianapolis. Cody Simon went in the fourth round to Arizona, who took Denzel Burke a round later, as the cornerback headed to his hometown team. Lathan

Ransom was picked by Carolina and Jack Sawyer by Pittsburgh. The Los Angeles Rams selected Ty Hamilton in the fifth round. Jordan Hancock went in the same round to Buffalo. The last of the 14 was Will Howard, who will remain teammates with Sawyer with the Steelers. If not for Seth McLaughlin being unselected because of his torn Achilles, the Buckeyes would have tied the record of 15 held by Georgia in 2022 for most players drafted from a single school.

Players would scatter around the country, but what they'd accomplished together would follow them forever.

30
What It Meant

The 2024 Buckeyes had gone through the lowest of lows and the highest of highs. The loss to Michigan had devastated them and put everything in jeopardy—their OSU legacy and possibly Ryan Day's future. Instead, the meeting afterward united the team. They confronted their failures and weakness. They resolved to redeem themselves in the playoff. It's an unanswerable question, of course, but would the Buckeyes have done what they did in the playoff if they had not suffered such a defeat against their archrival? It's sacrilegious at Ohio State to even ponder the possibility that a loss to Michigan could be a blessing in disguise. But it might have been.

"I feel everything happens for a reason," Donovan Jackson said. "I can't give you a what-if scenario. All I know is what happened, and it sucks that happened. I wish it didn't. But we were able to come together as a team, and the coaches were able to put together a great plan surrounding the strengths of our offense."

Cody Simon agreed. He said the defensive changes made after the October loss to Oregon and the lessons from the Michigan upset were instrumental in the postseason run. "I don't want to give an answer saying,

'No, we wouldn't have won it,'" Simon said. "I don't think that's true. I think we're the sum of all our experiences. If we win those games, you run the risk of believing your own hype a little bit. I don't want to say that we wouldn't have won. I think we were the best team, and we were capable of winning every single game we played. But certainly the losses were important for us because we really had to take a lot of time to reevaluate what we do and how we approach our daily life and our football and our practices and our game plans."

If Ohio State had beaten Michigan and won the Big Ten, the Buckeyes would have received a first-round bye, so the path to the championship would have been different. Would the same determined, angry team have showed up?

"I don't think we would have had as strong of a purpose as we did, if that makes any sense," Day said. "We still want to win. But when you go through something like that and you want to prove it to everybody and you get so hungry and starving, you almost start to play desperate. I don't know if that same desperation would have been in our eyes if we hadn't gone through that."

All the Buckeyes knew for sure was they had gone through the toughest path possible and mostly dominated. This team faced as much pressure as any OSU team ever has. Expectations are always high for Ohio State, but every other national championship in the modern era of Buckeyes football came unexpectedly. The 1968 "Super Sophs" team started the year ranked No. 11. The 2002 team was ranked 13th in the preseason. In 2014, the Buckeyes were ranked No. 5 in the preseason, dropped to No. 8 before the first game after Braxton Miller's season-ending injury, and were No. 22 following the loss to Virginia Tech.

Twelve times since 1969, Ohio State has started the season ranked No. 1 or No. 2. None of those teams won the national championship. The modern history of Buckeye football is mostly one of great teams that couldn't reach the finish line. The 24–12 loss to Michigan in 1969 ignited the Ten-Year War between Woody Hayes and Bo Schembechler.

The Archie Griffin–led teams of the 1970s fell short. So did several of the ultra-talented teams under John Cooper in the 1990s. Jim Tressel's teams lost the consecutive national title games in 2006 and 2007. Urban Meyer's most talented team was probably the 2015 one. Those Buckeyes lost in the rain to a Michigan State team using backup quarterbacks. Day entered 2024 with a sterling winning percentage marred by the heart-breaking losses to Clemson in 2019, Georgia in 2022, and to Michigan.

Seniors delayed their NFL careers to give winning a national championship one final shot, and they finally delivered. "It really meant everything," Josh Fryar said. "I knew it was my last year playing college football. Everything was a culmination from my freshman year to my fifth year at Ohio State. It was a lot of pain all the way up to my fifth year. We got hit with a little bit more adversity during that season, and then it all paid off in the end."

Lathan Ransom overcame the two serious injuries earlier in his career. He pushed himself and others to live up to their promise and then was instrumental in the championship run. "It's amazing," he said. "It means so much to me, just because of how much the guys and the relationships that I built on this team changed my life. It impacted my life on and off the field. It means a lot to me that through all the adversity that we faced being with coach Day, being here through all the ups and downs, and to finally do that for his family and for him, it's been special.

"I can't wait until 10-15 years from now when I have kids of my own to come back to Ohio State, especially being a dude from Tucson, Arizona, and be able to show them what their father had a chance to help accomplish."

Like Ransom, defensive end Mitchell Melton battled back from two devastating injuries. He wasn't a starter and didn't have the Ohio State career he envisioned, but that didn't lessen his pride in what the Buckeyes accomplished. "I'd be lying if I didn't say it was probably the best time of my life," Melton said. "Figuring myself out and who I wanted to be as a part of that team was very challenging at first, but especially this last year, it was a very fulfilling process. I've known those guys for what feels like a good chunk of my life. I knew I was going to war with my brothers. It's something I've never had before. It felt like youth league or high school. It just felt like fun. That's a testament to the guys in that room who made it fun and made it easy for me to be the best version of myself and strive toward that every day."

Tegra Tshabola remembers visiting Ohio State from Cincinnati and seeing the walls of the Woody adorned with pictures of past championship teams. Now he's a part of one. "This is probably one of the most memorable national championship runs in history," he said. "The fact that I'm a part of that forever, I'll always be forever grateful. Being a kid that would claim that he was going to play for Ohio State, to doing it and doing that on that stage, there's nothing more I could have asked for."

Will Howard took a chance by coming to Ohio State as a transfer from Kansas State. He wanted to make that "rocking chair" decision, and it came to fruition largely because of his play and his charismatic leadership. "It meant the world," Howard said. "Coming to Ohio State and deciding to be a Buckeye was the best decision I've ever made in my life. It was completely life-changing to be a part of this run this year, this team, this brotherhood.

"Obviously, being 16–0 national champs would be great, but I think it makes it even more sweet when you have to go through a bunch of shit and you get better because of it. It made us a lot closer as a team. It bonded us for life. We have this national championship for life. No one can ever take this away from us."

FOR FORMER BUCKEYE players James Laurinaitis, Tim Walton, and Maurice Clarett, helping to bring a title back to Columbus in a different role was almost indescribable. Laurinaitis lost in those title games in 2006 and 2007 and exhorted his players not to finish the 2024 season with that same feeling.

"I think you're just proud of the way the guys represented the university," he said. "I was proud of the way that the leadership handled the season."

The losses to Oregon and Michigan were hard to take, he said. "But the boys stuck together, and they were so mature," Laurinaitis said. "That really helped us down the stretch. I'm proud of the leadership, proud of the brotherhood."

Walton didn't come close to winning a national title as a Buckeye player in the early 1990s, a comparatively down era in Buckeye history. He left a successful career as an NFL cornerbacks coach to return to OSU.

"It's a dream come true," Walton said. "To get a chance to come back and coach at your alma mater is a big deal. To come back and win a national championship with a great group of guys, with one of the most amazing stories in college football history in one of the greatest runs ever, and to do something that hadn't been done [at OSU] in 10 years and only three times in the last 50 is a phenomenal feat. It will last forever and be forever etched in my mind and in the hearts of the Buckeyes."

Clarett, of course, did win the title in 2002. But he said he was too young and immature to appreciate that fully. He was doing it for himself back then. In 2024, he was doing it in service to others. Being involved with this team at 41 years old after two decades of estrangement from the program made the 2024 championship even more special to him than the one he won as a player.

"One thousand percent," he said. "[Back then], you think this is the way it's supposed to be. Then you realize this isn't an everyday thing."

He was thrilled for the players who'd endured so much. He was happy for Day for bringing him out of the OSU wilderness. He was impressed by the way the team responded to the adversity it faced. "It was just tears of joy on a lot of levels," Clarett said.

FOR THE TEAM'S coordinators, the championship was the culmination of decades of coaching. Jim Knowles had begun his career at Cornell when the Ivy League didn't even compete for a Division I-AA national title.

National championships were a pipe dream at most of his other stops—Western Michigan, Duke, Ole Miss, and Oklahoma State. He had come to Ohio State to fix the defense and win it all, and now he had.

"It's something that no one, no circumstance, event, or opinion can ever take away from that team," Knowles said. "All teammates are forever, but the ones that win it all get together more often and have no regrets."

Unlike Knowles, Chip Kelly had come close to the mountaintop. He had stunning success as a coordinator before becoming a head coach and sparking an offensive revolution at Oregon. His 2010 Ducks team lost to Cam Newton's Auburn 22–19 on a last-second field goal in the BCS title game. He'd been a head coach in the NFL. He'd won conference championships and prestigious bowl games. But he'd never been part of a national championship team. Now, at age 61, he was.

Kelly said he wasn't thinking about himself in the immediate aftermath of the game. He wasn't even thinking so much about Jeremiah Smith or Howard or the other stars of the team. He said he thought about below-the-radar or underappreciated players like Fryar, Tshabola, and Brandon Inniss. He said he thought about tight ends Patrick Gurd, Jelani Thurman, and Will Kacmarek, who along with Gee Scott Jr. had made good on helping that unit answer the challenge Keenan Bailey issued about toughness at the start of spring practice.

Kelly invoked the word *mudita*, used often in Buddhism to describe feeling joy in the success and happiness of others. "Everyone had a unique role and did everything they could in their role to win that thing," Kelly said. "So many guys contributed. That's the cool part of being in football because it's such a team sport. A lot of times, one or two guys get the accolades, but it takes so many of them for it to happen. Just to see the elation from those guys was pretty cool."

KELLY WAS HAPPY most of all for his protégé. Ryan Day had overcome so much in his personal and professional life. At times, he questioned whether coaching was the right path for him, given the sacrifice it required and the toll it took on him and his family. As competitive as he is, Day doesn't regard victory as the ultimate goal. He accepts that at a program like Ohio State, winning every game is important. If you lose more than a few, you won't remain its coach. But even more meaningful, he believes, is the impact he can make on his players as they become young adults. He understands the lessons they learn through the ups and downs of their careers will make them stronger for life after football. He considers himself a teacher, but he said he also learned from his players during the 2024 season because of the way they handled all the adversity they faced.

On January 20, Day tried to put thoughts about his father and the anniversary of his suicide out of his mind as much as he could during the championship game. After the victory, he found clarity that had eluded him for so long. "When you go through something like that at a young age, it doesn't make much sense," Day said. "It's just so confusing. Now, however many years later, it all made sense why I went through it. I think that was God's way of saying to me that you wouldn't have been able to accomplish this if you didn't go through this at a young age. It took all the way until I was 45 years old to realize why that was in my path.

"It went all full circle because of the resilience and the adversity, just during this year, that we had to go through. Maybe I wouldn't have been able to withstand it all if I hadn't gone through that at a young age."

From the Michigan game through the end of the playoff, he had worked almost nonstop, determined to do everything in his power to help his team redeem itself. In the weeks and months after winning the championship, Day carried himself like a man who'd had a boulder lifted off his shoulders.

"Almost everyone who sees us now comments that he's got a different look in his eyes," Nina Day said. "He's laughing and smiling. He lets his guard down a lot more. I'm not saying he's not focused now, but it was hard for him to really do anything besides think about football 24/7, 365 days a year. I think now he enjoys life a little bit more."

Day came to realize during the Ohio State's playoff run that it began to represent more than just the pursuit of a football championship. In an age when the loudest, nastiest voices seem to carry the day, his team's example of bouncing back resonated. After the title was won, Day noticed that when people approached him, many didn't say, "Congratulations." Instead, they simply said, "Thank you."

"It always felt like a great lesson," he said. "It's a good reminder that if you just hang in there and show some resilience, there are rewards. When you start a journey together, and with this group it started when they came in as recruits, and you see it all the way through, it justifies all the work and shows the type of people that did it."

It's remarkable how a championship can change perceptions. A 45-year-old coach who has never won a title can seem old. *He's already 45 and hasn't won it. Will he ever?* A 45-year-old who wins it all can seem young. *He's only 45 and has reached the pinnacle. How many more can he win?*

Shortly after the championship, Ohio State rewarded Day with a contract extension through 2031 that will pay him $12.5 million per year, second in college football behind only Georgia's Kirby Smart. With OSU's vast resources, a rich history, and a strong infrastructure in place, no one would be surprised if the Buckeyes add more championships under Day.

But it's hard to believe that any other could be more special than his first. It's hard to imagine a brotherhood being stronger than this Buckeyes team that hung together when it could have fractured and navigated the hardest path any college football team ever had to win a national championship.

Acknowledgments

I have been an Ohio State football beat writer for *The Columbus Dispatch* since 2011. This is my third book on a Buckeyes season, following *Buckeye Rebirth* about the 2012 undefeated season in Urban Meyer's first year and *The Chase* about the 2014 national championship. Every year, I have it in the back of my mind that my offseason might be consumed by another book. But every year after 2014, Ohio State's season was derailed. After the head-scratching loss to Michigan in 2024, I figured my 2025 spring would be free. Instead, Ohio State regrouped to run a gauntlet like no team in the history of college football ever had to win it all. Writing a book about the 2024 season was a no-brainer.

But I knew I'd have challenges. The biggest was getting cooperation from the players and coaches. Coaches are always swamped, and most of OSU's players started preparing for the NFL draft. I worried that many of the players were ready for the next chapter in their lives and might not want to rehash the season. Fortunately, almost all the players and coaches I asked were exceedingly generous with their time and insights. I ended up talking to more than 50 people, some for multiple hours.

Ryan and Nina Day are at the top of that list. My first interview was with Nina a week after the championship. Our two-hour conversation reassured me that this was a story worth undertaking, and she continued to be helpful throughout the process. I was fortunate with my two previous books that Urban Meyer was as helpful as he was. Ryan Day was just as essential for this one. Some of the topics we discussed had to be difficult and painful, particularly about his father, but he answered every question with honesty and insight. A head coach's time in the NIL/ transfer portal era is precious, and I'm so grateful that Ryan was so accommodating and candid. I hope readers now see the man and not just the coach. His is a remarkable story. The Days' teenage son, RJ, provided impressive perspective for someone his age—or really any age. I wish I'd been there when he finally beat his dad in that basketball game.

I'm also thankful to athletics director Ross Bjork, and his predecessor, Gene Smith, for helping me understand the season and the college football landscape from their perspective. Former coordinators Jim Knowles and Chip Kelly gave me their time and wonderful insights even though they'd moved on to new jobs. Knowles gets bonus points for talking to me for three hours while driving from Ohio to Pennsylvania during a snowstorm. Assistant coaches Larry Johnson, Brian Hartline, Tim Walton, James Laurinaitis, Carlos Locklyn, and Keenan Bailey were all generous with their time.

Others at or associated with OSU provided much help. Mickey Marotti was indispensable for the other two books and was just as crucial to this one. No one knows OSU players better than he does. Very few people know what it's like to be the head coach at Ohio State. Urban Meyer, in both the foreword and in the interview for the book, provided that unique perspective. Mark Pantoni, Logan Hittle, Brian Schottenstein, Jamey Houle, Maurice Clarett, Quinn Tempel, and Cardale Jones (buy his autobiography!) all provided context and information I couldn't have gotten anywhere else. Gee Scott Sr. helped share the remarkable turnaround story of his son. Ohio State sports information director Jerry Emig showed again why he's regarded so highly by helping facilitate interviews with players. Thank you also to Maddie Post for helping schedule interviews with Ryan Day.

Thanks also to the fine folks from New Hampshire who knew Ryan Day in Manchester and gave me the lay of the land there—Stan Spirou, Sean McDonnell, Mike Fitzpatrick, and Chris Day.

And then there were the players. I remember being so impressed with the perspective and maturity of the players from the 2012 and 2014 teams when I interviewed them for those books. The players on the 2024 team were just as good. I couldn't imagine having better interviews than the ones I had with Will Howard, Jack Sawyer, and Cody Simon. So many other players were generous with their time and gave me invaluable insights. Donovan Jackson, J.T. Tuimoloau, Denzel Burke, Sonny Styles, Jeremiah Smith, Lathan Ransom, Caleb Downs, Josh Fryar, Gee Scott Jr., Quinshon Judkins, Tyleik Williams, Ty Hamilton, Seth McLaughlin, Davison Igbinosun, Tegra Tshabola, Carson Hinzman, Luke Montgomery, Austin Siereveld, Jayden Fielding, and Mitchell Melton all helped make this book complete. To me, the stories of the lesser-known players like Fielding and Tshabola are ones I'm particularly grateful to be able to share.

I also want to thank *Columbus Dispatch* editor Michael Shearer, sports editor Brian White, and assistant sports editor Lori Schmidt for their support. A special thank you to my beat partner, Joey Kaufman, who picked up the slack to enable me to spend more time on the book and provided much-needed guidance and reassurance.

My Triumph Books editor, Don Gulbrandsen, was a great partner throughout the process. He was encouraging from the start and provided invaluable guidance and expertise. A good editor is hard to find, and Don is a great one. I always felt the book was in good hands with him. Thanks as well to Noah Amstadter, Bill Ames, Josh Williams, Jesse Jordan, and Stefani Szenda at Triumph, which has always been a great partner, and to Ken Samelson for his vigilant fact checking.

My family has always been incredibly supportive of me, particularly my dad. Born on the same day the Ohio State marching band first performed "Script Ohio" in 1936, he met my mom at Ohio State and taught me about OSU football as a kid growing up in Dayton. The Buckeyes won a national championship in 1954, his freshman year at Ohio State. I'm glad he got to see another national championship at age 88. My kids, Katie and Michael, are hardly the biggest football fans on the planet. But they have always been supportive and understanding of the sacrifices required of an OSU beat writer. My grandson, Atlas, born eight days after I submitted my manuscript, provided wonderful motivation not to slack off, just in case he came early. I'm so excited to watch that little boy grow up. I must also thank our faithful furry "daughter" Ellie for providing me company as I wrote. The biggest thanks of all, of course, goes to my wife, Erin. A wonderful journalist in her own right as a producer for WOSU's *All Sides with Amy Juravich*, Erin has always encouraged me and been my biggest fan. She put up with my book grumpiness and helped me see the finish line even when I wasn't sure I could. Just like Ryan Day couldn't have done what he has without Nina, I couldn't have done this without Erin.